THE CHILD WITHIN

Second Edition

THE CHILD WITHIN

Taking the Young Person's Perspective by Applying Personal Construct Psychology

Second Edition

Richard J. Butler

Consultant Clinical Psychologist in Child Health, Leeds Primary Care Trust and Senior Associate Lecturer, University of Leeds

David Green

Honorary Senior Lecturer in Clinical Psychology, University of Leeds and Consultant Clinical Psychologist in Child Health, St James's University Hospital

with a guest chapter by **Harry Procter**
Formerly Head of Child and Adolescent Clinical Psychology Services, Somerset Partnership NHS and Social Care Trust

John Wiley & Sons, Ltd

Copyright © 2007   John Wiley & Sons Ltd, The Atrium, Southern Gate, Chichester,
West Sussex PO19 8SQ, England

Telephone (+44) 1243 779777

Email (for orders and customer service enquiries): cs-books@wiley.co.uk
Visit our Home Page on www.wiley.com

Other Wiley Editorial Offices

John Wiley & Sons Inc., 111 River Street, Hoboken, NJ 07030, USA

Jossey-Bass, 989 Market Street, San Francisco, CA 94103-1741, USA

Wiley-VCH Verlag GmbH, Boschstr. 12, D-69469 Weinheim, Germany

John Wiley & Sons Australia Ltd, 42 McDougall Street, Milton, Queensland 4064, Australia

John Wiley & Sons (Asia) Pte Ltd, 2 Clementi Loop #02-01, Jin Xing Distripark, Singapore 129809

John Wily & Sons Canada Ltd, 6045 Freemont Blvd, Mississauga, ONT, L5R 4J3, Canada

Wiley also publishes its books in a variety of electronic formats. Some content that appears in print may not be available
in electronic books.

Anniversary Logo Design: Richard J. Pacifico

Library of Congress Cataloging-in-Publication Data

Butler, Richard J.
   The child within : taking the young person's perspective by applying personal construct theory / Richard J. Butler,
David Green ; with a guest chapter by Harry Procter. – 2nd ed.
       p. ; cm.
   Includes bibliographical references and indexes.
   ISBN 978-0-470-02997-8 (cloth : alk. paper) – ISBN 978-0-470-02998-5 (pbk. : alk. paper)
   1.   Personal construct therapy for children. 2.   Personal construct theory. I. Green, David, BA MSc. II. Procter,
Harry. III. Title.
   [DNLM: 1. Personal Construct Theory. 2. Child. 3. Infant. 4. Psychotherapy–methods. BF 698.9.P47 B986c 2007]
   RJ505.P46B88 2007
   618.92'8914–dc22

                                                                                                    2007013679

British Library Cataloguing in Publication Data

A catalogue record for this book is available from the British Library

ISBN 978-0-470-02997-8 (hbk) 978-0-470-02998-5 (pbk)

Typeset in 10/12pt Palatino by Thomson Digital, India
Printed and bound in Great Britain by TJ International Ltd, Padstow, Cornwall
This book is printed on acid-free paper responsibly manufactured from sustainable forestry
in which at least two trees are planted for each one used for paper production.

Dedicated to our children

Joe, Gregory, Luke

Rachel, Katie and Joe

CONTENTS

ABOUT THE AUTHORS

Richard Butler is a Consultant Clinical Psychologist with the child and adolescent mental health services in Leeds and an Honorary Lecturer at the University of Leeds. He qualified at Bristol University, undertook clinical practice at High Royds Hospital working alongside Don Bannister, participated as a sports psychologist with the British Olympic Association, worked with the World Health Organization on structuring assessment and treatment approaches for nocturnal enuresis and is involved with the Avon longitudinal Survey of Parents and Children in researching preventative strategies in child health. Throughout his work he has sought to draw on the principles of personal construct theory to help people enhance their psychological functioning. He is the creator of performance profiling, a method of enhancing sporting performance; co-author of the three systems approach to understanding and treating nocturnal enuresis; and more latterly developed the Self Image Profile as a means of understanding and assessing how children and adults construe themselves. Amongst his other interests is the active study of consistently poor golf, collecting vinyl records and suffering the trauma of supporting Huddersfield Town.

David Green is Clinical Director of the Doctor of Clinical Psychology training programme at the University of Leeds. He has worked with children and adolescents and their families for over 30 years and currently contributes clinical psychology support to the paediatric oncology service at St James University Hospital in Leeds. He is a long-standing Kellyan and has written and presented a series of papers on personal construct approaches to therapeutic work with young people on topics such as fixed role therapy and paediatric health care. He also has a keen interest in the processes of professional training, especially the role of clinical supervision.

INFLUENCES

Although we have been fundamentally moved and guided in our work by many salient theoretical notions within Personal Construct Theory, we are particularly indebted to three inspirational thinkers. The ideas and curiosity of these three leading lights within the field of Personal Construct Theory have, without doubt, provided the foundations upon which our clinical work with youngsters has developed. This book owes an extraordinary about to each.

GEORGE KELLY (1905–1967)

Born on his parents' farmhouse near Perth, Kansas, George Kelly 'consistently reflected the initiative, resourcefulness, self-reliance and courage of the American pioneer' (Thompson, 1968). Amongst his varied experiences in academia, he undertook a BEd at Edinburgh University in 1930 and in 1946 was appointed Professor of Psychology and Director of Clinical Psychology in the Department of Psychology at Ohio State University, Columbus. There he built his own house and patio, held regular Thursday night groups with students at his home to discuss his latest drafts and ideas and published The Psychology of Personal Constructs in 1955. He moved to Brandeis University in Massachusetts in 1965 and died at Massachusetts General Hospital, Boston on 6 March 1967.

DON BANNISTER (1928–1986)

Don was both a friend and colleague and widely acknowledged as instrumental in advancing the theory and clinical practice of Personal Construct Theory. He became 'a rallying point for new hope concerning what might yet be possible for a psychology that took personal experience seriously' (Mair, 1986). He came from a mining village in Yorkshire, worked proudly as a senior clinical psychologist at Bexley for 17 years and returned north in the mid 1970s to work at High Royds Hospital. There he continued work on children's construing, wrote novels and awkwardly played goalkeeper for Psychic Rovers, splendidly wrapped in the red and white colours of his boyhood team, Doncaster Rovers. Don was truly a fighter for what he valued. He died of cancer on 11 July 1986 in Ilkley, West Yorkshire in sight of the moors he used to croon about at Christmas parties bar t'at.

TOM RAVENETTE (1924–2005)

Tom borrowed 'the Psychology of Personal Constructs' from Don Bannister whilst a student at the University of London and 'immediately found it a rounded set of ideas which he could carry forward into the practice of educational psychology' (Neimeyer, 1985). Whilst working as an educational psychologist Tom always sought to make a difference to the children he met. He developed a myriad of techniques and probing questions to aid clinicians, teachers and others to understand how youngsters made sense of their worlds. Don Bannister first introduced us to Tom's work, knowing of our interest in understanding children. Tom's work, like that of Kelly before him, was feverishly passed in dog-eared grubby carbon copies between clinicians eager to discover his views. You see Tom wrote as a practitioner for fellow practitioners. As he memorably said: 'Research psychologists seek to find a significant difference. Applied psychologists (like himself) strive to make a significant difference.' Eventually these ideas were put together as a published collection of papers in 1999. Tom's work was innovative and exciting. He readily gave his time to present workshops for trainees in clinical psychology, playfully having them sit with crayons and inviting them to both draw themselves and their opposite. He remained keenly interested in others' ideas and was prepared to deliver a timely challenge to students that effortlessly bridged a generation gap of some 50 years. He was just as charitable with his attention to those of us who were maybe not quite that much younger than him. Tom was an active conference participant who listened carefully to other presenters' views and would always find time for the encouraging comment and indeed take the opportunity to put you right on a few things if he felt it necessary! And what Tom thought of your work mattered. . .

FOREWORD

This foreword appeared in the first edition of our book *The Child Within*. As we were about to ask Tom for his thoughts regarding a new extensively elaborated edition we heard of his unfortunate death. Hopefully his comments on the first edition remain apposite.

I was highly honoured to be invited to write a foreword to this book but I have to confess that this for me was a novel venture, never before having written one for another's book. Nonetheless I had dim recollections of other 'forewords' and presumed that this would provide an adequate briefing for this occasion. The nearer I got, however, to putting pen to paper and the greater the number of possible comments I had scribbled down as raw material, the more ignorant I felt as to what would be fitting for this particular text. How long? What kind of structure? What tone? I know of no 'scientific studies' on the writing of 'forewords', perhaps that subject does not qualify as suitable for investigation, so in default I decided to carry out a mini-project on the subject using the books on my own shelves as a normative sample. Looking at some 25 non-fiction texts, although there were prefaces in abundance, I came across only one 'foreword'. Are Personal Construct Psychology books any difference in this regard? No, the proportion was just the same. So the result of asking this simple question is the remarkable outcome that the practice of eliciting 'forewords' is rather rare (p value approximately 0.5!). Why then such an invitation?

It seemed to me on reflection that a 'foreword' was not just a form of programme notes in advance, preparing the reader for what is to come. Rather it was a delicate way, at one and the same time, of (1) validating the writer of the 'foreword' by effectively saying 'You are just the person who really does know all about these matters', and (2) inviting validation of the book, and thereby its writers, by implicitly saying 'We offer something original and of value. Your recognition of this will confirm both us and the contents.' Under (1) the text itself offers validating messages by way of the generous quotations from my own writings and I take this opportunity of expressing my warm appreciation of the writers' generosity. My observations under (2) will come later and I can say in advance that they certainly will be validating but I hope will also point beyond. Be that as it may, I like both the delicacy and the implicit messages of the invitation.

As the title says, the theme of the book is *The Child Within* and is an account of the use of Personal Construct Psychology (PCP) in resolving problems where a child is presented as the focus. The context within which this work is carried out is the hospital. This needs to be pointed out rather than taken for granted, since the resolution of comparable problems may take different forms when carried out in other contexts, for example child guidance clinics in the community, schools and social service departments. In particular, development in the uses of PCP may also take on different forms according to the context. It is a part of my credentials that my passport into professional practice as a psychologist was by way of the Maudsley Hospital, thereby giving me some notion of the hospital as a context but, more importantly, by being present at the birth of PCP in England. Although the odyssey of my developments of PCP in relation to child-focused problems started there nearly 40 years ago, it was continued in these other contexts eventually finding expression in Ravenette (1997), a text which in some ways parallels *The Child Within*.

I do not propose to go through the text chapter by chapter but rather to isolate some of its themes, both explicit and implicit, starting with the title itself. It is a matter of history that it is the adults who have spoken for, and on behalf of children. The essence of this book, mediated through its title, is that the child has his/her own individual meanings, and ways of making sense of themselves and their circumstances. Without finding ways of exploring these ways we are likely to fall seriously short in understanding those matters which lead to a referral. Even in some forms of 'therapy', designed to explore 'the child within', the meanings and interpretations are frequently alien to the child's implicit theories. The title points the way, in theory and in practice, to restoring the balance back from adult-centred to child-generated meanings, a most valuable corrective.

But the title does much more. Within Personal Construct Psychology the use of contrast suggests other, but related, issues consideration of which provide further balances against too one-pointed a stance. And these will probably be important when the child is presented as 'a problem'. Thus *The Child Within* suggests immediately a variety of contrasts: 'the world without', 'child versus peer group, or family, or parent, or school' each or any of which might well be important in understanding 'the problem' itself, in its broader perspectives, over and above the proper concern for 'the child within'.

My second theme is about theory. The value of theory lies in finding alternative ways of conceptualizing phenomena such that they will be of greater value in dealing with those problems for which that theory is relevant. The grasp of a theory by the practitioner is measured by his/her skill in communicating its concepts in everyday language. The theory under consideration here is personal construct theory and the authors demonstrate their real mastery not only by communicating in the way I have just described, but also in demonstrating its value and application in the presentation of actual case material. The book is not for theorists but for practitioners, a matter of some moment since such books very rarely appear.

My third theme is that of context. As I said earlier, the work reported in this book was carried out in a hospital context. Therein lie potential hazards insofar as the communications are aimed as much to the outside world as to a hospital readership. A hospital has its own jargon which is taken for granted. 'Illness', 'disease', 'suffer', 'cure', 'treatment' and 'syndrome' are all common expressions in medically oriented contexts and may indeed be very proper in the case of physical disorders. They raise question marks, however, when they are carried over to the area covered by psychiatry, and child psychiatry in particular, since they reflect a style of thinking, knowing and action which may be less appropriate in dealing with the vaguer complains about children. Moreover the great attention given to finding 'diagnostic' labels to fit the child who has been referred, rather than the circumstances which the referral reflects, may carry the risk of looking in irrelevant directions if we are concerned with the circumstances as sensed by 'the child within'.

My final theme makes references to the therapeutic work that was carried out with each of the cases. The writers demonstrate that a range of Kellian strategies are well within the possibilities of children despite the frequent argument that a high level of verbal ability is a necessary prerequisite. But I have a reservation about the word 'therapy'. I am aware that the expression has a long and honoured usage, yet implicitly it has the undertone that there is something wrong and it is the therapist's task to cure it. My own preference is to use the expression 'constructive intervention' which accurately reflects both the nature of the theoretical stance and the purpose of one's involvement in a case but without the framework of 'illness' and 'cure'.

It is, I think, necessary to say all of these things, in order to make the point that the book is almost completely free of the hospital, or medical, atmosphere which might so easily have been communicated in the writing. I count this in itself to be a major triumph. I have to concede, however, what I consider to be one small fall from grace but, and I say this somewhat cryptically, had the authors used the term 'dyslexia' in italics, I might have complimented them on a neat way of communicating doubt. Many, perhaps, might not agree with the validity of my observation.

All that I have written up to this point has been at a professional level but I plead licence, by way of concluding comments and at a personal level, to point to two special sources of delight. The first is to say how pleased I was to read short italicized quotations linking 'the text within' to 'thoughts from without' as elaborative subtitles for so many chapters.

My second source of delight is the reference to the TV detective Columbo and his 'naïve' style of interviewing. Here I would also add my own favourite detective, G.K. Chesterton's Father Brown. And why? It seems to me that underlying all his successes is his implicit question 'Under what circumstances might this just make sense?' a truly Kellian thought.

It is my hope that this book will penetrate all those establishments where children are presented as a cause for concern by those adults who carry responsibility for them.

Tom Ravenette
(1924–2005)

ACKNOWLEDGEMENTS

So many good folk have encouraged and supported us through the writing of this book. We would especially like to thank Aileen Kennedy for her endeavours in typing the manuscript, Gil Rhodes for his enthusiasm and appetite with some of our 'scientist' projects and Jon Heron for his statistical expertise. We are also indebted to Nicole Burnett for her invaluable editorial assistance. Finally we are grateful to the many children and young people with whom we have worked and who have unreservedly trusted us with their construing.

CHAPTER 1

FUNDAMENTAL PRINCIPLES

What we take to be our knowledge of things is actually only an opinion.

(Plato)

Although Franz Epting (1988) regards children to be amongst the most elusive, perplexing and enigmatic of all the creatures we might seek to understand, they continue to intrigue and fascinate us. There is a truism about mystery fostering a desire to make sense. However, grappling with the vagaries and challenges of children can invite a sense of helplessness. Parents customarily feel exasperated, incompetent and culpable whilst teachers may feel provoked, defensive and reproachful. Undoubtedly children often confound those to whom they are brought for help, be they a doctor, therapist, psychologist, mentor, nurse, social worker, probation officer or solicitor.

Nevertheless in seeking to understand children, impressions and judgements are frequently and unnervingly made about them. Indeed the operative word here is 'made' as such views tend to be just that – 'made' by an observer of the child, employing their own framework of understanding. Not until we contend with the protagonist's own view – the child's perspective – can we be considered to have anything other than an incomplete and jaundiced comprehension of the child. A major theme throughout this book is a search for ways to grasp the child's perspective. Through so doing it aspires to make a difference in the way professional practice frames the struggles of childhood and more generally to hopefully promote improved ways that adults might approach, appreciate and comprehend youngsters.

1.1 PERSONAL CONSTRUCT THEORY

Primarily our approach is guided by George Kelly's ideas, comprehensively elaborated in the theory of personal constructs (Kelly, 1955). As with the first edition of *The Child Within* (Butler and Green, 1998), our fundamental aim is not to summarize the theory, given the notable reviews provided by Don Bannister and Fay Fransella (Bannister and Fransella, 1986; Fransella, 1995, 2003), but to explore the theoretical implications for understanding children's experiences and the practical applications of the theory in fashioning change with young people.

Don Bannister (1985) set a backdrop from which personal construct theory (PCT) can be viewed in contrasting relief. He posed the question as to why psychologists, in their typical snobbery, offer contrasting explanations of the behaviour of scientist–psychologists on the one hand and their subject matter – ordinary mortals – on the other. Some cursory reflection reveals that although psychologists often convince themselves they are thoughtful theorists and bold experimenters, the rest of humankind is depicted as 'flotsam, pushed hither and yon by the vagaries of genetics or unconscious infantile conflicts, or environmental stimuli'. George Kelly determinedly set out to depict all persons, including youngsters – psychologists and non-psychologists – as scientists. This became known as his root metaphor. He heralded a theory in which people might be considered a mixture of creative guesswork and co-operative venturing, something we formally call *science* and informally call *living*. In portraying people as akin to scientists in reaching out to impose meaning on the events that confront them, Kelly was proposing that each individual constructs the dimensions of their own reality.

PCT proposes fundamentally that a person's functioning can be perceived as a means of understanding the world. World here is taken to be inclusive in referring to phenomena, themselves included, with which the person comes into contact. The theory intimates that people strive to make sense of events, experiences and themselves by detecting repeated themes (known as constructs) that enable them to anticipate what is likely to happen with future events. People act, in Kellyan terms, as if they are scientists, in eagerly searching to understand. PCT is, thus, essentially a meta-theory in the sense of being a theory about the theories people have about themselves and the world.

Kelly's engagement with children has often been thought to not amount too much. However, as George Thompson (1968), a colleague and lifelong friend, suggests, Kelly's formative years as a budding researcher and psychologist were spent in a variety of contexts, trying to fathom out young people. Within academia Kelly received a BEd at the University of Edinburgh in 1930 for work on predicting teaching success and a PhD in psychology at the State University, Iowa, in 1931 for a thesis on common factors in reading and speech disabilities. At a clinical level Kelly began a travelling clinic in Kansas where he would drive from town to town offering psychological services to youngsters. According to George Thompson, although Kelly often employed psychometrics with children, he rarely cared about the test scores – interviewing the child, parent and referrer for him made eminently more sense. 'I think I might have a little creativity' he once commented to George Thompson.

PCT has a particular language, a raft of definitions, many familiar concepts with alternative meanings and a structure embodied by a set of corollaries. Written in 1955, Kelly's mammoth work *The Psychology of Personal Constructs*, now over half a century old, remains powerful and insightful, though is not the easiest of reads. Drawing from the theory, this chapter highlights the base assumption and some of the major principles that have particular relevance for working with children. The chapters which follow take up these themes to examine childhood experiences in a broad array of contexts.

1.2   AN UNDERLYING ASSUMPTION

A fundamental assumption underpinning PCT is the notion of constructive alternativism, which essentially proposes that all our current perceptions, insights and understandings are open to question and reconsideration. For therapists engaged in the task of helping others change and reframe their experiences, such a premise could hardly be more heartening and optimistic. Change is always considered a distinct possibility.

Kelly went so far as to conjecture that even the most obvious occurrences of everyday life might appear utterly transformed if we were inventive enough to construe the situation differently. We constantly create and recreate our own experience so that any aspect of our lives from the most momentous to the most mundane is potentially open to reinterpretation. This splendidly liberating, but somewhat awesome, principle is as applicable to the child's understanding of self as it is to adults' attempts to understand children. Perhaps children need little convincing that there is always another avenue to be explored, another angle of attack to be considered. It is undoubtedly adults who are more likely to try and persuade themselves that they have discovered the 'real' meaning of events.

Such a sense of conviction is crucial to our capacity to act as effective decision-takers, but it has a downside. If in our analysis we have come to the conclusion that a particular phenomenon can be sensibly understood only in the terms of our favoured explanatory model, it is but a small step to believing that said phenomenon is 'nothing but' what we see in it. If the phenomenon in question is a child, pre-emptive construing of this nature can trap youngsters in somewhat rigid categories that concerned adults devise to help them with their problems (e.g. hyperactive, maladjusted, dyslexic). Kelly's message is a reminder that scientific construing, be it of the personal or the professional kind, is provisional in its nature. We formulate hypotheses to test. Good scientists live out their experiments, but always with a view to revising their theories in the light of experience.

1.3 THE ESSENTIAL PRINCIPLES

1.3.1 If You Want to Know What's Wrong, Then Ask

This is George Kelly's infamous first principle. Although making eminent sense, there are, of course, many ways of asking questions, though not all facilitate better ways of understanding youngsters. Social pleasantries yield humdrum stereotypical responses. Polite requests promote acquiescence. Closed questions render closed answers. Many strategies of 'asking' are loaded in the sense that certain answers are presumed or expected. We may, for example, assume we have asked children about their circumstances but often this turns out to be a projection on our behalf. We tend to put forward our theories of the child rather than asking the child their theory or version of events. Thus as bad scientists we ask questions which confirm the view we have of a child. 'You did that on purpose, didn't you?' is perhaps a classic example of an adult seeking endorsement for their theory, leaving children little room for relating the events as he or she might construe them.

Adults in the position of caring for children often seek to understand a child, by inadvertently implying a form of interrogation. Whenever children are asked about their version of events with a question beginning with 'Why...?', the inevitable response appears to be a blank stare coupled with a mumbled 'Don't know'. Because 'why...?' questions are generally asked in the context of confrontation, it seems hardly surprising that the child baulks at the prospect and avoids a considered response. Questions framed in the context of genuine inquiry, such as 'How come...?' or 'Can you tell me...' are more likely to be met with thoughtful reflection on the youngster's behalf.

A gathering convention amongst professional ranks is to ask by rote – swamping the individual with a host of prepared questions, either in questionnaire format, structured interview or psychometric assessment so as to determine an appropriate category of 'abnormality' or level of functioning. Inquiry of the form: Is the child's behaviour abnormal?; Does the child realize their actions are socially inappropriate?; Is the child's cognitive capacity typical for their age? are illustrative. Such exploration characteristically bears answers that relate to the inquirer's frame of reference, not the participant's perspective. The results enticingly offer an understanding of the child, compared to others of their age, but tempt us to consider the child pre-emptively and exclusively in such a way. These methodologies unfortunately continue to be the adopted yardsticks by which children are understood.

However, we might consider such approaches as ways of understanding children, but not as Tom Ravenette (1977) cogently argued, as ways of understanding children's understanding. That requires us to appreciate and fathom young people from the inside looking out, rather than from the outside looking in. Franz Epting (1988) depicts the logical extension of such investigations by illustrating how many textbooks on child psychology remain silent on the topic of the child's psychology or personality, but offer 'intricate descriptions of cognitive development 'as if it were the same thing'. Our failure to understand an other, as Bannister and Fransella (1986) note, inevitably derives from asking people to answer our questions rather than noting the nature of the questions they are asking. And interestingly, young people often pose their questions, not in a verbal form but, as discussed later, as a behavioural narrative.

Tom Ravenette (1980) invited us to consider that the basic tool of anyone charged with helping children solve problems and issues is the question, and that what is crucial for the professional is 'the capacity to 'invent better and better questions'. He elaborated 'better' to mean facilitative for the child and penetrating for the interviewer. Epting (1984) drove this message home by his insistence that any techniques and procedures we may adopt should 'always be in the service of 'a feasible portrayal of the human experience'. Kelly's first principle judiciously invites us to take the other's perspective into consideration, rather than seeking to studiously fathom out complexities, jump to spurious conclusions or wildly interpret other people's behaviour.

Good questions, in a Kellyan sense, invite a youngster to present their perspective. They foster a climate of shared knowledge. They inspire the one doing the asking to develop an understanding of the other's understanding. Individuals are after all experts on their own understanding. They are the authority on their own self. An inquiring process characteristically highlights the individual's construing. Through careful listening, elicitation of constructs, seeking contrasts and elaboration of construing a picture of the child's ways of making sense, characteristically emerges. To this end, later chapters offer a number of facilitative processes.

1.3.2   The Child is an Architect of Reality

Kelly, and more recently, Ronen (1996) suggest that children, like adults, rather than reacting *to* the environment around them, act *on* it. They decidedly grapple to understand the world, their experiences in it and themselves. It is as if the world as given to all (reality) becomes represented uniquely to the child by the way he or she seeks to make sense of it. Events do not reveal meaning but, rather, how we represent the event to ourselves imposes meaning on the world. Thus we know the world only through our perceptions of it. Our knowledge and understanding is anchored in our assumptions, not in the bedrock of truth itself, whatever that may be. Youngsters are, therefore, in a very substantial sense, architects of their own unique reality.

Kelly's root metaphor of the human as the scientist or, in this context the child as scientist, portrays the essence of the encounter. A youngster, like any other, cannot possess a copy or mirror image of reality, but rather a constructed version based on his or her experience of it. Kelly (1955) supposed the aspirations of the scientist are essentially the aspirations of all folk and proposed that their paramount characteristics involve:

- a *curiosity* about the events before them

- a desire to *question the truth* of anything

- *predicting* the meaning of events and forecasting what may subsequently happen – Kelly intimated that by formulating constructs, scientists were aided in their predictive efforts

- *formulating a theory* – a body of constructs with a focus and a range of convenience.

- bringing the constructs (theory) up for *test* against subsequent events, thus enabling an assessment of the accuracy of the forecast

- *modifying the theory* according to the outcome

- a concern not with accumulating and cataloguing knowledge but an *understanding of the principles* or the abstractions that strike through events. In this way, Kelly argued, the scientist is able to penetrate a bewildering mass of concrete events and come to grips with an orderly principle.

Kelly proposed the personal construct as the basic unit of analysis, as the means by which an individual accesses the world. The characteristics in italics hint at Kelly's construing of the scientist. Interestingly they bear little relation to how youngsters tend to construe a scientist. A sample of 12–16-year-old schoolchildren from Cardiff, when asked to describe three characteristics of a scientist, produced a rare selection of constructs, loosely categorized in terms of:

- physical appearance – skinny, old, short
- appearance – wild hair, high trousers, wears glasses, scruffy, geeky
- being antisocial – not having friends or a social life
- being committed to their work – hardworking, sensible, serious, patient, careful and dedicated
- being cognitively adept – brainy, intelligent, good memory, nerdy
- having a tendency towards eccentricity – scatty, mad, lost the plot.

Little wonder then that few youngsters turn to science as a profession. And hardly in tune with Kelly's intention in proposing the scientist as a metaphor for how we make sense of the world. However, the same group of adolescents elicited a number of other characteristics which Kelly might have felt more compatible with his intention, declaring that scientists:

- *search for meaning* through doing experiments, studying events and investigating things
- *reflect on events* by analysing things, having lots of ideas and being a lateral thinker
- *find solutions* by making discoveries, solving problems, inventing things and sorting things out
- *disseminate results* by being a good communicator and sharing ideas.

Construing is an act of discrimination arising from an awareness of similarity, theme and repetition in the events encountered. Noticing that benevolent acts in others match our own sense of hospitality fosters a view of generosity. Kelly further suggested that constructs are bipolar, with meaning arising by way of the contrast. Thus generosity might contrast with being 'mean', 'tight-fisted' or 'stingy' implying a fiscal aspect; or 'selfish' suggesting notions of charitableness. Being aware of both poles of a construct promotes an improved understanding of the youngster from their perspective and reduces the likelihood of misinterpretation.

Once discriminations are formed the child is better equipped to anticipate. As Mancuso and Adams-Webber (1982) describe, anticipations are the schemata that are assembled to incorporate, integrate and assimilate incoming information. The child's understanding of events thus enables him or her to anticipate how future events might unfold and in traditional scientific manner check out how well those anticipations helped the child make sense of the event.

1.3.3   Construing is Non-Judgemental

Constructs are not viewed in terms of being right or wrong, just as emotions are not evaluated as good or bad. Construing is regarded as a search for meaning. How individuals come to understand themselves, through the process of making sense, is value-free. Thus a socially removed adolescent may construe being on their own as independent and self-sufficient. Evaluative judgements arise from a 'goodness of fit' model (McCoy, 1977) whereby acts (ours or another's) that meet our expectations are evaluated positively, whereas acts that fall short of anticipations may create negatively loaded evaluations. The socially isolated individual may remain content with himself, preoccupied in solitary activities. However, should the youngster wish for friendliness and social activity, but remain awkward in social encounters, he is likely to remain ill at ease and dissatisfied. Being stuck in repeatedly validating a socially inept view of self, which may act to protect the person from perceived criticism, remains value-free as it reflects the person's acts of construing. It becomes value-loaded once the youngster becomes aware that acting in such ways is at odds with how they would like to be.

1.3.4   The Way We Construe Determines the Way We Act

This principle elaborates the anticipatory aspect of construing. Developing an understanding of events, through the process of construing, provides a hint of how things might go in the future. Such anticipatory inklings provide the basis of our actions. Tom Ravenette (1980) suggests however, that construing lies at a low level of awareness such that an individual may not 'know' his or her constructs until a situation is provided whereby they are asked to produce them. Individuals, according to Ravenette, do not appeal to their construct systems in order to act but, rather, they *are* their construct systems. Thus behaviour can be seen to have direct relevance to a youngster's construing. Indeed all behaviour might be viewed as a testing out of the construct system. We check the validity of our construing by behaving. Thus behaviour may be conceptualized as a question and framed as an experiment.

On the whole children are insatiable experimenters. They test out rules, customs, boundaries, social conventions and the like. They check out notions of themselves through their actions. Youngsters may be viewed as seeking to understand their world through their actions which will increase their ability to understand and anticipate events. Constance Briscoe (2006), the first black female judge in the UK, tells a story of how, when she was a child, her mother abused her for bed-wetting. 'I went into the bathroom, removed the top from a bottle of bleach, diluted it with water, drank it and went back to bed. I chose

Domestos because Domestos kills all known germs and my mother had for so long told me that I was a germ. If the bleach worked, I would die' she wrote. Constance Briscoe's identity determined her actions. Children also act in ways that define what they perceive themselves not to be. Many young-sters construe themselves as not good at drawing, maths, being on their own, or music. 'I just had it in my head that I couldn't sing' said Renee Zellweger after being told to shut up by her brother when she was singing Beatles songs in the shower. We tend to consistently seek to validate the way we are, even when this denies us the opportunity to try something new. Thus construc-tions of self can be a barrier to preventing what we would like to be. Lack of change or success lies not in a lack of talent, but that such notions lie outside our self-image of who we are and what is for us appropriate.

If children's behaviour reflects their construing it may thus be possible to infer their experience or construing from their behaviour. Seeking to put ourselves non-judgementally into the 'child's shoes' can enhance our understanding of conceivable reasons for their actions. Our inferential tools, however, re-main unsophisticated and Epting (1984) has urged for developments in useful procedures for what he called this 'reading behaviour backward'. In Chap-ter 6, laddering is explored as a means of understanding the links between behaviour and more superordinate psychological and core constructs.

1.3.5 Children Behave in Particular Ways Because it Makes Sense to Them

The actions of others often appear bemusing. Youngsters may act in ways that stir discord, opposition or contention in others; appear fully absorbed in unusual or idiosyncratic behaviours; or display considerable unease in situations others may find exciting, engaging or commonplace. We tend to understand others through interpreting their behaviour and actions in our terms. Thus should our moral construing take precedent when we see a group of young people vandalizing property we may take the view that they are being antisocial. However, acts and behaviour begin to make sense once we seek to construe the world in their terms. For these youths, their high spirits in destroying property might be construed as sociable in that it maintains their status in the group or helps to curry favour with peers.

Although not always immediately apparent, all actions serve a useful pur-pose for the actor. This principle emerges as a logical and related extension of the thesis that a child's behaviour reflects the way they construe. The no-tion that a child's behaviour makes sense to the individual no matter how bizarre, deviant or self-defeating it may appear to the onlooker, is a pivotal theme arising from personal construct theory. Don Bannister's seminal work with individuals incarcerated on the long-stay wards of psychiatric institu-tions, who were diagnosed as suffering with schizophrenia, was perhaps the ultimate expression of this core assumption of the theory (Bannister, 1962, 1963). Bannister sought to discover the personal sense in the construing of individuals deemed to be displaying classic thought disorder. He endeavoured to make an understandable link between their views of the world and their often seemingly bizarre behaviour. As a result of Bannister's investigations, he surmised that these patients employed such loose systems for understanding their social worlds that they could not reliably anticipate events. In consequence, their own actions seemed unpredictable and senseless to those around them.

In returning to the arena of childhood, it is precisely those children who most frustrate our efforts to help that we need to make the most conscious effort to understand. Otherwise we are tempted to give up and justify our ineffectiveness by resorting to hopeless explanations of human nature that locate responsibility firmly within the child, such as 'plain evil', 'lazy', 'thick as two short planks' and so on. However, gaining convincing access to a youngster's private perspective is far easier said than done, especially when children rarely have the awareness to deliver their understandings like the morning newspaper on the doormat, even if they had the inclination. None the less, implicit in personal construct theory is the faith that the child's behaviour is valid, that it represents a search for meaning and there is always a potentially comprehensible relationship between an individual's actions and their constructions of the world.

Although a pretty sizeable task, making sense of a child's conduct would be enhanced if it were possible to see the world through their eyes. In such a vein, PCT encourages us to metaphorically put ourselves in the youngster's shoes. From such a vantage point, we may perceive how things are from their perspective. The process of understanding someone else therefore calls for us to suspend our usual ways of construing. Once another's behaviour becomes understood in their terms, light is often shed on the reasons they may be stuck. Behaviour which appears problematic can be understood sometimes as a solution for the individual, an idea elaborated by Tom Ravennete (2003) in the educational setting. From a more clinical setting, bedwetting maybe maintained because, as one child suggested, it ensures that the smell will prevent burglars from breaking into the flat. Because behaviour makes sense to the protagonist, it is always useful to ask for what problem the behaviour is a solution.

A preparedness to investigate the motives behind even the most deviant and dangerous activities of young people is not an intention to excuse. On the contrary, if public policy towards juvenile delinquency, for example, is not informed by proper scientific curiosity about the inner world of those who misbehave, it is unlikely to meet its stated aims. As surely as correct diagnosis needs to precede effective medical treatment, so an understanding of each individual child's experience should precede psychological intervention in their life.

There is nothing inherently wrong with labels. We need to categorize and make discriminations. Problems arise if the adhesive on our labels gets too sticky by half. What begin as useful propositions may end as unalterable opinions as we slowly succumb to what Kelly described as the dread condition of 'hardening of the categories'! What we need is the psychological equivalent of those clever little yellow notelets that can be stuck on most surfaces to convey some helpful message, but are easily removed once they have fulfilled their purpose. The alternative may mean caging children for infinity in the pigeonholes we have constructed for them.

1.3.6   Acknowledgement of Individuality

PCT celebrates individuality through acknowledging uniqueness in how people make sense of their encounters with the world. While we may confront common difficulties or share similar backgrounds, we invariably experience life uniquely. Individuals differ from each other in terms of how they perceive and interpret situations before them. Further, by advocating that people enduringly strive to comprehend events and by doing so develop a framework of understanding, the theory invites us to consider the person as active in relation to their environment; not, as some theories suggest, reactive to it. Kelly proposed a psychology that celebrated the singular way in which we appraise our existence. He recognized the different priorities individuals bring to bear in their personal analysis of the world around them and appreciated the far-reaching implications of the interpretative framework we each evolve in our continuing efforts to make sense of our situation (Bannister and Fransella, 1986).

Kelly proposed that the uniqueness of an individual arises from the unrivalled and distinct way in which they anticipate experience and make sense of their lot. People hold views, perceptions, assumptions, opinions and understandings about themselves, others and the environment within which they live and it is these notions that determine individuality. From such perceptions people anticipate how things might unfold, again in unique and idiosyncratic ways. Thus it is the distinctiveness of construing which heralds individuality. That is not to deny that there are certain commonalities in our experience which are important to acknowledge. PCT is also interested in similarities between ways a group of individuals are viewed by the world. For example, twins may look identical; their parents may choose to dress them in similar outfits; their friends and family may be unable to tell one from the other; and yet they will each have a singular opinion of the school they attend, the home they live in and even the very business of being a twin. It is quite credible that when it comes to construing the world around them they might find they have more in common with another child than with their apparently identical twin. Rather than be surprised at this psychological divergence, families with twins tend to recognize the key role this 'personal' construing plays in the development of an autonomous sense of identity.

The respect for the uniqueness of individual experience that is enshrined in PCT places a significant responsibility on adults wishing to use Kelly's ideas in their work with children. While at other times we may want to teach young people to use our language and appreciate our particular view of events, when following the personal construct tradition the job of the senior partner in the discussion is to get to grips with the children's perspectives. This means using their words, investigating their idiosyncratic theories and respectfully checking to ensure we have properly understood what they intended to tell us; above all, never assuming we already know what we need to discover. Exploring the personal constructs of children is undeniably a serious undertaking.

1.4   CONCLUSION

The sceptical reader might by now be wondering why, if this personal construct theory is so optimistic and helpful, have they not heard of it before? This puzzlement might be further aggravated by the realization that George Kelly, the author of the theory, first published his ideas as long ago as 1955, with 2005 marking the centenary of his birth.

There is no mysterious tale of undiscovered manuscripts or arcane scholarship needed to explain our decision to write the first edition of *The Child Within* in the late 1990s, or this later elaboration of personal construct theory with children some 50 years since Kelly's original work. George Kelly, unlike several renowned American psychologists, did not market his ideas in the usual manner in which novel psychotherapies are sold to fellow professionals. He wrote at an abstract theoretical level, providing an integrated model of human understanding which could inform and enrich the practice of clinical psychology, education, child care and human relationships in general. Kelly did not, however, tend to be procedurally specific in describing quite how his ideas could best be translated into effective operation. It is unlikely that this omission from Kelly's writing was mere oversight on his part. Rather, he preferred to invite those who chose to follow the personal construct way to work out the implications of his ideas for themselves.

Within clinical psychology an increasing body of published research illustrates how productively Kelly's successors have taken up this challenge (Winter, 1992). However, relatively few clinicians have explored the possibilities of using the personal construct approach with children. Our aim, therefore, in writing this book is to provide an accessible introduction to Kelly's theory as applied to the challenge of trying to help children in trouble. It is written in the expectation that the reader will have both an active interest in ideas and a pressing need to apply them.

The style and format of this book have been designed to mesh theory and practice by using a series of case studies to demonstrate how sometimes abstruse ideas can be translated into a workable intervention in a child's life. We have not, however, tried to produce a compendium of tried and tested recipes. To push the culinary metaphor a little further, we do not see ourselves as master chefs sharing our expertise. Instead we aim to provide enough stimulus and structure to encourage interested readers to cook a little something up for themselves.

CHAPTER 2

ADOPTING A CREDULOUS APPROACH

At first glance it might seem we are over-egging the pudding by devoting a full chapter to Kelly's advocacy of the 'credulous' approach when conducting psychotherapy. After all he didn't make this recommendation particularly with the treatment of young people in mind. And what's the big deal about believing the stories people tell you anyway? Don't all decent therapists start from that assumption? Since Kelly regularly exhorted psychologists to 'transcend the obvious', we also invite our readers to consider more closely the still risky and radical implications of being truly credulous in our dealings with children.

2.1 APPROACH, METHOD AND TECHNIQUE

The British family therapist John Burnham has helpfully proposed a hierarchical model for differentiating between different schools of psychotherapy (Burnham, 1992). At the heart of any theory is the approach that defines its fundamental character and should inform the manner in which practitioners orient themselves to all aspects of their work with clients and colleagues alike. The level of method is best understood by considering how a devotee of a therapeutic school might describe their everyday working practice to an interested enquirer. So methods are indicators of what might be termed 'the approach in action'. Techniques are construed as trademark interventions that are unique to a particular model and therefore need to be operationalized in enough detail for an observer to recognize their special character.

In this book we aim to describe the application of personal construct principles to understanding and assisting young people in trouble at each of these three levels – approach, method and technique. In so doing we hope to counteract some of the frustrations that childcare professional are apt to experience when they first encounter Kelly's writings. Very interesting but what exactly am I supposed to do with these ideas? However, our wish to provide illustrative examples of personal construct methods and techniques should not disguise our view that an appreciation of the implications of the credulous approach lies at the core of everything we advocate.

Among his many other professional activities Kelly was a trainer of clinical psychology students and well understood the appeal of 'how to do it' cookbooks that prescribed technical interventions and promised sure-fire therapeutic success. He, however, was wary of being too directive as an educator. In his own words he felt that teaching 'should free students' concepts as well as fix them'. Nonetheless he was determined to instil one pre-eminent ethical attitude in all his young charges. They should adopt a credulous approach in their work.

2.2   AN UNUSUAL WORD TO CHOOSE

'Credulous' sounds like a word whose meaning we ought to grasp immediately. Surely it's something to do with trust and belief. This sounds a wholly admirable characteristic – just the kind of quality we'd like others to see in us. But a reviewer of the satirical author Francis Wheen's book *How Mumbo Jumbo Conquered the World* (Wheen, 2004) commented pithily that 'it is not nice to mock the credulous and foolish, but it is funny'. Did Kelly really intend his followers to run the risk of appearing gullible chumps? Well, probably yes . . .

Even if we choose a less pejorative synonym for 'credulous' than 'gullible' – perhaps 'unsuspecting' is a more neutral term – it is clear that Kelly wished to realign the traditional power relationship that had existed between therapists and their clients. Psychologists and their ilk should be prepared to be 'taken in' by those whom they presume to help because being credulous means taking seriously everything – but everything – your patient or pupil chooses to tell you. As Kelly put it 'from a phenomenological point of view the client, like the proverbial customer, is always right'. This is a risky stance to adopt and not one that is generally typical of the way professionals deal with the public they ostensibly serve. Doctors don't tend to communicate with their patients like this. Adults don't often relate to young people this way either.

2.3   CONCEPTIONS OF CHILDHOOD

PCT was never intended to be a psychology reserved for fully formed minds. Kelly wrote of human passions and ambitions and his model of humankind has implications for us all, big or small. So the notion of people as personal scientists who construct and test their evolving theories about themselves and the worlds they inhabit applies to young and old alike. As Salmon (1985) noted, this contrasts markedly with the traditional tenets of developmental psychology. 'We think of childhood as essentially entailing incompetence. Children's lack of competence forms the constant basic theme of psychological research, which typically focuses on what a child cannot do rather than on what she or he can. More generally we view the young in the perspective of helplessness, ignorance, neediness – as requiring to be guided, taught, brought up.'

Such pathologizing of the young has been splendidly satirized in a spoof medical paper penned by Jordan Smoller entitled 'The etiology and treatment of childhood' (Smoller, 1987). His po-faced account lists the defining clinical features of this unfortunate condition of childhood as:

- Congenital onset
- Dwarfism
- Emotional lability and immaturity
- Knowledge deficits
- Legume anorexia (aka refusal to eat up your veg!).

The author wryly observes that despite the seriousness of these symptoms almost all sufferers seem to recover in time. It's a playful thought that conveys a very important message. If the dominant story we tell ourselves about young people emphasizes their limitations and immaturity, there is a danger that adults will struggle to recognize and respect the pertinence of children's understandings of their lives. They will inevitably fail to adopt a credulous approach.

2.4   CULTURAL MARKERS

The TV series *Star Trek* has a long-standing record of inventing plots set in unlikely future worlds inhabited by implausible aliens that offer a convincing sideways commentary on life on Earth at the present moment – or at least life in contemporary USA. One such episode, entitled 'Rascals', centres around an accidental transformer malfunction (a dramatic device much loved by *Star Trek* scriptwriters) that has a freakish effect on Captain Jean-Luc Picard and three other members of his crew. Their bodies have become rejuvenated to such an extent that all now have the physical appearance of 12-year-olds but, crucially to the plotline, retain their full 'adult' mental capacities. In a series of nicely observed scenes the remainder of the grown-up crew members of the Starship Enterprise are portrayed as struggling ineffectually to take their captain at all seriously in his new youthful guise. In very short order Picard is obliged to resign his leadership role as he too cannot envisage anyone with his boyish appearance carrying the authority required of a commander.

This brief entertainment has been carefully deconstructed by a theoretical physicist called David Deutsch (1997) in a paper provocatively entitled 'The final prejudice'. Deutsch notes how the circumstances aboard the ship have been carefully arranged like some elegantly designed psychological experiment so that only one variable has been manipulated. All that has changed about Captain Picard is his physical appearance. In all other ways he is precisely the man he was prior to the transformer malfunction. Furthermore beneath their Starfleet uniforms the crew of *The Enterprise* have far from uniform bodily characteristics. One senior staff member is an android. We also know that during their many inter-galactic adventures these selfsame individuals have managed to develop courteous ways of communicating with all manner of odd-looking creatures. However the point of this conceit is that, as Deutsch observes, 'there is one shape, and one shape alone only, that disqualifies a person from receiving the respect of his fellow human beings. And that is the shape of a human child.'

As ever this cautionary tale is intended as a commentary on our culture. The 'Rascals' episode inevitably ends happily. The youthful appearance of Picard works to his advantage as he is able to outwit the loathsome Ferengi who have invaded *The Enterprise*. The resourceful ship's surgeon Dr Crocker finds a 'cure' for the captain's malaise and he and his colleagues are returned to their former age-appropriate appearance. All's well, that ends well. However, Deutsch is not convinced that our culture's prejudice against recognizing the competence of children will be so readily righted. Taking a credulous approach in communicating with young people still unfortunately runs against the cultural grain.

2.5   SOCIAL CONSTRUCTIONIST EXPLANATIONS

Personal construct theory, as its name unambiguously announces, has a focus on the unique manner in which individuals make sense of their experience. The allied field of social constructionism (Burr, 1995) has, by contrast, placed a greater emphasis on the common belief systems held by communities and the cultural origins and social implications of those shared understandings. Adopting an openly political stance, rarely revealed in Kelly's writings, authors in the social constructionist tradition argue that the explanatory ideas available to members of any society are subject to considerable cultural constraints. While in theory the meaning of anything that exists can be reconstrued, in practice we tend to draw upon a limited number of socially sanctioned ways of looking at our world. One consequence of this common cultural heritage is that these dominant narratives serve to uphold the social status quo within a community. So men from a strict Muslim tradition might cite religious scriptures to justify denying their womenfolk equal political rights in their society. Men in Victorian England used different arguments, perhaps invoking beliefs about the inherent frailty of the female constitution to support their position, but the point of their discourse was identical. Those who are currently in charge, should stay in charge!

One widely established power dynamic in human relationships is that adults in general and parents in particular make decisions on behalf of children. Social constructionist theory would predict that we have a number of popularly supported justifications for adopting this blatantly undemocratic position. We probably do. Try the following personal construct experiment designed using Denis Hinkle's notion of the Resistance-to-Change grid:

Here are two provided constructs concerning what we might broadly term good parenting. We will assume that the preferred poles (i.e. how we would like to see ourselves and be seen by others) are obvious.

Enable your children to make their own decisions

VERSUS

Discourage your children from making their own decisions

Protect your children from possible harm

VERSUS

Fail to protect your children from possible harm

Hinkle (1965) devised an uncomfortable question that he anticipated would reveal which constructs matter most in an individual's particular scheme of things. First of all position yourself on a seven-point scale where a score of one represents the positive pole and seven the negative pole on the two constructs provided. If you are not a parent yourself, rate your own parents in the same way. Now here's the rub. You are invited to make an awkward choice. You must alter your view of yourself (or your parents) on one of these two dimensions in the direction of the non-preferred pole. The construct on which your resistance to change is stronger is judged to be 'superordinate' in

Kelly's terminology. Which is worse for a parent – to see themselves as failing to help their offspring think for themselves or failing to protect them from danger? The prediction is that the latter option will win (almost) every time.

If our predominant conception of childhood is that youngsters experience a lengthy period when their relative immaturity and incompetence render them vulnerable to mishap, it follows that we expect responsible adults to ensure their continued safety. The public opprobrium that is heaped on any parent who ignores this powerful social injunction, by for example nipping down the pub and leaving an infant unsupervised, is an indicator of its cultural importance. Sometimes the State is even prepared to remove children from their parents' care if they are considered to be inadequately protected from risk. In the UK the relevant legislation – The Children Act (Department of Health, 1989) – directs courts to pay heed to young people's preferences in these situations, but ultimately to act 'in the best interests of the child' – as perceived by the adult community. Fortunately there are few contexts in which parents are faced with having to choose between respecting their child's opinions and ensuring their well-being. Healthcare settings can prove a notable exception.

2.6 THE SERIOUSLY ILL CHILD

Although therapeutic outcomes in paediatric oncology have improved markedly in the last 20 years, families are well aware that a significant minority of those suffering from childhood cancer do not survive into adulthood. We can reasonably assume that parents will feel highly protective towards their children in these circumstances. There will also be several complicated treatment decisions to be taken – sometimes urgently. Do the adults involved in these tense discussions tend to communicate in a credulous manner with the young person whose future is in such evident jeopardy? An observational study conducted in Leicester (Young et al., 2003) suggested that in this time of crisis parents and oncologist made minimal efforts to involve the young patient in their conversations. 'Relegated to non-participant status' is the blunt term the researchers chose to describe this recurrent dynamic. Of course there may be practical rather than cultural reasons why the young person played such a peripheral role in these consultations. The symptoms of the illness itself or the side effects of powerful drugs may have temporarily diminished both their competence and confidence. However, a systematic overview of research conducted on communication patterns between paediatricians and families across a wide range of contexts (Meeuwesen and Kaptein, 1996) provided evidence that the sidelining of young people in medical discussions of their cases is likely to be the norm rather than the exception.

Sceptical readers may find themselves reflecting that there is nothing surprising in the one-sided nature of any doctor–patient communication. Children are just getting the same treatment as everyone else! There have, however, been political pressures on the medical establishment to recognize the wisdom that comes from long experience of illness. The 'Expert Patient' movement seeks to mobilize the knowledge and understanding of sufferers from a wide variety of complaints so that the design and delivery of health services can be informed by the user's perspective (Department of Health, 2001). This explicit recognition of consumer competence is entirely in line with Kelly's previously quoted assertion that 'the customer is always right'. We will return to the theme of expertise in clinical practice later. In the UK the Department of Health has organized a nationwide training programme to recruit potential 'expert' patients and train them for this new and influential role. Nobody under the age of 18 need apply . . .

2.7   OLDER AND WISER?

This sudden acknowledgement of capability once a young person has 'come of age' happens again and again. You become eligible to drive a car; buy an alcoholic drink; consent to sexual relations; get married; have a credit card; and vote – the ultimate responsibility in a democratic society. These transformations occur instantly. Yesterday you couldn't. Today you can. To paraphrase Cole Porter: 'How strange the change from minor to major . . . '

Of course young people don't change overnight when they reach their eighteenth or twenty-first birthdays, but society's construal of their competence does. It therefore follows that this reconstruction is itself open to revision. A multidisciplinary team of researchers in the USA has recently argued that social and economic changes in Western industrial societies have altered expectations that individuals will consider themselves to have entered adulthood in their twenties (Settersten, Furstenberg and Rumbaut, 2005). They have therefore proposed that a new developmental stage of 'emerging adulthood' should follow adolescence in the textbooks of life-cycle psychology. The old markers of feeling grown-up – becoming financially independent of your parents and starting a family of your own for example – seem neither as achievable nor as salient to the current generation of twenty-somethings as they were to the 'baby-boomers' who bred them. As a consequence participants in Settersten's research had developed alternative criteria by which to gauge their progress in life, such as their capacity to establish and maintain satisfying personal relationships. However, even when adopting this contemporary yardstick many young Americans in the twenty-first century apparently continue to construe themselves as in some senses 'immature' adults well into their thirties. The implications of this stance contrast vividly with the personal and social expectations of young adults in previous generations, as illustrated by the following story:

> A psychologist colleague told of the satisfaction he had gained from suddenly getting to know his father-in-law some thirty years after having married his

daughter. In the intimate setting of his local pub the older man had dropped his past reserve and started to disclose some of his wartime experiences. As well as poignantly recalling lost comrades-in-arms, he also casually revealed that at the age of 22 he had been fighting as a gun-spotter in the Royal Artillery supporting the allied advance in Northern France. A large group of Luftwaffe airmen had become isolated behind the front line and, wary of vengeful reprisals from the local French resistance, wished to surrender to the British army. As the senior British officer in the town it fell to this young captain to accept the surrender and ensure the subsequent safety of his prisoners – which he did.

At the time of writing the authors of this volume have three sons in their early twenties. Without being disloyal to our lads, we struggle to imagine them shouldering any comparable responsibilities. Trusting them to take a phone message seems challenge enough on occasions! Young men probably do not change much across the generations, though our constructions of their capabilities undoubtedly do.

2.8   CULTURAL VARIABILITY

As the old adage goes 'the past is a foreign country; they do things differently there', and we do not need to look backwards in time to note conceptions of childhood that differ markedly from our own. We could look around to the child-rearing practices of other contemporary cultures that challenge our 'West is best' assumptions. The anthropologist Michelle Johnson noted how much Fulani families in West Africa expect of their daughters (Johnson, 2000). By the age of four girls are expected to care for their younger siblings and to fetch water and firewood. By the age of six they will be adept at pounding grain and producing milk and butter.

There will be other settings in which necessity demands that young people make significant social and economic contributions to their communities at a much earlier stage than we consider normal, or even healthy, from our particular cultural standpoint. When we read of the mental health problems of child labourers in Ethiopia (Fekadu, Alem and Hagglof, 2006) or the tragic lives of boy soldiers in the Angolan civil war the moral superiority of the values underpinning our notion of childhood may seem self-evident. However, a recent report jointly produced by UNICEF and Save the Children has argued that traditional Western psychology's inattention to the 'evolving capacities' of young people has resulted in a widespread failure to respect their fundamental human rights (Lansdown, 2005). The paper proposes that a new balance be struck between our continuing wish to protect children from harm and our ethical responsibility to give them an age-appropriate voice in the many decisions that affect their lives.

2.9   WINDS OF CHANGE

There is something inexorable about cultural change. As individuals we are continuously caught up in a tide of subtle but powerful social influences that we struggle to understand, leave alone resist. The clothes we choose to wear; the names we give to our children; our political ideologies; all these apparently autonomous personal decisions are largely determined by the 'zeitgeist' of our times. So the attitudes we adopt in our communications with young people will likely go with the prevailing cultural flow. But there is always some room for manoeuvre. We can 'position' ourselves slightly differently in our conversations (Davies and Harre, 1990) so the hierarchy of our exchanges is flattened. When a parent's account of their offspring's conduct is in danger of becoming a ceaseless catalogue of complaint we can deliberately search out stories of competence and success. Above all we can listen carefully and credulously to what our young charges have to say for themselves. It is from these small incremental shifts that significant social change is fashioned.

The remainder of this book contains, we hope, a variety of suggestions about how adults can engage in credulous conversations with children and why it might prove worth their while to do so. Those wishing to conduct formal psychological research can also consult a number of contemporary publications with innovative suggestions for recruiting young people into their enquiries (Fraser *et al.*, 2004; Greene and Hogan, 2005). Creative feedback systems have been established whereby children's opinions as service users (be they patient or pupil) can inform the quality of their future care (e.g. Ross, 2003).

There remain nonetheless many circumstances in which young people are not routinely 'taken at their word'. Alexa Hepburn published an account of research into conversations between young callers to a child protection helpline in the UK and the social workers who staff the service (Hepburn, 2005). Two discussions between young female callers (aged 12 and 13, respectively) and their allocated telephone counsellor were closely analysed. Both girls had contacted the helpline because they were worried that a close friend was being sexually abused. The verbatim recordings of these conversations illustrate how hard the young callers have to try to justify their concerns in the face of what they interpret as disbelieving responses from the adult at the other end of the phone. Both their motives for calling and the adequacy of the evidence on which their fears are based seem to be called into question. The study does not attempt a comparison with the discourse between the counsellors and adult callers to the NSPCC helpline. However actions, such as referral to the police, occur disproportionately more frequently in response to adults' as opposed to children's concerns.

The paper is entitled 'You're not takin' me seriously' ...

CHAPTER 3

THE FRAMEWORK OF PERSONAL CONSTRUCT THEORY

It has been mooted on a number of occasions that George Kelly was some-what ambivalent about the publication of his two volumes entitled *The*

Psychology of Personal Constructs. Those who knew him personally, such as Don Bannister and Fay Fransella, felt Kelly himself was unsure about the wisdom of seeking publication, although he remained passionately committed to his theory. He spent many years elaborating the theory through discussion of his ideas and chapters with his students at 'Thursday night' groups held at his house in Columbus, Ohio. Fransella (1995) discussed Kelly's reservations about publication, suggesting that he felt the psychological community in 1955, dominated by the contrasting themes of environmental determinism of behaviourism and the intra-psychic musings of classical psychoanalysis, was not ready to accept the radical nature of his theory.

Fay Fransella (1995) further noted that Kelly felt his theory would 'sink or swim in British waters', a prediction fascinatingly confirmed by Robert Neimeyer's socio-historical account of the early development of PCT (Neimeyer, 1985). Kelly's work remained largely overlooked by the wider psychological fraternity until Don Bannister stumbled across it on the dusty shelves of the University of London library, whilst searching for a psychological theory that made sense to him in his endeavours to pursue a PhD. Staying with the seafaring metaphor, it is appealing to wonder if Kelly's ideas would have remained sunk without trace had not Bannister conducted such a thorough trawl of the library shelves.

Don Bannister sought to test Kelly's ideas rigorously, particularly his principle that behaviour, however perplexing to an observer, represents the individual's search for meaning, in the field of schizophrenic thought disorder. Rather than judge or diagnose the individual on the basis of his sometimes 'bizarre' behaviour, Bannister ventured to see the behaviour as an experiment. He wished to know what experiment the person was engaged in which made him behave in such a way. Bannister's mode of enquiry was fundamentally based on the notion of understanding the person from the person's perspective, not seeking to fit him into a nosological category or a pet theory we may have about why others behave in the ways they do. Bannister's impetus slowly gained momentum, and workers in a range of professional settings began to test out the usefulness of the theory on issues pertinent to them.

Kelly meticulously described the structure of his theory. According to Fransella (1995), this tallied with one aspect of his own psychological functioning which she described as his 'almost obsessive concern for detail'. Whether Kelly's own background as a physicist and mathematician contributed to this remains open to question. His immersion in methodology and precision did, however, seem to influence his metaphorical notion of the person as a scientist. Kelly invited the clinician or therapist to regard the person 'as if' he or she were a scientist. As Fransella (1995) suggests, this leads us to consider that it is the person who 'conducts his or her own personal experiments to test out their construing of events' and the test we use is our own behaviour.

3.1 FORMALITY OF THE THEORY

Kelly (1955) presented his theory in the form of a fundamental postulate and 11 corollaries (Bannister and Fransella, 1986). The fundamental postulate states that *a person's processes are psychologically channelized by the ways in which he anticipates events*. Essentially Kelly was viewing the individual as striving for personal meaning. He argued that individuals grapple to understand their world. They perceive similarities and themes in the events before them, propose theories about such events, foster anticipations about the future and seek to test continually how much sense has been made of the world through their behaviour.

The world, it might seem, is composed of events. These are the objects or happenings with which we are continually faced. Kelly preferred to call them *elements*. They make up both the physical and psychological world within which we function. Quite how we make sense of the myriad of elements is the question Kelly was seeking to address in his formal description of the theory. He chose to outline this carefully with 11 corollaries, summarized here (Figure 3.1) in the form of a diagram.

By way of illustrating the corollaries, the case of Robert, a 10-year-old boy, will be explored. He was referred by his general practitioner because of concerns over 'hyperactive' behaviour. A school report told of Robert's difficulty in maintaining concentration, with his mother expressing concerns about the way he was 'always on the go'. A brief interview with Robert highlighted something about how he made sense of himself. He was invited to 'tell me three ways that best describe the way you are', a credulous invite, given the first interview. Such questioning proved undemanding for Robert who eagerly suggested 'active', 'arty' and 'helpful', in that order. Perhaps, given the primacy of 'active', he too construed himself, as others had labelled him, as possibly overactive.

'Active', 'arty' and 'helpful', can be considered as *emergent poles* of three constructs. Kelly described the emergent pole of a construct as *the one which embraces most of the immediately perceived context*. Asking Robert to describe the contrast to these poles by suggesting he might describe how someone *not* active, *not* arty and *not* helpful might be, produced the *implicit* or contrasting pole of each construct. Robert offered:

Active _____ Boring

Arty _____ Writer

Helpful _____ Sit around and don't do anything

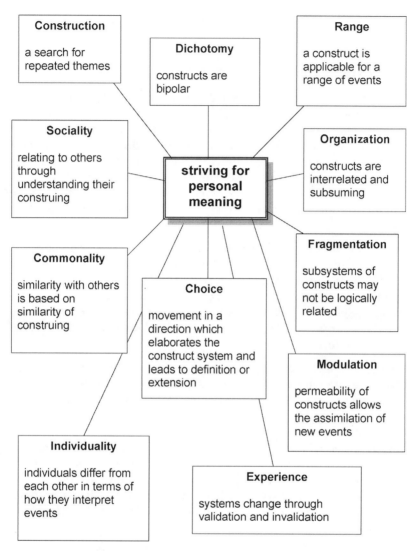

Figure 3.1 A diagrammatic summary of Kelly's corollaries.

Kelly considered the building blocks of his theory to be constructs. His *di-chotomy corollary* suggests that *a person's construction system is composed of a finite number of dichotomous constructs.* Robert had eagerly produced three on request, but probably had a whole lot more in his repertoire of self-descriptions (although interestingly Kelly stated a finite number), that enabled him to anticipate events before him. Robert was next invited to elaborate the meaning of these three constructs. Two questions pertaining to each construct often prove fruitful in furthering an understanding of a youngster's construing:

- 'Which end (of the two poles of the construct) would you prefer to be at?' This is marked with *P*.

- 'When you are active (taking one pole of a construct) could you tell me three things that you are doing?' Alternatively the question can be phrased in terms of what other people do when they are being active. This form of questioning is called *pyramiding*. It seeks to understand the actions or behaviours that underpin the construct. Robert's responses for each construct were as follows:

Active _____ Boring
P
Playing games a lot
Running around
Playing sport
Arty _____ Writing
P
Building things
Drawing
Painting
Helpful _____ Sit around doing nothing
P
Tidy up
If someone is stuck, try and help
(Robert only provided two responses here)

With Robert's responses there is a suggestion that rather than perceiving himself as hyperactive, he construes himself more of a boy of action. Robert adopts an active mode, by which he means playing, tidying up and helping others, rather than be engaged at the contrast end of the constructs which imply boredom and sitting around doing nothing.

3.2   CONSTRUCTS

The properties of a construct can be understood in terms of the following:

- An abstraction arising from an awareness of a similarity and a contrast between events. Robert had formulated this construction about himself by noticing repeated themes in the way he was behaving and contrasting this with the actions of others who did not behave in a similar way. Kelly summarized this in his *construction corollary*, which suggests *a person anticipates events by construing their replications*.

- Constructs are bipolar. The relationship between the two poles of a construct is one of contrast. Robert's three constructs contrast boring with active, writing with arty and sitting around not doing anything with helpful. It is such contrast, insisted Kelly, which provides meaning. Thus 'thoughtful' might, for example, be contrasted with 'impulsive' (a dimension concerned with contemplation) or alternatively, with 'inconsiderate' (concerned with attentiveness and caring). The contrast to 'sad' may be 'happy' (emotion) or 'cool' (presentation); whereas the contrast to 'stupid' may be 'bright' (intelligence) or 'sensible' (behavioural). Seeking the contrast for any elicited construct therefore crucially enhances an understanding of the child's construing.

- Constructs arise out of an individual's personal experience and as such are considered to be fundamentally their own. Robert's constructs are his alone. They are his discriminations about the world and remain unique to him. Anyone else, in a similar situation, might have perceived different themes, similarities and contrasts.

- Constructs are a means whereby an individual discriminates the events with which they come into contact. On meeting other children, Robert might construe them as active if they play sport, boring if they don't. He might also anticipate that those children he construes as active will also be interested in playing games. When he comes across someone who tidies up, Robert's means of construing suggests he would anticipate that he or she is also helpful. On a similar theme, a child entering a library is likely to be drawn to a section from which they have previously found books that are riveting reads and ignore sections they anticipate hold books which are boring. Such a theory about books, hinged on a construct 'riveting–boring' operates to 'simplify' the environment. The same child might then employ a whole series of other discriminating constructs to help them decide which particular book to borrow. Chapter 7 describes how intricate patterns of construing can be built up around subject areas through ever more elaborate discriminations, in ways that herald the individual as an expert or connoisseur. Although books are considered to be physical elements, the same applies for psychological elements. Thus a youngster's previous contact with librarians might lead them to be construed as helpful, respecting of literature, quiet, intelligent and likely to wear glasses. If, however, the child hits upon one who grimly admonishes them for returning a book late, he or she is faced with having to re-construe their understanding of librarians.

- Individuals do not appeal to their construct system in order to act, but they *are* their construct system. Robert's notion of himself as helpful would move him, for example, towards someone he perceived was stuck. He wouldn't refer to his construing before acting. Ravenette (1997) has suggested that asking children to consider their means of construing, as Robert had been asked to do, might be the first time they are consciously aware of their means of construing. Much of a child's construing might therefore be considered to lie at a low level of awareness.

- The abstraction may or may not, have verbal markers. Robert was effortlessly able to provide verbal labels for the elicited constructs. However, constructs are foremost the discriminations we make, not the labels we attach to them. Kelly referred to 'unlabelled' constructs as *preverbal*, possibly emerging before the child has command of speech and which continue to be employed even though the individual has no consistent word symbol.

- Should a youngster take another person's verbal markers as a basis for a construct, he or she will invest it with their own personal meanings. Robert's notion of being active seemed categorically different from the pathological vision of activity that adults conferred upon him. Kelly's *individuality corollary*, which states that *persons differ from each other in their constructions of events*, stresses the uniqueness of each person's construing, even where they may attach similar verbal labels to their discriminations. The contrast end of a construct helps define the meaning. Thus Robert contrasted active with boring, whereas many adults might perceive the contrast in terms of a lack of energy, laziness or indeed 'normal' activity levels. From a sentence completion task of over five hundred adolescents asked to consider how they would describe themselves, we found a number of descriptions that occurred only once. What is interesting about many of these 'unique' constructs – competitive; difficult; disobedient; dreamer; impulsive; motivated; outspoken; patient; self-centred and untidy – is that such construing is often employed by adults such as parents and teachers in their observations of such youngsters.

3.3   ELEMENTS

Constructs, according to Kelly's *range corollary*, are *convenient for the anticipation of a finite range of events only*. Robert's construct 'arty–writing' might well prove useful in approaching school work, constructional play and homework, but is perhaps less fruitful in mending a puncture, playing the one-armed bandit, fishing for sticklebacks or negotiating with his parents a raise in his pocket money. Would it matter a jot to Robert whether he addressed these activities as an artist or as a writer?

A construct thus has a range of convenience, best suited to a particular set of events or elements. The range may, of course, be very wide or very narrow. Young children's constructs tend to have a wide range of convenience where events and eventualities are 'good' or 'bad', 'fair' or 'unfair', to be 'loved' or 'hated'. Such overarching constructs seem applicable to most events with which young children are confronted. Robert's construct 'active–boring' has a similar feel in being potentially applicable to numerous events. The range of a construct appears to narrow as an individual develops an expertise or connoisseurship in a particular area.

Constructs of course are never fixed. They vary in terms of how permeable they are in accommodating new events or elements. Were Robert to try drama, cycling or fire-setting and these were accommodated as either active or boring, then his construct would be considered permeable. Kelly encapsulated this idea in the *modulation corollary*, which states that *the variation in a person's construction system is limited by the permeability of the constructs within whose range of convenience the variants lie*. A construct is permeable if it admits new elements, and impermeable if it rejects elements on the basis of their newness.

3.4   STRUCTURE

Constructs rarely stand alone. Kelly suggested they are both interrelated and subsuming. He described this in the *organization corollary*, which states that *each person characteristically evolves, for their convenience in anticipating events, a construction system embracing ordinal relationships between constructs*. There is a hint in the contrast poles of two of Robert's constructs – boring; sit around doing nothing – that these two constructs are closely aligned to one another. Were Robert to feel like tidying up (a behavioural expression of his helpfulness) after a game, the construct *active* might become more closely aligned to *helpful*. Thus for Robert helpful might come to imply active.

Kelly's notion of constructs subsuming other constructs is described in terms of superordinacy and subordinacy. Pyramiding is one way of elaborating subordinate constructs. Thus 'building things' for Robert is subordinate to being arty. When engaged in construction tasks Robert would perceive himself as arty. One implies the other. Laddering, on the other hand, is a means of eliciting superordinate constructs. Usually, with youngsters, this requires asking 'how come?' one pole of a construct is preferred. Robert, with some hesitation, said he preferred to be active because 'If you're bored, you don't do much', arty because he didn't like writing a lot, and helpful because it was boring to sit around not doing anything. Robert had struggled to expand a more superordinate level. With youngsters this is not unusual. Many children hold very permeable superordinate constructs often of a moral nature such as 'good–bad', enabling most events to be extrapolated as good or bad. Not being allowed an ice cream means a child perceives his mother as bad; a teacher who listens to the latest music is ace. With development emerges a more hierarchical structure, with psychological constructs such as Robert's active, arty and helpful sandwiched between subordinate behavioural notions and superordinate maxims. This will be elaborated further in Chapter 6.

As a construct system grows and evolves, subsystems of construing develop. Thus Robert might have a very different set of constructs when it comes to coping with his awkward and resentful brother. Helpfulness might not play any part in Robert's construing of such an event. Further, were Robert to take up trainspotting, for example, he might discover a new set of constructs which service this occasion better, including perhaps the benefit of 'sitting around doing nothing'. Kelly described this aspect of construing in the *fragmentation corollary*, which states that *a person may successfully employ a variety of construction systems which are inferentially incompatible with each other*. Fascinatingly, a darts player may have a superordinate view of self as innumerate but can calculate the best way 'out' in nanoseconds.

3.5   COMPARISON WITH OTHERS

Diagnostic ventures intrinsically seek to fit a perception of the child's problem into a predetermined category of disorder. Much research also aims to select participants by adopting thorough inclusion and exclusion criteria, assuming homogeneity of the sample is secured. Such procedures, argued Kelly, are crucially flawed. The *commonality corollary* suggests that *to the extent that one person employs a construction of experience which is similar to that employed by another, his or her processes are psychologically similar to those of the other person*.

Youngsters are thus similar, not in terms of an 'outsider's hypothesis, but in terms of their own typical ways of construing. Whatever the 'outside' consensus of Robert's hyperactivity, any similarity with other children given a comparable diagnosis is wide of the mark. An understanding of Robert's self-construing gives this away. This is not to say that Robert cannot be understood as like other children. He might be considered similar to other children (or adults) who are guided by a sense of action, a wish to be involved and a distaste of boredom. Commonality is being 'like-minded'.

The approach employed to understand how Robert construed his self has been applied across large groups of children and adolescents in non-clinical contexts in two major cities (Leeds and Newcastle) in the north of England (Butler, 2001). In response to being invited to 'tell me three ways that best describe the way you are', something about how youngsters employ constructs both commonly and uniquely is being illuminated. Table 3.1 presents the 'top ten' most frequently elicited constructs to this self-description inquiry, by gender and age band with children (7–11 years) and adolescents (12–16 years).

Frequency of elicitation is one means of harnessing constructs that are shared by the population and which therefore may be considered to have a sense of

Table 3.1 Top ten most frequently elicited constructs by age band and gender

Children (7–11 yr) (n = 118)		Adolescents (12–16 yr) (n = 533)	
Male	Female	Male	Female
Funny	Happy	Funny	Friendly
Happy	Funny	Friendly	Happy
Sporty	Friendly	Kind	Kind
Kind	Helpful	Sporty	Funny
Nice	Kind	Stupid	Loud
Helpful	Shy	Happy	Quiet
Friendly	Cheeky	Trustworthy	Trustworthy
In trouble	Sporty	Nice	Nasty
Cheeky	Brainy	Boring	Nice
Hard-working	Moody	Helpful	Shy
		Fun to be with	Fun to be with

commonality. 'Funny' was found to be the most frequently elicited construct for boys at all ages whereas for girls, 'happy' and 'friendly' are consistently elicited very frequently throughout childhood and adolescence. Males are more likely to refer to themselves as 'sporty' whereas girls more likely to construe themselves as 'shy'. Children frequently construe their self as 'cheeky' whereas adolescents think of themselves as 'trustworthy'. Those constructs realized by particular aspects of the population include 'in trouble' and 'hard-working' with male children; 'brainy' and 'moody' with female children; 'stupid' and 'boring' with male adolescents; and 'loud', 'quiet' and 'nasty' amongst adolescent girls.

3.6   RELATIONSHIPS WITH OTHERS

A central tenet of Kelly's theory and one particularly salient for those in a profession designed to help others, is the notion of sociality. Kelly stated in the *sociality corollary* that *to the extent that one person construes the construction process of another they may play a role in a social process involving the other person*. This suggests that the success of any interaction with another person is based on the degree to which each person understands the other. Had we sought to understand Robert by way of a behaviour checklist, observation of his behaviour in class, an interview with his mother and a school report, a framework or 'external' description of his behaviour would no doubt have been attained. However, such accomplishments would depict nothing of how Robert considered his own behaviour. The sociality corollary suggests an understanding of the other person's construing best fosters a relationship. It does not imply that the two individuals have similar construct systems, but that they are prepared to take a leap in understanding how each ticks. It may be that Robert's cat made a better stab at understanding him than adults who sought to impose a diagnostic framework upon his behaviour. His cat was able to detect when it was advisable to pester Robert for food and a stroke and when, during his arty times, to leave well alone.

3.7   MOVEMENT

Bannister and Fransella (1986) describe people as 'in business to anticipate events and if they do this by developing personal construct systems, then they will move in those directions which seem to make most sense'. This means in directions which seem to elaborate their construct system. Thus it might be predicted that Robert would endeavour to be active, arty and helpful and seek to avoid boredom and writing. Kelly chose the *choice corollary* to define the direction of a person's movement. This states that *persons choose for themselves that alternative in a dichotomized construct through which they anticipate the greatest possibility for the elaboration of their system*. In electing to pursue a direction, 'being active' in Robert's case, a child is also clarifying and confirming a view of himself as active (Kelly called this *definition*). Thus each time Robert elects to play sport he asserts, in ever greater detail, his notion of himself as active. Additionally the choice, in Robert's case, to be active may lead to further elaboration of the system through what Kelly called *extension*. Should Robert be tempted to tackle his homework or clean out the rabbit hutch in his active way he may, as it were, be reaching out to increase the range of his construct system by exploring new areas. Thus, a choice to act in a certain way elaborates the construct by increased definition and possible extension.

Construct systems are continually developing and changing. They change in relation to the accuracy of the anticipations. Predictions will sometimes be correct. Robert might take to a new sport, such as rugby, in his active mode with an anticipation of enjoyment and evasion of boredom. His anticipations might prove correct and his notion of self as active and sporting would therefore be validated. Sometimes, of course, predictions can be found wanting. Should Robert take up snooker, for example, with the same anticipation, he may well be invalidated. Robert might thus attach snooker to the boring pole of the construct, active–boring. He might re-construe snooker as not a sport at all or redefine his notion of 'playing sport' as those activities which involve a degree of running around.

Kelly employed the *experience corollary* to describe the change in a construct system. This states that *a person's construction system varies as he or she successively construes the replication of events*. All change necessarily involves a change in self-construing. Robert might have a greater sense of himself as sporting should he enjoy rugby and a more selective view of self as sporting were he to find snooker boring. Change within a person's construct system, Kelly argued, leads to the experience of emotion.

3.8   EMOTIONS

Whilst a youngster's construing of self, others and the world they inhabit is constantly changing and developing, there are times when validational fortune makes change or resistance to change a matter of concern. We may determinedly seek to avoid change, opting to secure further evidence of the way we are. Alternatively we seek the challenge of new experiences and fresh elaboration of our self. We may become conscious that our way of construing is becoming unhelpful or discover that significant others assuredly value our way of being. We may be challenged by a realization that we have acted in a manner we would not have expected of ourself or sense something troubling in having to face situations we perhaps don't feel easily equipped to deal with. In such predicaments, construing comes into question. Kelly postulated that consequent reverberations in the construct system give rise to feeling. Hence emotions have been conceptualized as arising when constructs are in *transition*.

Although emotions remain phenomenological experiences, typically expressed in terms of 'I feel ... ', folk often consider or construe themselves in emotional terms. A survey of self-descriptions with children, adolescents (Butler, 2001) and adults (Butler and Gasson, 2004) revealed many 'emotional' terms in reference to the self. Happy, moody, easily upset and bad-tempered were amongst the most frequent self-descriptions elicited with children; happy, sad, moody, easily upset and worrier were frequently elicited as adolescent self-descriptions; whilst happy, cheerful, shy, warm, anxious, worrier and calm emerged as frequent descriptions amongst an adult population. Perhaps recurrent experience of emotional states leads individuals into making sense by construing themselves in emotional terms.

There prevails the thorny issue of what constitutes an emotion. Some feeling states, such as happy, sad, guilty, angry and anxious appear universally accepted, whereas others, such as humour, worry, invention, love and wonder survive as mysteries within psychology because they make no sense viewed as either 'cognitive' or 'affective' (Bannister, 1977) and as such tend to remain free from the shackles of psychological experimentation.

Emotions within a PCT perspective are regarded as

- *Phenomenological experiences* being internal events, concerning predictions one makes regarding the self in certain circumstances. They do not refer to an observer's assessment of what a person may be experiencing. Thus within PCT, terms such as hostility refer to the experience of the person, rather than how others may be affected by the person's acts.

• Defined in terms of '*awareness*' that the construct system is in a transitional state. Being in a state of awareness of some fate of the construct system is the essential aspect that distinguishes behaviour regarded as emotion from behaviour regarded as non-emotional (McCoy, 1977).

• *Psychological processes*: Emotions are hypothesized as emerging from a sense that one's construct system is in need of revision, elaboration or change.

• *Value- free*: The process is resultant on construing and in itself carries no positive or negative valence, although the experience is appraised by the individual usually in such terms.

Kelly intriguing sketched only six emotions, framed in terms of the following dimensions:

• validation versus invalidation of construing

• anticipated change in the construct system

• goodness of fit between actions and self-construing

• adeptness of the construct system to meet new events

• a means of elaborating or preserving the construct system.

Mildred McCoy (1977) sought to elaborate Kelly's original model of emotional experience, without undermining his expressed intention that the experience of emotion arises when the person is undergoing a change to the construct system. She both fleshed out Kelly's dimensions and proposed another – the fit between the person's construct system and another person's system – in expounding a further 13 emotional states. In the following brief discussion a further expansion of emotions are presented with Kelly's original definitions marked (*) and McCoy's elaboration marked with (**).

3.8.1   Validational Issues

Validation might be understood in a variety of forms – an anticipation that turns out the way we expected; a perceived acknowledgement from others confirming the view we have of ourself; or an active striving to confirm the way we are (a Kellyan choice to define our self in a particular way). The contrast to validation appears to be both invalidation, where anticipations turn out not to be the case, and the loss of validation, where the source of previous validational experiences disappears. When considered in relation to the organization or structure of self-construing – core, psychological and behaviour – a flavour of differing emotional experiences may be outlined:

Structure	Validation	Loss of validation	Invalidation
Core	**Love –* validation of one's core structure	*Grief, dejection, despondency –* loss of validational experiences	*Rage, fury –* invalidation of core construing
Psychological	**Happiness –* validation of one's psychological view of self	**Sadness, misery –* loss of an element that may otherwise have validated important aspects of self	**Anger –* invalidation which leads to hostile behaviour
Behaviour	**Satisfaction –* validation of a non-core structure	*Pensive –* opportunity to engage in tasks that may prove validating is denied	*Tantrum, temper, annoyance –* invalidation of a person's behaviour

Love (**) in essence amounts to validation of a person's sense of identity. It is the feelings associated with an acceptance of one's core construing, by a significant other, such as a parent. Love is the phenomenological experience, the sense arising from an acknowledgement of one's core construing, not one's feelings towards another, although a significant other may be 'loved' as the source of one's validational experiences. Because love is phenomenological it may not necessarily be reciprocated. One individual may experience love through being validated yet may not be a validational source for the other. Happiness (**) is the sense of feeling good, elated or joyful and arises, according to McCoy (1977), when a part of the core construing is validated. It may alternatively be considered to arise from validational experiences at a psychological level. Good performances for the sporting, making others laugh for those with a sense of humour or, in Robert's case, successfully helping someone who was stuck or complete a drawing to his satisfaction, would validate his vision of self as respectively helpful and arty. Satisfaction (**) arises with the sense of fulfilment after the completion of an activity, particularly one which challenges the view of self. A finished painting, a completed jigsaw, a computer game solved, a satisfactory piece of homework concluded, all invariably lead to a sense of achievement and sometimes a feeling of relief. A youngster may feel satisfied if an event turned out negatively, provided they predicted it would. Thus the 'I told you so' feeling experienced by children when demonstrating their predicted incompetence.

Grief, along with the associated feelings of despondency, despair, dejection and hopelessness may be understood as arising from a sense of loss, in which a significant source of validational experience disappears. Bereavement, being removed from the family and loss of functioning as a result of illness may all reduce the opportunity of core constructs being validated. Sadness (**) according to McCoy (1977) may arise from invalidation although it may also arise from feelings of loss where important elements fail to remain within the range of convenience of a person's constructs. Thus losing a friend reduces the potential for validation of sociability; fun, being outgoing, trustworthy and so forth. No longer feeling special to some other person is the loss of an element that may otherwise have validated important aspects of our self. A feeling of pensiveness or wistfulness occurs when the opportunity for engaging in tasks that may prove validating is denied us. Being prevented from watching a favourite television programme, being thwarted by the weather from playing sport, or being stood up on a date are all examples of foiled potential validating experiences.

Rage emerges when core constructs are invalidated. When abruptly confronted by experiences that undermine our fundamental understandings of self, we frantically seek to defend our core construing. Rage and fury imply an active search for preservation in the face of potential chaos and disorganization. It is the core structure which, when challenged, leads to rage, not events that invalidate the way we think of ourselves. Thus invalidation of 'the need to see our self as competent' or 'the need to avoid disapproval' will lead to rage and the forceful desire to protect that fundamental construing. Anger (**) results from invalidation of psychological construing. The anticipated response to friendliness might be affable for those who perceive of themselves as 'approachable'. However, cold, unfriendly and aloof reactions to such friendliness lead to anger. Thus Robert might become angry were he to discover that his attempts at art seemed always to lead to disasters. The person's sense of self is invalidated. As with rage, anger implies a determined effort to assert the status quo. McCoy (1977) reflects this with her definition of anger as an awareness of the invalidation which leads to hostile behaviour, where the person seeks to force events into conformity so the prediction does not fail. Tantrums, temper and annoyance result from invalidation of a person's behaviour, where behaviour is the active search for meaning. Invalidation may arise through the acts of others, where a reasonable request is denied. A child fails in his attempt to persuade a parent to alter bedtime or an adolescent is refused extra clothing allowance. Invalidation may also occur in the face of a person's anticipations of their own behaviour or performance. Thus missing a penalty for the football team, forgetting lines in the nativity play or making an error on a simple maths task may lead to annoyance.

3.8.2   Anticipated Change in the Construct System

When again considered in relation to the organization or structure of self-construing – core, psychological and behaviour – an anticipated change in the construct system leads to the following emotional experiences:

Structure	
Core	*Threat* is the awareness of imminent comprehensive change in core structures
Psychological	*Fear* is an awareness of an imminent incidental change in core construing
Behaviour	**Bewilderment* is an awareness of imminent comprehensive change in non-core structures

Threat (*) occurs when a person becomes aware that to continue to make sense of events before them they need to shift or re-evaluate some of their core construing. There arises a need to construe the self in a new manner. The means whereby a person currently understands their self may need to shift. It is not the event itself, but the potential impact on a person's construing of self. The birth of a younger brother or sister may necessitate a change in how a youngster construes herself. Were Robert to find that he failed to succeed or enjoy his rugby ventures, he might be faced with a necessary revision of himself as an all-round sporting individual. Fear (*), according to Kelly, arises when events challenge our construing of ourself. He suggests core constructs are involved but more subordinate constructs are inevitably likely to be implicated. Fear is not as pervasive as threat. Being fearful, frightened or scared is the realization that one's current view of self needs to change in order to resolvedly make sense of events. Bewilderment (**) arises when faced with novel events that require alteration in construing in order to make sense. Events become unpredictable with the familiar construct system. According to Kelly (1955), the permeability of constructs allows the incorporation of new events. McCoy (1977) uses the example of entering a different culture with new architecture, transport, cuisine and landscape that requires the present construct system to accommodate. Bewilderment is that feeling of being at odds in a new situation, with a realization that one's current construing may leave one feeling awkward and out of place. The first day at a new school is a potentially bewildering, disorientating and puzzling experience.

3.8.3   Goodness of Fit between Actions and Self-Construing

In refining 'goodness of fit' as an explanatory dimension of emotions, Kelly (1955) elaborated the notion of a role. Role, it is assumed, is structured in relationship to the significant people in one's life. Within one's construct structure, according to Kelly, there are 'frames' which enable one to predict and control the essential interactions of self with other people and with societal groups, which altogether constitute the individual's conceptualization of his core role. Role is an ongoing pattern of behaviour that follows from a person's understanding of how others, who are significant or associated with his task, think. It is both a social interaction frame of reference and the basis of identity (McCoy, 1977).

Social roles for youngsters include brother, sister, friend, playmate, scapegoat, musician, pupil, monitor, leader, joker, prefect, captain and so forth. Core roles may be understood as what the individual regards as fundamentally important for them in undertaking this role. Thus a mother may feel the need to nurture and protect as a core construct, a friend may value the need for approval, whereas a 'good' pupil may seek to elaborate competence. At a psychological level, a role may be understood in terms of the attributes an individual feels are important. Thus friends are to be regarded as trustworthy whilst the good pupil seeks to be hard-working. Finally at a behavioural level, a role will be played out by the behaviours and actions the youngster considers makes most sense.

Structure	Goodness of fit	Dislodgement
Core	*Self-worth, pride* is an awareness of goodness of fit with core role structures	*Guilt* is the perception of one's apparent dislodgement from core role structure
Psychological	**Self-confidence* is an awareness of goodness of fit with attributes of the core role	*Frustration* is an awareness of dislodgement from attributes considered important in the core role
Behaviour	*Self-belief* – anticipation that the person can undertake the behaviour necessary for a performance	*Vulnerability* – anticipation that the person is unable to undertake those behaviours necessary for a performance

Self-worth or pride may be conceptualized as a perception that one remains 'true to oneself'. The way we portray ourselves fits with our social role or identity. Self-confidence (**) arises from a perception that a person adopts attributes they consider important in undertaking a social role. Thus the artist anticipates their creativity and colour balance on their next piece of work; the leader anticipates their adeptness at persuading other children to act in certain ways and the scapegoat feels certain they will be blamed. Robert might be confident of doing well with constructional tasks given his liking and expertise in such areas and equally confident of doing badly with a piece of writing, given his notion of self as not very good in this area. It is important to note that a sense of confidence is related to an anticipation of goodness of fit, not judgement about how well you might do. Thus children often show as forceful a demonstration of confidence for tasks they anticipate failing (e.g. 'I'm no good at this' or 'I can't do that'), as they do for tasks they anticipate succeeding with. Should events turn out as expected, then the youngster experiences confidence. Self-belief may be viewed as task-orientated and refers to a person's anticipation that they can undertake the behaviour necessary for the performance. Butler (1996, 1999) has structured this in the sporting context with the Performance Profile, a means whereby sports people can identify behaviours considered important in their performance. Bandura (1977) chose the term self-efficacy to describe a similar concept which is defined as an estimate of one's ability to execute a task successfully.

Guilt (*), an emotion Kelly fleshed out, is an awareness of acting in ways at odds with core role construing. Guilt is experienced when we act in a way we would not have expected of ourselves. A therapist who fails to listen to their client, a mother who fails to protect her child, an antisocial youth who assists someone in trouble all invariably experience guilt. Guilt, as with all emotions, is value-free and arises from the perceived discrepancy between self and the core role. Thus acting with disregard for others will create guilt with those who consider themselves caring but not cause guilt with those of an antisocial persuasion. An act of generosity by someone very careful with their money would engender guilt in the same way as someone on a diet eating a creamy chocolate cake. Robert might experience guilt were he to slob in front of the television as he would be acting in a way which contradicts what he would expect of himself. Frustration is an awareness of dislodgement from attributes considered important in the core role. It is sensed when the attributes considered necessary are denied expression. Frustration arises when as an agitator there is a wish to contribute but an opportunity fails to arise; as a leader, there is a desire to influence or dominate but the context prevents it. Vulnerability is task-orientated and refers to a person's anticipation that they are either unable to or fail to undertake those behaviours necessary for a performance.

3.8.4   The Ability of the Construct System to Meet New Events

How well the construct system functions when confronted by new events gives rise to a raft of emotions, again linked to structural levels within a person's construct system:

Structure	Unable to meet new events	Able to meet new events
Core	*Dread, trepidation, shock* is a sudden awareness of the need to construe the self differently	*Fulfilment, exhilaration, awe –* anticipated validation of a new social role
Psychological	**Anxiety* is a recognition that the events with which one is confronted lie mostly outside the range of convenience of the construct system	***Contentment* is an awareness that events with which one is confronted lie within the range of convenience of the construct system
Behaviour	***Surprise* is the awareness of a sudden need to construe events	*Comfort, being at ease* is an awareness that the person is ably equipped to deal with events with which they are confronted

Dread is the feeling of facing an event for which you have no available constructs to make sense of the situation. It is like suddenly feeling completely like a fish out of water. Anxiety (*) is the awareness that events with which the child is confronted lie outside the range of convenience of the construct system. There is a feeling of being unable adequately to make sense of events. Events are unpredictable. Anticipation is also important here so that anxiety may result where an individual is unsure they have the means (or constructs) to deal with the event. What may lie outside of the range of convenience is how the outcome of an event may affect the self. Thus interviews, tests, exams, public speaking, performing and so forth may create anxiety because the person is unsure of what failure might mean in terms of future performance, how others will construe them and the effect on self-construing. Asked for the first time to roller-skate, Robert might feel ill-equipped in terms of his construing to grasp such an event. There may be further implications in that Robert might feel unsure about how potential failure will affect his construing of self. It is the inability to grasp the unknown which creates anxiety. Surprise (**) is a transitory state arising from being confronted with an unexpected event. Humour, teasing, jokes, tricks and fun rely on an element of surprise where recipients have to briefly review their means of construing in order to grasp the meaning of an event.

Fulfilment arises from an anticipated validation of a new social role. Becoming a new friend, for example, may validate a core sense of approval. Contentment (**) or excitement arises when anticipated or actual events are meaningfully construed by the current construct system. Feeling comfortable or at ease is an awareness that the person is ably equipped to deal with events with which they are confronted. Robert could contentedly spend time with paper and paints creating pictures with a sureness that he had the ability to face the task.

3.8.5   The Fit between the Person's Construct System and Another Person's System

The sociality corollary lies at the heart of this raft of emotions, which call for a need to be able to subsume another person's construing. The youngster, by 'reading the mind', or believing they can detect what others think (a significant individual, a social group or society) is able to match themselves with other people's constructions of them.

	The fit between self and the perceived opinion of self	The fit between self and other
Core	**Shame** is an awareness of the dislodgement of the self from another's construing of your role	**Contempt** is an awareness that the core role of another is comprehensively different from one's own
Psychological	Shy – the anticipation that another will hold an opinion of you that may be at odds with what you would wish of yourself	Jealous – awareness that someone else's social role is validated at the perceived expense of your own
Behaviour	Embarrassment – awareness of other people's evaluation of your behaviour is at odds with one's own	

Shame (**) or humiliation is the awareness of dislodgement of self from another person's construing of one's role. Shame is the result of behaving in a way that the child perceives is not expected of him or her. It involves both an awareness of another person's construing, thus involving the sociality corollary, plus a sense that one's behaviour has not been as the other predicted. Robert might experience shame were he to perceive that his mother was disappointed in him as a good pupil for not putting time aside before bed to improve his writing, but instead choosing to use this time to play computer games. Shyness or self-consciousness is an anticipation that another will hold an opinion of you that may be at odds with what you would wish. Thus Robert may feel a sense of shyness were he to consider other people would disapprove of him being 'arty'. Embarrassment or awkwardness is a sense that your acts are under the scrutiny of others and that you will not do yourself justice or you will meet with their disapproval.

Contempt (**) according to McCoy (1977), arises when we surmise that another's essential construing of themselves is dramatically different from ours. It stems from a perception that the philosophies, principles or beliefs of individuals within a social role are at odds with our own construing. The other person is positioned at the contrast end of a construct we value strongly. At an individual level, for example, we might consider a person's self-centredness to be in contrast to the view of ourselves as generous, altruistic and accommodating. That another is shallow whilst we value depth; flippancy in others when seriousness is personally valued. In terms of social roles, disdain may be felt over teachers who show little concern for their subject whilst the youngster is keen to learn. Jealousy might be considered to arise with awareness that someone else's social role is validated at the perceived expense of your own. You may feel envy of someone picked in the team at your expense or looked over during selection in favour of someone else.

3.9 BEHAVIOUR

Kelly described two behaviours – hostility and aggression – which typically arise when an individual's construct system is under threat or requires elaboration. As with emotional experiences, Kelly also attempted to define these behaviours from the protagonist's perspective rather than in terms of other people's reactions to the child. It might be postulated that there are also emotional experiences arising from such behaviour.

Aggression (*) is regarded as the active elaboration of one's perceptual field. It is the experience of pursuing a way of construing, actively experimenting to check the validity of our construing. It is about seriously wishing to know. Aggression surfaces in seeking out areas of confusion and actively experimenting with solutions; in our willingness to risk in order to find out things. Essentially aggression describes the pursuit of putting constructs to the test; trialling constructs to judge which might best fit. It is noticeable in risk-taking and being adventurous. Aggression is the means whereby a person widens their understanding. Were Robert to throw himself into a new series of artistic endeavours in pursuing his notion of himself as arty, this would be construed as aggressive. In contrast, frustration may be considered as the thwarting of active elaboration. An awareness of aggression – the active elaboration of one's perceptual field – arguably gives rise to feelings such as being energetic, alert and alive. In contrast feeling tired and worn out are associated with an awareness of choosing not to engage in active elaboration.

Hostility (*) was regarded by Kelly as the continued effort to extort validational evidence in favour of a type of social prediction which has already been recognized as a failure. Hostility has thus a self-preserving function. It is about seeking to prove you are right. When invalidation of construing appears unremitting, re-construing to enhance meaning is one option. Alternatively, if the person has invested heavily in the prediction or alternative theories seem too bleak, the evidence may be doubted, the person may rationalize, 'cook the books' or delude themselves that their construing is good. Under threat of invalidation the person may seek to maintain a current way of construing by trying to alter events to conform to original expectations or predictions. Were Robert to find his artwork marked constantly low by his teachers and yet it remained important to him in construing himself as artistic, a hostile reaction might be to disregard the marks because the teacher 'doesn't like me'. Forcefully searching for validation may give rise to manipulation, seeking to control others and 'bullying' others into validating our beliefs.

3.10   CONCLUSION

Personal construct theory is a 'complete' model of how individuals function psychologically, providing a framework for clinicians to better grapple with the complexities and dilemmas that children and young people present. Don Bannister once presented the complete theory, with the main tenets, definitions and all, on a side of A4 paper in order to demonstrate the concise yet comprehensive nature of the theory. Although enjoying instant appeal, the theory has drawn criticism from some quarters, noticeably in terms of intellectual isolation and particularly around the relationship with cognitive behavioural formulations.

The intellectual isolationism, according to Bob Neimeyer (1985) has its origins in Kelly's dismissal of early psychological models as if they were wholly irrelevant to his own theory-building efforts. Whilst this may have left Kelly vulnerable to both philosophical criticism and hostility (in a Kellyan sense) from the mainstream psychology of the time, it highlighted the distinctiveness and therefore attractiveness of his own ideas. Currently the dominant models within clinical psychology rotate around cognitive-behaviourism, which has often implicitly and explicitly credited Kelly's personal construct theory as having contributed importantly to their work (e.g. Beck et al., 1979).

The word 'construct', by which Kelly sought to describe how individuals abstract meaning from events, has confusingly come to mean something 'cognitive' to many psychologists. Regrettably this has to personal construct theory being considered a cognitive theory, something Kelly was fully aware of and had set about determinedly rewriting his book with an 'emotional' flavour before his untimely death in 1967. Most proponents of PCT, as noted by Neimeyer (1985), view the essence of Kelly's theory as an attempt to transcend the cognitive–emotion–behaviour trichotomy, something this chapter has sought to illustrate by fully embracing the emotional experience of individuals. It is therefore not surprising that those working within a PCT model should feel ill at ease being identified with an explicitly cognitive movement.

The continued rejection of cognitive therapies and thus the continued intellectual isolation of those working within PCT, is not so much prompted by technical differences, but by their fundamental theoretical incompatibilities. This is astutely observed by Phil Salmon (quoted in Neimeyer, 1985) who, in taking issue with cognitivist assumptions with realism, suggested 'behaviourism a priori defines reality independent of the perspective of the individual and since cognition ought at least to be in some sense phenomenological, I see cognitive behaviourism as a doomed approach'. Kellyan theory, on the other hand, with its assumptions explicitly stated, is optimistic in framing individuals as active, interpretive beings seeking to make sense of the world they inhabit.

CHAPTER 4

DISCOVERING CHILDREN'S CONSTRUING

At the very heart of Kelly's theory of personal constructs is a pressing insistence that if we are to understand a youngster's actions or assist them in resolving their problems, we must first make a determined effort to see the world through their eyes. Though we can chart, through careful observation, the objective challenges they face, or infer through informed guesswork how they might feel in specific situations, we should be necessarily wary of assuming we know how any child is making sense of their particular experience. Should we inadvertently assume an understanding of the child, from an 'outside' perspective, we are in danger of deferring to a sense of our own expertise. We may boldly assert many a judgement concordant with our particular framework, but inexorably wide of the mark in terms of the youngster's construing. Thus a therapist concluded a child's inquisitive acts demonstrated that he was 'impulsive and overactive, like a live wire that's not earthed'; a teacher, bemused by a boy's behaviour, reported that 'he acts in strange ways and if he continues to behave in this way, he is likely to end up there – in Strangeways' (this being the name of a prison in Manchester); and the pastor for Victoria Climbe, a young girl who died after horrific acts of abuse involving forcing her to sleep in the bath because of her bed-wetting, suggesting 'her incontinence was due to her possession by an evil spirit that could be solved by prayer'.

Where youngsters present with troubling and troublesome behaviour, it is unlikely that the vacuum of understanding is addressed solely by the opinion of experts. Experts unquestionably know much about their field of interest, but they tend to make assumptions and interpretations derived from constructions as an observer, not protagonist. Thus the opinion they may give has a fair chance of being totally at odds with the youngster's issue, leaving any well-intended advice ungrounded and unlikely to be assimilated or acted on by the young person in question. The clinician of course has an armoury of investigative procedures at their fingertips – psychometrics, checklists, diagnostic categories, case notes, reports, structured interviews and so forth – to help formulate views of a child. However, we need to ask whether such practices are predominantly an aid to answering our questions rather than assisting youngsters to express their unique perspectives.

If we all essentially construct our own realities, we cannot begin to appreciate the psychological world of a young person unless we become aware not only of the raw objective facts of their life and their observable reactions to what confronts them, but also how they interpret their existence. This chapter explores some approaches we have found helpful in developing an understanding of how youngsters construe their world.

4.1   DEVELOPING KELLY'S FIRST PRINCIPLE

Kelly devised a common-sense principle to guide enquiry. Highlighted in Chapter 1 , it suggests that 'If you want to know what's wrong with a child why not ask them? They might just tell you.' A widespread reaction to such an invite might go something like 'Well, what else would you do?' Kelly's seemingly banal suggestion contains, however, a number of implications which may not be immediately obvious.

First there is an implicit reminder that the child is the expert on their own experience. No matter how disaffected, rebellious, stupid, immature,

ill-mannered or disinterested they may appear, each young person is the ab-
solute world authority on themselves. They have expertise regarding themselves. Such sentiments do not deny the expertise or validity of parents, teachers, psychologists or other adults caring for the youngster. They surely also
have a deep sense of knowing about parenting, teaching and so forth borne
from their constructions of their experience in the role. They have, in Kelly's
reflections, a broad understanding of childhood issues whereas the particular youngster has a detailed, if unvoiced, understanding of the events as
they effect him or her. There is mileage in conceptualizing this relationship in
terms of a model of equal expertise (Butler, 1997) where child, adult (parent or
teacher) and clinician, although inhabiting different worlds, are considered
all to be experts in their own right and where the views of all are treated as
credible and helpful in seeking to explore solutions.

Secondly Kelly hoped to rehabilitate the question as a helpful way of discovering something about the inner world of children. Not all questions open
up enquiry. Some questions may have a quite contrary effect, conveying a
sense that the questioner already knows the 'right' answer and is merely
trying to trick or humiliate the person he is quizzing. 'Come on, boy, we
haven't got all day. Why did the Spanish Armada fail so manifestly to achieve
its aims?', might reflect a conventional, if somewhat caustic, approach to
accessing a child's knowledge. 'What in heaven's name possessed you to
do such a thing?', is a frequently overheard adult style; bemused investigation on being confronted by a child's puzzling behaviour. When adults
pose rhetorical questions or inquire with accusation, the likelihood is that
the prospects of mutual exploration of meaning are killed in the egg. However, when a question is posed because the questioner genuinely wants to
discover something of which he or she is ignorant, and is prepared to listen intently to try and learn from the reply, the process opens up appealing
possibilities.

Kelly's third lesson is a timely faith in the importance of 'keeping it simple'.
Psychologists have a formidable repertoire of complex tools for investing the
human psyche – lengthy questionnaires, convoluted interpretations, galvanic
skin-response monitors, sophisticated statistical packages and so on – yet such
an array of gadgetry is not required in order to listen carefully to what a young
person is trying to say. Whisper it quietly, but there is a school of thought that
says you may be better off without it.

Kelly's support for uncomplicated principles of communicating with children does not mean we can discount matters of technique entirely. All of us,
children included, have a wealth of implicit knowledge that we may not easily articulate. We know more than we can say. Constructs, as Tom Ravenette
(1977) proposed, often lie at a low level of awareness. Moreover, those ideas
to which we do have reasonable access are not neatly organized like some

exemplary stamp collection, carefully indexed to help the casual observer find what he's after. Perhaps a more fitting analogy is the 'it's in here somewhere' frustration we encounter when trying to retrieve a mislaid letter from a desk strewn with a compost of correspondence! Thus we need to develop some enabling strategies to allow children to begin to tell us their stories. Personal construct theory has fostered some fresh and inviting approaches in this respect.

4.2   CHECKING OUT THE CONTEXT

If children and young people are to be encouraged to reveal and explore their ideas about themselves it is important to create a climate in which such atypical reflection is experienced as a safe undertaking. Given our shared expectations that most of the questions adults ask children have right and wrong answers, we probably need to emphasize that, in our enquiries, there are no correct ways of making sense of events. We are undoubtedly inviting personal opinions, wishing to respect the uniqueness of each individual's views and experience. 'Dare to be different' might be the invitation to convey. Overall the enquirer's message is that, above all else, we aim to try and understand what the child is getting at – what they mean to say in their own terms.

Although Kelly's straightforward maxim for finding out about issues and problems makes eminent sense, when we have before us a child or young person, our adult-framed questions, rather than eliciting a sound understanding, often lead to curtailed interactions and cul-de-sacs. Youngsters are often less than careful when responding to a question with a 'don't know'. They may genuinely be faced with a query that sits outside their powers of construing; they may not readily have access to constructs which would otherwise enable them to shape an answer, or they may present the 'pat' response by way of avoiding engaging in conversation. Acknowledging the validity of a 'don't know' response is important and it is sometimes heartening for youngsters to realize that clinicians too are faced with many situations they have uncertainty about. Remaining propositional encourages open-mindedness. Occasionally it is helpful for a youngster to be invited to consider questions they might ask to test what the clinician might know and not know.

It remains a rare luxury for any person to be afforded the time and respect to feel properly understood by another. For an adult to pay such privileged attention to a child is perhaps an even more exceptional occurrence. We might therefore anticipate that our carefully crafted questions may initially be treated with suspicion. One way that adolescents, in particular, may be tempted to test out how convincingly an adult – be they teacher, therapist, or parent – plays this role of understanding investigator, is to 'con' or deliberately mislead this apparently concerned grown-up to see how they will react. The adult then faces a familiar dilemma. Do they accept as trustworthy some evident falsehood and run the risk of being dismissed as some easily duped dunderhead not worthy of being taken seriously? Or, do they challenge the accuracy of the account the young person has provided and so stand accused of crass hypocrisy in claiming to respect the adolescent's opinions and then call him a liar in the next breath? Get out of that!

Kelly advocated that we try to set aside our fear of being deceived, and adopt what he termed a 'credulous' approach to the young people with whom we work (see Chapter 2 for extended discussion of this still revolutionary notion). Believe what they tell us. Even if faced with what appear implausible accounts of events, the listener responds in good faith in the expectation that this exchange will ultimately make sense once the speaker's scheme of things is more fully understood. So, for example, a troubled school pupil who denies he has any learning problems may need to know that it is his view of events rather than his teacher's opinion which is going to be validated, before he can acknowledge his areas of difficulty. When Peter Falk played the TV detective Columbo he seemed to convey just this sort of trusting bemusement as he scratched his head and asked suspects if they would kindly go through their stories 'one more time' so he could make sure he understood properly what they wanted to convey to him. Youngsters, as active meaning makers, appear eager to help clarify any apparent 'misunderstanding' when faced by clinicians who just wish to check they have correctly captured the child's ideas and theories.

When exploring areas of concern the issue may become ever more problematic, as it may be the concern is meaningful only to the parent bringing the young person along for help. As Sharon Jackson and Don Bannister (1985) discovered, a youngster may be problematic to others but see themselves as easy to understand. The problem as seen by others may not be meaningful for the child. Thus questions directed at the 'problem' may be perceived as nothing but irrelevant (Ravenette, 1977). In terms of Kelly's sociality corollary, the clinician would be failing to construe the construction processes of the child, and in so doing fail to grasp an understanding of the child.

Understanding youngsters then is a matter not of squeezing the child into our means of construing (through diagnosis, categories and so forth) but of understanding the child's understanding. We need to discover the ways children view the world and themselves in their own terms. Taking the metaphor of PCT, the youngster is viewed as if they are a scientist, having theories about the world. Behaviour, though sometimes remaining a puzzle to us, can be seen as the child's means of testing his particular theory. As therapists it is usually imperative to understand how the child is making sense of the world.

Personal construct theory holds that constructs are the means of making sense with individuals having a unique but limited set of discriminations which they use to define their experience. Interestingly by seriously listening to children's verbalizations they will reveal their means of making sense. Broadly constructs might be considered the evaluative component of a statement whereas elements are objects contained in that same utterance. Thus:

Statement	Construct	Element
'It's not hard to hit the ball'	Hard – easy	Ball
'I hate cabbage'	Hate – love	Cabbage
'I'm good at reading.'	Good – poor	Reading
'That CD is ace'	Ace – awful	CD
'Do you like Scarface?'	Like – dislike	Scarface

4.3   TRADITIONAL CONSTRUCT ELICITATION

Constructs are considered to have two poles, with contrasting meaning, which flexibly enable the individual to make sense of a restricted range of phenomena. So a construct such as 'diligent – lazy' might describe an attitude to work, but would, in all probability, not be relevant to a consideration of the different curry dishes on the menu of a favourite Indian restaurant, where 'blows your head off – mild as milk' would arguably fit the bill much better.

Conversations with children might appositely seek to discover which constructs they employ in relation to key issues in their lives. When learning to speak their language we aspire not just to use their words but also to grasp their meaning. Kelly devised a straightforward sorting system to elicit constructs relevant to particular concerns. Traditionally this involved taking three elements, or events, such as the names of family members, subjects studied at school, or possible holiday destinations, and asking an individual 'in which way are two of these people (subjects, places or whatever) the same and therefore different from the third?' This form of triadic questioning might elicit a reply like 'My mum and sister like to talk a lot but my granddad doesn't say much'. Thus 'talk a lot' might be taken to be the emergent end of a construct this youngster employs in making sense of family members with 'doesn't say much' forming the contrast end of the construct. Conveniently the triadic invite generally reveals both poles of the construct.

Sometimes however, especially for young children, such three-way comparison can prove conceptually difficult. Inviting contrasts between a pair of elements is a less demanding request in such circumstances yet, as Reid Klion and Larry Leitner (1985) discovered, can prove extremely effective in eliciting constructs from children as young as five years. Sometimes referred to as a dyadic or sorting method, it involves inviting a youngster to consider how two elements compare, either in their similarity or difference. A child might perceive a similarity between themselves and a friend in terms of them both 'playing good tricks on others', which represents one pole of a construct to do with relationships amongst peers. The contrast pole is likely to emerge by inviting the child to describe, in this case, someone who doesn't play tricks on others, revealing the opposing end as 'boring'. A child focusing on the difference between two elements such as sleeping in your own bed and staying overnight at a friend's house might perceive the difference in terms of sometimes being scared when waking up away from home, in contrast to feeling safe in your own bed. Means of discovering children's construing in these ways have been discussed fully by Salmon (1976) and Butler (1985).

4.4   ALTERNATIVE MEANS OF CONSTRUCT ELICITATION

Perhaps a more conceptually relevant means of eliciting constructs with young people is to consider not three or even two elements, but just one. Sometimes this has been called the free response method (Klion and Leitner, 1985). Although there are many forms, a starting point is usually to develop a list of elements or events which are embedded in the youngster's perceptual field. Thus a child may be asked 'Who do you think knows you best of all?' A list of individuals significant to the child is consequently assembled, and may include, in addition to themselves, family members, friends and teachers, the child's favourite cartoon figure, esteemed sporting hero, television star, imaginary friend or the family pet. Through employing such a list, constructs may then be elicited in a variety of ways:

- *Description:* Taking the elements from the list one at a time, the youngster is invited to recount three important ways they might describe the significant people in their life. A fruitful line of enquiry might start with an open-ended invitation such as: 'Tell me three things about the other kids in your class'; 'Could you give me three descriptions of what this sister of yours is like?' or 'So you have a pet dog called Rascal – tell me three things about him'. Although these remain descriptions of 'another', the constructs employed by the child are their own, thus revealing something of how the youngster makes sense of people. Since it is highly unlikely that individuals develop one system for making sense of other people and an entirely separate system for making sense of themselves, such constructs also reveal something of the youngster's own self construing.

- *Who are you?* This represents a direct request to the young person to say who he or she is. In Chapter 3 Robert was invited to respond to such an inquiry. The question runs along the following lines: 'If I were to ask you to tell me three things that best describe you, what would you say? Who are you?'

- *Self-evaluation:* A favoured, and usually unintimidating, line of questioning suggested by Ravenette (1977) is to ask the child to evaluate themselves as they think others see them. Taking the list of elements, the child is asked, 'If I were to ask (e.g. your mother) to describe you, to tell me the three most important things he or she could say about you, what *three* things would he or she say?' In metaphorically trying to stand in another person's shoes the child feels perhaps less apprehensive about describing him- or herself. However, given Kelly's notions about the individuality, uniqueness and ownership of constructs, in endeavouring to respond to this question the child is doing so by means of their own construct system.

As with all forms of construct elicitation, the contrast pole of each description needs to be sought, usually by asking the child to describe someone who is not like the emerged pole. Importantly contrasts are considered to be personal, not necessarily logical and say something about how the speaker is making sense of their predicament.

After seeking the contrast pole to each description, constructs may be elaborated in various ways. The child can be asked which end they would prefer to be at. This indicates the degree to which the child is content or dissatisfied with him- or herself. The child might be invited, as Tom Ravenette suggested, to describe what is important or special about the preferred end of a construct. This elaborates the personal meaning. It may also produce higher order or more superordinate constructs. If a child comes up with a series of physical constructs such as 'stocky', 'black hair' or 'spotty', such questioning about the importance of such descriptions for the child can lead to the emergence of more psychological constructs.

Moving in the opposite direction, a child might be invited to describe the behavioural constituents of a construct through the process of pyramiding. This was undertaken with Robert in the preceding chapter, and essentially requires asking the child to describe what a person typically does when they are described by the construct. Thus an intricate elaboration of 'moody', for example, can be discerned by asking the child to describe what a person tends to do when they are being moody.

A theme common to all these forms of construct elicitation is a request for the child to find three responses. Asking for three descriptions or characteristics holds many advantages. Firstly it challenges a 'pat', superficial or off-the-cuff response as the youngster is invited to consider a more comprehensive consideration of the elements. Whereas pat answers may serve as a defence against revealing what is personally meaningful, asking for three may challenge the child to search for thoughts and feelings which are the beginnings of a personal self-assessment. Secondly asking for three responses directly validates for the child that there is not just one correct answer.

Tom Ravenette found another way of using the fascinating number three in eliciting children's constructs. He invited the child to express their view on events, situations and problems which are located onto an imagined other child. Thus a child is asked,'Tell me three things about . . . (e.g. the sort of girl who worries about going to school)'. This might be met with the following reply:

1. She doesn't like sums.

2. She loves her mummy.

3. She hasn't got any friends.

Immediately revealed are emergent poles of constructs such as 'like – dislike', 'love – hate' and 'lacking friends – having friends'. There is of course no magic about the number three, nor any law about extracting a third construct if a youngster can easily produce only two. The purpose of the exercise is to pose a question in a form with which schoolchildren, in particular, will be familiar and to set a manageable challenge.

4.5   SELF-PORTRAITS

Children who enjoy words often participate eagerly in the playful interrogations described above. Others, however, prefer to express themselves visually, and find it easier to show or draw an image of themselves. Drawings enable children to make statements about themselves without being put in a potentially embarrassing position of talking about their self in the first person. The drawing in Figure 4.1 is by a six-year-old boy eager to display his sporting prowess. 'That's me scoring' he claimed proudly.

The drawing in Figure 4.2 is by a nine-year-old boy whose mother saw him as something of an invalid because of an inherited calcium deficiency. In contrast, the impression his self-portrait gave was of a robust, active youth, a view confirmed by his commentary on the picture: 'I'm one of the strongest boys in my class. Nobody pushes me around.'

Sometimes simple stylized portrayals of faces with a variety of facial expressions can open up fruitful conversations with children. Presenting a sketch of a child's face, for example looking angry, can encourage a child to describe their own feelings. The enquirer might ask:

• 'How do you guess this person's feelings?'

• 'Do you ever feel like that?'

Figure 4.1 Scoring a goal: the drawing of a six-year-old boy.

- 'What might make that person feel this way?'
- 'What thoughts go through your mind when you feel that way?'.

Where children show an inclination to draw, Ravenette has suggested that they might be invited to sketch their feelings as in a 'portrait gallery'. Figure 4.3 shows the portrait gallery of a nine-year-old boy, Tom, who was struggling emotionally to cope with a foster placement with foster parents who were undertaking this care for the first time. Tom was asked firstly to draw a happy face. He was then asked about times that made him feel happy. This was followed up by an inquiry as to whether Tom knew any other feelings and, as before, he was asked to draw the face and comment on his own experiences of the feeling. He came up with eleven faces, his responses to each being:

- happy – 'When I do things right.'
- sad – 'When I fight with my big brother and get told off.'
- angry – 'When people call me names; when I argue with my brother; when I shout at Mum.'
- frightened – 'Never feel frightened.'

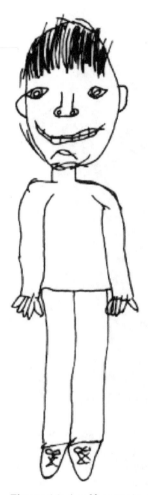

Figure 4.2 A self-portrait of a boy with inherited calcium deficiency.

- embarrassed – 'Never.'
- bored – 'At school when I've finished work; on holiday when I've nothing to do.'
- cheeky – 'When I argue with Mum.'
- worried – 'About being fostered.'
- excited – 'When I win things; when I'm going on trips and to the caravan.'
- bad-tempered – 'When I get sent to bed.'
- proud – 'When I'm good at school; when I get an award.'

Figure 4.3 A portrait gallery drawn by Tom, a nine-year-old boy.

It has often been suggested both theoretically and empirically that children lying within the 'autistic spectrum' have difficulty, not so much in making sense of the physical world in which they inhabit, but in understanding the psychological world. This has been termed a difficulty in 'mind-reading'. The youngster with autistic tendencies, it has been argued, is all at sea when it comes to deciphering or construing the emotional world of themselves and others. It is as if more abstract, psychological events remain outside the range of their construing and thus they tend to struggle with social relationships, preferring the 'safe' world of objects. Figure 4.4 shows a self-portrait gallery for a 10-year-old boy, Simon, for whom there had been serious questions concerning the possibility of Asperger's syndrome. His responses both in terms of drawing and subsequent verbal elaboration give a sense of the pedantic nature and lack of both self-reference and emotional 'depth' that is characteristic of such children's functioning.

In the traditional manner both a happy and sad face were drawn and Simon asked to identify which was which. Appropriately labelled, he was then asked 'What three things might make this face happy?' Simon said:

- 'Doing jokes to them.'
- 'Tickle him.'
- 'Get a pet for him.'

When then asked what kinds of things might make him happy, Simon replied 'Got a toy from the shop.' In a similar vein Simon was then asked about the sad face. He suggested the three things that would make the face sad were: 'Throwing a bucket of water over him'; 'If one of his friends has died'; and 'A thump on the face'. He would have a sad face if he was 'crying'. Next, again in traditional fashion, a roundish circle was drawn to represent another face and Simon was asked 'I wonder what other faces we can have. How else can we feel?' to which he replied 'Laughing'. Simon was then invited to draw a 'laughing' face within the circle (see Figure 4.4) and when asked the customary questions, suggested that what would make the face laugh would be 'Tickle him', 'Do jokes to him', 'When Christmas comes' and 'When Easter comes – get an egg'. Simon could not suggest a time he might laugh. In a similar vein, Simon suggested 'crying' as another feeling, which might arise 'If one of his pets die', 'If someone thumped him in the face', 'When he's drawn a picture and can't find it', and 'Gets a computer for Christmas and someone steals it'. He would cry if 'Someone gangs on you at school'. Finally in response to other possible feeling faces, Simon was able to hazard only two others – 'Chinese' and 'Japanese' – which he drew and reflected upon only in that with the former the 'eyebrows slant', whereas with the latter the 'eyes slant', an abstraction exclusively reflecting physical construing.

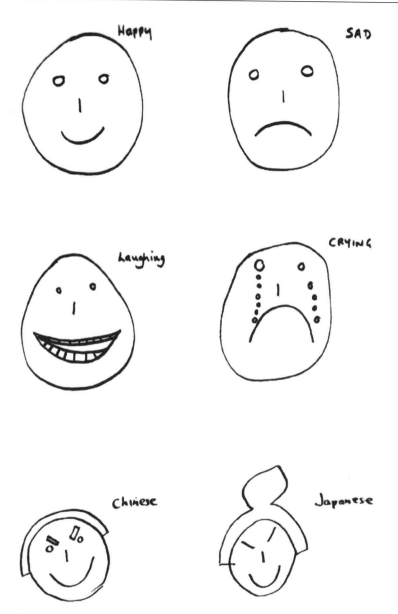

Figure 4.4 A portrait gallery produced by Simon, a 10-year-old boy with Asperger's syndrome.

4.6 DRAWINGS IN CONTEXT

Drawings may also provide an effective stimulus to enable children to give a more detailed account of their construing in particular settings. Ravenette (1977) pioneered the use of artfully vague cartoons that convincingly set a scene without making explicit exactly what's going on between the characters portrayed. His 'Trouble in school' caricatures offer the young person a range of educational scenarios from which to select three particularly appealing pictures; the example in Figure 4.5 is one of Ravenette's sketches. A child may be engaged in conversation with the enquirer along the following lines:

- 'Someone in this picture is feeling troubled. Which character do you think it is?'
- 'What do you think is happening?'
- 'What do you imagine they are thinking?'
- 'Why are they feeling this way?'
- 'What do you guess would make a difference to the way this person feels?'

Questions serve many functions and at their most profound they may enable the respondent to search for meanings at deeper levels of awareness than usual. Being asked to respond to drawings through such questioning may

Figure 4.5 'Trouble in school' sketch.

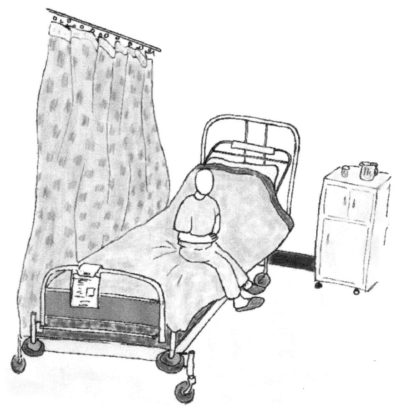

Figure 4.6 'Someone's suffering' sketch.

have an advantage of gaining access to a different range of experience from that elicited through purely verbal enquiry. With a little invention, the notion of sketching in a background, on which the young person can impose a more personal sense, can focus discussions on other situations with particular importance for individual children. For example, the scene in Figure 4.6 is from a series of illustrations unoriginally entitled 'Someone's suffering' developed to encourage children with chronic illnesses to articulate what they make of their various medical encounters.

4.7   ELABORATION OF COMPLAINTS

It is, of course, possible to provide a focus for a conversation without the use of pictures. Kelly, for instance, took advantage of the familiar observation that human beings seem to enjoy nothing better than complaining about each other. The 'elaboration of complaints' approach (Ravenette, 1997) invites the individual to air their misgivings on a chosen issue (which might be parents, siblings, teachers, grandparents, bullies and so forth) by inviting a youngster to complete the following series of statements:

- 'The trouble with most . . . (brothers, parents, teachers, etc.) is . . . '
- 'They are like that because . . . '
- 'It would be better if . . . '
- 'The difference that would make is . . . '

Such a sentence-completion format enables the youngster to highlight what he or she sees as the issue, explore their reasoning and understanding for why that might be, offer some solutions and hints as to what difference any change would make. Ravenette notably suggested that clinicians are in business to help make a difference whereas academics, through statistical analysis, search to find a difference. The sentence-completion format may of course be tailored to the special interests and problems of particular children. The following extract is from a personally designed series of questions completed by a 10-year-old boy with leukaemia who seemed to 'act out' his feelings about his illness but could give no explanation to his mother as to why he behaved as he did:

- 'What Leeds United needs is . . . *a new good player.*'
- 'The worse thing about having cancer is . . . *getting my needle put in my portacath.*'
- 'My mum . . . *always does the washing.*'
- 'I wish . . . *I did not have cancer.*'
- 'I get angry when . . . *my needle gets put in my portacath.*'
- 'The best thing about school is . . . *I like doing art.*'

4.8 STORYTELLING

There are evident similarities between the way Ravenette uses pictures to provide the structure around which a youngster is invited to weave a story, and the range of 'projective' tests that psychoanalytically inclined psychologists employ to encourage children to display the 'inner world' of their experience. The Children's Apperception Test (CAT), for example, uses cartoon drawings of various animals (lions, monkeys, dogs, even kangaroos) which are depicted in various scenes intended to promote discussion of potentially problematic issues within the family (such as sibling rivalry or parental conflict). The user of the CAT expects the child's accounts of what's going on in the picture to reflect what's going on inside the child. The material produced is then analysed within the psychologist's framework of Freudian child development theory.

The personal construct approach to the analysis of children's stories is significantly different. Certainly a personal construct psychologist designs what they hope will be personally salient cues to enable a young person to tell their particular tale. They may use pictures to establish a context, or provide prompts to maintain the momentum of a spoken account. However, there is no assumption that the experience of any character described in the story parallels precisely the experience of the storyteller. Rather the expectation is that, in telling their tale, the child will employ constructs that they use in their understanding of other people.

There is, further, an expectation that the range of ideas a child has evolved to try and make sense of those around them is also likely to form the foundations of a developing theory of self. It is nonetheless awfully tempting to check out with some children whether their responses to a storytelling exercise are, in fact, a thinly veiled autobiographical account of their own experiences. We might therefore suggest to a child that 'We're really talking about you here, aren't we, Katie?' Such smart-alec attempts at confirming the adult's hypotheses can sadly bring an enjoyable experiment to an abrupt and clumsy conclusion. An alternative way of pursuing the same hunch might be to ask:

- 'Are there any ways in which you think you are similar to the girl in the story, Katie?', and

- 'What about the ways in which you think you and the girl are different from each other?'.

Such wording emphasizes more of an interest in the child's theories about human nature, rather than the psychologist's theories about children! In trying to create a psychological model that reflects the complex ways in which a young person's views 'fit together', there is a search to explore the intricacy of the *child's* construct system, rather than slot the child conveniently into any of the *enquirer's* predetermined diagnostic categories.

4.9   SELF-CHARACTERIZATION

Very often we are primarily interested in what children make of themselves compared with their views of other young people, with the person they would like to be or with the person they imagine their mum or dad would like them to be. Kelly, ever the creative soul, devised an approach termed self-characterization, which invites the young person to describe themselves as if a character in a play. Sharon Jackson (1988) provides a full account of this technique, the idea being that by writing in the third person an individual can step back from themselves a little and draw a pithy portrait of what they consider the essential elements of their personality. The only other instruction to the creator of a self-characterization is to write with an intimate and sympathetic understanding of your subject. Sometimes this simple framework helps people produce a candid and powerful précis about how they construe themselves. For example:

> Neil is 15 years old and goes to the King's High School. He is taking GCSE examinations in June this year. He is shy and is always vulnerable and finds it very difficult to communicate and get over ideas and very often is lost for words and as a result is laughed at regularly. Neil finds it difficult to make friends and, as he is vulnerable, he always makes mistakes when talking to a large group of people, e.g. in class discussions at school. The worst problem is getting across ideas, and instead he says stupid things.

> Neil is very shy and appears queer and he is also very boring. He appears upset and as a result he usually makes a fool of himself.

This account was written by a 15-year-old lad who evidently understood the task well enough, though significantly he elected to emphasize his perceived failings despite the invitation to be gentle on himself. He raised a series of constructs concerned with a sense of shyness, vulnerability and a difficulty in communicating. Neil also highlighted some implications of being like this, including being lost for words, saying stupid things and being laughed at.

Younger, or less able, informants sometimes struggle to grasp the 'official' format of the self-characterization. They may feel ill at ease with the artificiality of writing about themselves in the third person. Offering to act as secretary and writing down the child's account can help younger, more reserved or intimidated children to voice an account of themselves.

4.10   ELABORATING CONSTRUCT SYSTEMS

Once a young person has been able to articulate some of the ways in which they make sense of their world, there may be a wish to consider how such constructs relate to each other. Kelly proposed that individuals organize their constructs in a loosely hierarchical fashion with a limited number of what he dubbed 'core constructs' that are of central importance to their comprehension of events. In Chapter 6 this will be covered in more detail. One of Kelly's last PhD students, Dennis Hinkle, developed a number of neat ways of investigating these ordinal relationships between constructs. Hinkle (1965) devised a method of questioning, which he termed 'laddering', that rapidly leads to the heart of a person's belief system; 'Why?' and, particularly for younger children 'How come?' questions are useful in this respect.

Neil, at 15 years of age, readily employed a host of psychological constructs in his self-description or characterization. However, when engaging young children, in particular, in exercises to elicit constructs, they may struggle to move beyond concrete, physical descriptions (such as their clothes, colour of hair, where they go to school and so forth) and not produce the psychological constructs which older children typically employ in elaborating their sense of identity. Inviting the younger child to ladder a physical description may evoke meaningful psychological constructs. Laddering with youngsters usually consists of asking them to reflect on the importance of the construct for them. Thus the elaboration of a physical construct may go something like:

Enquirer 'Is it important that some children have freckles?'

Child 'Yea.'

Enquirer 'How come it's important?'

Child 'Well, kids with freckles are always telling jokes.'

In such ways more psychological constructs ('tell jokes') are revealed. Further laddering, through asking about the importance of such psychological constructs, tends to unveil more superordinate or core constructs. Returning to Neil's self-characterization (above), questions which might lead towards his core constructs are

- 'How come it is better to be tough than vulnerable?'
- 'Why do you believe it's important to be able to communicate your ideas?'
- 'How come it is difficult to make friends?'

At other times the enquirer might find he needs more detail to grasp the meaning of certain statements in a self-characterization. Hinkle developed an alternative style of questioning, which he called 'pyramiding', for checking out what a construct implies in practice. This tends to rely on 'What?'. Ways of developing a better understanding of what Neil means by particular expressions in his self-characterization might include:

- 'Give me an example of a time when you felt you made a fool of yourself.'
- 'What sort of person do you think makes mistakes when talking in a large group?'
- 'How would I know you'd said something stupid?'

Such forms of elaboration are also freely available in exploring how adults make sense of youngsters. Thus asked to describe a child, a parent may say he is disruptive, defiant and aggressive. Such descriptions reside at what might be understood as a 'psychological 'level' in the hierarchy, and to grasp the details of such behaviours we might pyramid or ask what the child does when being 'aggressive' or 'disruptive' and so forth. For example, disruptive may imply excessive talking and not letting others settle; defiance may mean a verbal refusal to do as asked; and aggressive may mean verbally taunting a sister.

4.11   IMPLICATIONS GRIDS

One indication of superordinacy, in Kelly's parlance, of one construct over another is if the individual considers that changing their view of themselves in one respect (e.g. becoming less popular at school) would automatically result in their revising their opinion of themselves in some other way (e.g. feeling less confident). These interrelationships can be mapped using an implications grid (another of Hinkle's ideas) but a simple clinical example serves to illustrate the principle:

> Brian, at 17 years old, had a chronic problem of encopresis. His soiling was a source of friction in his relationship with his mother. Moreover, he had few friends and was more dependent on his family than most boys his age.
>
> He was offered admission to a residential treatment unit for adolescents. Staff in the unit were undecided about whether to focus the treatment regime on encouraging Brian to become more age-appropriately autonomous, or to concentrate on relieving his 'symptomatic' problem of soiling.
>
> When Brian was consulted he was able to clarify the relationship between these two issues in his own mind. If he became more independent that would be fine but it would not, in his judgement, have any necessary influence on how likely he was to continue soiling. If, however, he were to become clean Brian reckoned there would be a veritable domino effect on other ways in which he construed himself, such as feeling more grown-up, attractive to girls, and more independent of his family.
>
> The unit took Brian's opinion seriously and organized a treatment programme designed to tackle his soiling problem directly. As Brian had predicted, movement on this symptomatic construct set up a virtuous circle and boosted his self-esteem no end.

This positive outcome illustrates how shifting position on a superordinate construct has a substantial knock-on effect on the rest of the system. Because such movement has so many implications, revisions of core construing can also prove to be the most resistant to change.

4.12   GRIDS

Personal construct theory is strongly associated with the use of the repertory grid technique devised by Kelly as a mathematical means of defining the relationship between elements and constructs. The practical application of employing grids with youngsters is fully explored in Butler (1985). A number of more or less straightforward statistical packages are available to analyse significant patterns in a person's responses to grid investigations. For example they enable clinicians to determine if certain constructs cluster together; how elements relate spatially to constructs and whether a particular pair of constructs is used in a similar fashion. Computing power multiplies exponentially the number of calculations that can be made on the basis of a quite limited data set.

However, the purpose of inquiry is to listen closely to what young people have to say. There is a danger that the unwary might be fooled into thinking that the messy business of understanding children can be subcontracted to a computer software program. It is possible to use the inventive structure of repertory grids without needing an advanced degree in mathematics. Again a case illustration makes the point:

> Jack (6) and Jill (7) are brother and sister who have lived in a series of foster homes since being admitted into the care of their local authority social services department as a result of concerns that they had been neglected by their own parents. Long-term decisions were now to be made about their future care arrangements. Their father (now remarried) had applied to have his children returned to live with him; Jack and Jill's current foster parents wished to make a long-term commitment to their care; Social Services' preference was to place the children with adoptive parents. The Children Act, under which their case was to be heard, demands that wherever possible the children whose well-being is under consideration be given a voice in proceedings.

> Both Jack and Jill completed a very simple repertory grid. The elements they were asked to think about were the five homes they could remember living in. These were:

Mum and her partner.

Dad and his new wife.

Ron and Mary – first pair of foster parents (emergency reception).

Nick and Carol – second pair of foster parents (short-term allocation).

Andy and Ann – current foster parents (for more than a year).

> Neither Jack nor Jill could recall the time when they lived with both their natural parents.

> The names of each couple were written on postcards and Jack and Jill added small drawings to remind themselves of who was who. They then completed a ranking grid by placing the elements (the five homes) in order of preference regarding the following questions:

- 'Who did you feel most safe with?'

- 'And who did you feel next most safe with?', and so on.

Jack and Jill undertook this task separately. The patterns of their replies were internally consistent, and they also showed a broad consensus in their preference. The structure of the repertory grid allowed them to express their views on their future care in a way that the court could both trust and respect.

Further discussion of the design, application, analysis and interpretation of various forms of grid are found in Fransella and Bannister (1977).

4.13 DEPENDENCY GRIDS

Kelly devised one further specialized grid which can prove particularly pertinent to understanding children. The 'situational resources' grid maps the problems that confront a person against the sources of help that they can call upon for assistance. The theoretical underpinning of this matrix is Kelly's assertion that we are all dependent yet what matters is how we disperse our dependencies. A healthy situational resources grid will indicate a range of people to whom a young person might turn for help and a strategic sense of which person is best equipped to help with a particular sort of difficulty. So a teenage daughter might happily seek her father's advice on possible career options, but would infrequently canvas his opinion on her choice of make-up!

Research into the intriguing phenomenon of 'resilient' children who manage to survive potentially damaging experiences of deprivation or disadvantage without suffering long-term harm to their psychological development has pointed to the importance of social support systems as a primary protective factor promoting the capacity to cope under duress. 'Born survivors' seem to make good use of extra-familial supports and show an ability to recruit concerned allies to their cause. Conversely, children who keep all their

Table 4.1 Peter's dependency grid

Task	Me	Mum	Dad	Sister	Gran	Friend
Cleaning teeth	4	5	6	0	0	0
Tidying my room	2	6	5	3	0	0
Taking my tablets	4	5	0	0	4	0
Buying and choosing my clothes	4	5	3	0	0	0
Spending money on me	3	4	0	0	3	0
Checking 'the bag'	4	5	2	0	1	0
Changing 'the bag'	4	7	0	0	3	0
Doing my homework	4	0	5	2	0	0

emotional eggs in one basket and exhibit an undispersed pattern of dependency may struggle to cope when confronted with problems, if their sole source of support is either unavailable or ill-suited to provide some specialist form of help. School-phobic children sometimes find themselves in precisely such a dilemma.

The following case example illustrates how well a dependency grid can display the pattern of a young person's reliance on others. Peter, age 12, had had a urostomy as an infant and so is required to use a urine bag which needs fairly careful management. His family and physician considered he was of an age when it would be appropriate for him to take more responsibility for his own health care. As the dependency grid in Table 4.1 shows, Peter felt far from prepared for such a promotion. Also of interest is that his willingness to delegate responsibilities was not restricted to issues surrounding 'the bag'. For example, he does not see either doing his homework or cleaning his teeth as exclusively or even primarily his job.

4.14   CONCLUSION

Personal construct theory does not provide a recipe book of techniques to guide us in designing our interventions in the lives of children. Kelly reckoned that the question 'Why?' needed to be answered before the question 'How?' could be properly considered. This principled position can prove damnably frustrating for the hard-pressed practitioner wanting to know what to do next. This chapter has introduced readers into a range of ways in which they might tap the 'inside story' of a young person's experience. The remaining chapters will hopefully provide some insight into how this approach can be employed in putting this hard-won understanding to practical use.

CHAPTER 5

THE EXPLORATION OF SELF

Other people could not understand me unless they knew me.

Such a perspicacious statement from a 14-year-old girl, Lucy, reveals something of the many experiential dilemmas surrounding the concept of 'self'. Firstly the girl is able to reflect upon herself. She holds a notion of self which she recognizes others need to access in order that she is understood. It has been suggested that we are invariably the only species to have the ability to reflect upon the self (Andrews, 1998). Indeed the renowned grandfather of modern psychology, William James, noted the 'duality' embedded in a person's reflection of their self (James, 1892). The 'I' in 'I am honest' suggests that at one level (the core) the person is able to analyse and reflect on another (less core) facet of themselves – the 'me', which in this case is their 'honesty'. As Don Bannister (1983) boldly illuminated, reflexivity is the ability to distinguish the self that screams from the self that ponders why it screamed.

Secondly, there is an assumption that the self is created. Lucy has developed ideas about her own self, a notion absolutely in keeping with Kelly's theory whereby people actively create theories about the world including the construction of a theory of self. Thirdly, Lucy implies, in her statement, something of the fundamental need to maintain the view she has of herself. There is a flavour of a ready acceptance that this is how Lucy is, warts and all, and other folk, in their dealings with her, might just need to understand that. The self, as Kelly intimated, is at the hub of psychological functioning and the person will thus determinedly preserve and sustain the view they have of themselves. The construction of self is rarely up for grabs. You hold on to what you have and there are apparently a host of means whereby this is accomplished.

How the self is constructed influences which environmental stimuli are selected for attention. It also influences the contexts with which we engage. Thus a youngster who sees herself as shy is likely to turn down invites to parties and avoid putting herself in the limelight. An adolescent who considers himself lazy is more likely to loaf around the house at a weekend than opt to join the local jogging club. In such ways the self-image becomes a significant regulator of the individual's behaviour. It organizes the individual's interpretation of the world, fosters actions in line with that view of self and ultimately enhances the probability of validation. A youngster who construes himself as kind, will in all likelihood act towards others in kind ways, thus validating such a definition of self. Identity continually seeks validation. Lucy may construct a view of herself as academic, cool, a hippie and decidedly not a hooligan, ballerina or shallow, and her behaviour, in expressing such notions, will consequently confirm her identity.

The self preserves itself also through:

- Comparison of behaviour against the view of self. Thus acts that are out of kilter with what people expect of themselves will evoke Kellyan guilt. Viewing himself as uncaring and unsympathetic, in helping the old lady across the road a youth would feel awkward and ill at ease with himself.

- Comparison of behaviour with how others might perceive the self. The tendency to predict how others think of the self and tune into the feedback from others which validates the person's own construing of self is known as reflected appraisal, a phenomenon initially postulated by Charles Cooley in the early part of the twentieth century. The search for others' acknowledgement of self is ubiquitous. Thus a child with a developing notion of himself as mischievous looks for confirmation from peers, parents, teachers and other adults in the youngster's social environment.

- Possible invalidation. The prospect of the view one has of the self being disconfirmed is likely to result in Kellyan hostility. Individuals tend to distort information or events so as to verify or sustain the prevailing view of self. Thus should a parent's exasperated reaction to the child's behaviour be considered disconfirming of the self, the child is likely to consider the parent as moody, too demanding or a persistent nag.

The determined efforts that folk go to in preserving a particular view of self suggest inflexibility and intransigence in self-construing. The choice corollary also indicates that people may perpetuate a view of self by making repeated decisions to act in ways that define a particular view of the self. Robert Hartley's fascinating study (Hartley, 1986) further intimates that people adopt a stance regarding their self despite knowledge of other possible selves. His work with children considered 'overactive' (discussed further in Chapter 10) shows that when asked to complete a task *as if* they were 'clever' or 'not clever' they adjusted their behaviour and reactions to the task accordingly. Hartley suggested such youngsters had the behavioural repertoire to act in alternative ways but chose to act in ways that validated their view of self. In sympathy with Kelly's fundamental postulate, youngsters are able to take on alternative constructions, yet predominantly favour familiar forms of construing.

However construing is not static. Young people embody Kelly's idea of people being a 'form of motion', with their active search for meaning. The choice corollary highlights how constructs are elaborated through being acted on, how youngsters 'flesh out' their construct system and ultimately begin to modify the view they have of themselves. Sometimes children are troubled by the way they construe themselves and seek help to change their construing. Therapy, after all, assumes change is feasible. On the other hand, children may be considered troublesome by others, who then seek to have the child's construing altered.

5.1   THE SELF AS TROUBLING TO OTHERS

A final consideration with respect to Lucy's statement concerns a striving to be understood. In harmony with the sociality corollary, Lucy contends that it is only when other people know something of how she makes sense of herself, that they will be fully able to relate and understand her. Sharon Jackson and Don Bannister (1985) carefully elaborated the idea that youngsters may appear confusing to other people (in that it seems difficult to understand them) but are perfectly able to derive an understanding of themselves. So where parents might feel like pulling their hair out in being unable to fathom why a child won't stop fighting his siblings, the child himself may knowingly take this stance, given fighting elaborates a particular combatant view of self.

So being troublesome sometimes revolves around misunderstanding. A sense of being misunderstood weaves its way through many youngsters' dilemmas with parents, teachers and the wider social culture. They may be in conflict with what is expected, but they have at least, usually, a tentative understanding of their actions. A survey of over 500 adolescents revealed many examples

Table 5.1 A sample of responses from a sentence completion survey with 533 adolescents (aged 12–17 years)

No one sees me as I really am
Everyone thinks they know me but they don't
I feel as if no one really knows me
No one sees me as I really am
No one considers me to be the person I really am
Everyone considers me to be a person I'm not
Other people wonder what I'm really like
Everyone sees me as a bitchy person which I'm not
Other people wonder what I am like
Other people could not know what I feel
Other people could not see who I really am
No one sees me as I want to see me
Everyone sees me as the person who I am
No one sees me as a caring person but I am
No one considers me to be what I am
They think I'm a tramp but I'm not
No one believes me to be different when I am
Everyone considers me to be strong-hearted when really I'm not
No one sees me as who I am
Everyone thinks I'm a swot but I'm not
No one sees me as who I am
No one sees me as I really am inside
Other people could not believe what I am like
No one sees me as I really am
No one sees me as myself
Other people wonder who I really am
No one sees me as sensitive as I am
No one sees me as the real me; I never give all of whom I am
No one considers me to be who I really am – quite serious and thoughtful

of how young people sense they are misunderstood by others, some of which are depicted in Table 5.1. A straightforward solution, to paraphrase Kelly's first principle, is that if youngsters' actions perplex us, why not ask them about it – they might just tell us. We might further wish to gather an understanding of the way they see themselves through the self-image profile (discussed later). As Tom Ravenette (2003) implies, such exploration not only helps the youngster portray their view of self to the clinician, but it can also foster a better understanding of their own self.

5.2 THE SELF AS A MYSTERY

Harry was eight years old when he first entered the clinic, somewhat shy, perhaps intimidated and naturally hesitant. Referred by his general practitioner

because of poor concentration at school and 'general behaviour out of character for him', it seemed he was becoming something of a concern to others.
Two avenues of exploration seemed immediately apposite – an understanding of his 'character' (his sense of self) and equally a formulation of the perceived change (being 'out of character') was required. With reference to the
latter, Kelly's proposition that behaviour may be viewed as an experiment
suggested Harry was engaged in a fresh enterprise, being aggressive in the
Kellyan sense, of actively elaborating some aspect of himself. That others were
construing Harry's change of behaviour with concern did not necessarily imply that Harry perceived it in this way.

Harry's family had something of a complicated history. His father never married his mother. His mother had subsequently married another man, had
another son and divorced him. For the last three years, Harry's father had
been again, somewhat turbulently, living within the family. Harry suffered
with occasional bouts of migraine and asthma, but nothing else medically of
note. Harry's reticence evaporated fairly rapidly over the first few sessions as
he began to describe his predicament and the struggle to be understood. As
his story unfolded he demonstrated remarkable and astute observations of
himself. His powers of self-analysis appeared all but fully fledged. Reflection
is an interpretative act, a means whereby we construe the way we are.

At school Harry was described as very quiet, preferring his own company,
his concentration likely to wander especially when required to listen, and
showing a vulnerability to 'distraction by other classroom activities or things
outside the classroom which catch his eye'. An assessment of cognitive functioning illustrated both Harry's high level of ability across a broad spectrum of
intellectual activity and literacy and also, in marked contrast, his unease with
visuo-motor tasks and consequent struggle to master mathematical concepts.
A difficulty in assimilating visuospatial information frequently seems inex-
tricably to hinder a child's command of mathematics. A dilemma for Harry,
and children like him, was not the issue of being dim at maths – indeed many
children come to such a conclusion relatively easily, and sometimes with relief
– but that his inability in this one area stood out in stark contrast to his assessment of himself in pretty much all other academic areas. Indeed Harry would
experience much validational support for his notion of himself as bright, but
would have found himself at sea in terms of validation when it came to maths.

Harry might have been considered not only a source of perplexity for others, but also something of a puzzle to himself. The flipside of Jackson and
Bannister's thesis is that some children can be both confusing to others and
confusing to themselves. Our failure to anticipate some of our own actions or
make sense of them retrospectively assures us that self, like the world at large,
is a mixture of the known and the mysterious. Harry had certainly grasped
this. He had fathomed the meaning of much of his behaviour, and yet despite

his ponderings some aspects remained a mystery. A catalogue of confusing experiences (such as Harry's mathematical ability, his illness, his father's return, the change in parental reactions to him, his social isolation and so forth) could invalidate a child's self-construing to such an extent that the child becomes both a mystified and mystifying psychologist. Harry's construing of self became a central issue.

5.3   SELF-CONSTRUING

The notion of self is something of a theoretical and conceptual minefield. Definitions of self and facets of self abound. Many are esoteric, ill-defined and the interchangeability of terminology is perhaps unsurpassed in psychological literature (Butler and Gasson, 2005). Notions such as self-image, self-concept, self-worth and self-esteem are customarily used synonymously and indiscriminately.

Personal construct theory postulates the notion of self is, like any other conception, an act of construing. We make sense of ourselves in the same manner we determine meaning in other events. Given other people play such heightened and significant roles in an individual's life, the means by which we elaborate our construing of self must be essentially similar to how we refine our construing of others. Self-construing is an integral part of our total construct system. Whether we contrast or align ourselves with others, we inevitably accept that 'without' and 'within' are perceived in the same terms. Thus we construe ourselves on constructs we also employ to construe others. As Bannister (1983) portrayed, our 'self-picture and world picture are painted on the same canvas and with the same pigments'. Such a metaphor implies that the self, in addition to being a scientist, may also be equated with artistic endeavour. The active search for similarity (e.g. 'That's just like me') and contrast (e.g. 'You'd never see me like that') generates a sense of differentiation in self-awareness. As the individuality corollary states, people differ from others in the way they construe events, and also therefore in the way they construe themselves. Such views led Bannister (1983) to define self as not a haphazard collection of autobiographical data, but what you believe yourself to be.

Tapping a child's view of their self has traditionally been accomplished through standard self-concept/self-esteem scales, of which there is a vast array to choose from. However, most are one-offs, used in idiosyncratic research studies and appear only fleetingly in the professional literature. Butler and Gasson (2005) reviewed the available scales for children and adolescents, noting that:

- Most lack a distinct theoretical stance, although there are a priori claims either of unidimensionality or implicit recognition of multidimensionality in structure.

- Most have been developed and psychometrically validated on small geographically limited samples, usually in the USA, with arguably little correspondence with a national census, thus creating significant problems in generalization.

- Generally, and perhaps of most concern, there is a widespread reliance on author-generated items in the composition of scales. Hughes (1984) astutely made the point that only instruments composed of individuals' own descriptions of self should be considered as valid measures of self-concept.

5.4 THE SELF-IMAGE PROFILES

Recently the self-image profile (SIP), founded on the maxims of personal construct theory, has been developed to systematically represent a youngster's vision of self (Butler, 2001). In deference to developmental notions of construing, there are now a range of SIPs covering childhood into adulthood with the child version (SIP-C) for age range 7–11 years, the adolescent form (SIP-A) for 12–16 years (Butler, 2001) and recently an adult version (SIP-AD) for 17–65 years published based on similar principles and format (Butler and Gasson, 2004).

Developmentally there is compelling evidence to suggest self-construing progressively elaborates both in structure and content, as the individual moves through childhood and adolescence into young adulthood. With age, constructs increase in number, range of convenience and variety of implications, with a sense of self typically moving from physical to more psychological construing (Bannister and Agnew, 1977; Butler, Redfern and Forsythe, 1990). In tandem, there appears to be increasing discrimination and organization in how the self is structured. 'Concrete' verbal representations of self give way to more psychological self-reference as the individual matures. Butler, Redfern and Forsythe, (1990) found, for example, that young children with nocturnal enuresis perceive their problem in non-psychological terms with concerns over the immediate consequences, hygiene and the contingencies following wetting. As children with enuresis grow older they are more inclined to construe their bed-wetting in psychological terms such as the social and emotional consequences.

Figure 5.1 shows a SIP-A completed by James, a 12-year-old, attending clinic because he had started 'bunking off' school, causing disruption in lessons and avoiding homework. He was genuinely concerned and frustrated by his recent 'avoidance' of school endeavours, suggesting that only being a valued member of the football team kept him attending at all. The SIP has a set of self-descriptions (psychological constructs) down the left-hand side. Items 1–12 are loosely of a positive nature whereas items 13–25 have a more deprecating flavour, a layout which through a quick glance enables the clinician

		Not At All					Very Much		DISCREPANCY
		0	1	2	3	4	5	6	
1	kind						☆		1
2	happy							☆	3
3	friendly							☆	1
4	funny							☆	2
5	helpful					☆			1
6	hard-working						☆		2
7	talkative					☆			1
8	confident						☆		2
9	sporty						☆		0
10	intelligent						☆		3
11	fun to be with						☆		2
12	good looking							☆	2
13	feel different from others				☆				1
14	lazy			☆					1
15	annoying			☆					1
16	moody		☆						1
17	mess about				☆				1
18	shy		☆						1
19	cheeky			☆					0
20	loud				☆				1
21	sarcastic / bitchy		☆						1
22	worry a lot		☆						1
23	bossy	☆							1
24	short-tempered		☆						1
25	get bored			☆					1

The Self Image Profile is published by Butler (2001) and reproduced with permission from Harcourt Assessment.

Figure 5.1 A Self-Image Profile (SIP-A) completed by James. Source: The Self-Image Profile is published by Butler (2001) and reproduced with permission from Harcourt Assessment.

to appreciate the young person's view of self. The youngster is informed that the SIP is a way of helping us understand something about the kind of person they are. It is further suggested that the scale is a survey, not a test, with there being no right or wrong answers. Youngsters are then invited to:

- Consider each item and shade the box according to 'how you think you are' using the 0–6 scale, where 0 means 'not at all' like the description, up to 6 which means 'very much' like the description. Youngsters are reminded that they can use any number along the scale to show 'how you think of yourself'. Only one pole of the construct is shown which facilitates the individual in making ratings.

- Then consider each item again and place a star in the box according to '*how you would like to be*' (an ideal).

5.5 PRINCIPLES UPON WHICH THE SIP IS BASED

Personal Construct Theory has traditionally turned to the repertory grid as a method of exploring how people make sense of themselves, yet as Bannister and Fransella (1986) emphasize, construct theory is potentially rich as an inspiration for new 'instruments'. The attraction of the SIP perhaps lies not so much in its mathematical properties, but in its root assumptions, which stress the importance of items being generated by the population for which it is designed, not by the experimenter who wishes to observe the population. In David Winter's terminology, the SIP concerns itself with the client's, not the clinician's yardstick (Winter, 1992).

All SIPs are composed of items generated by the target population. In contrast to most scales relating to self, where items emerge in line with the author's conceptualization of what determines self-concept, the SIP endeavours to ensure items are relevant and meaningful for the population for whom the scale is intended and representative of events in the child or young person's life. A comprehensive pool of constructs were gathered by inviting large samples of the population to give typical descriptions of themselves in line with customary elicitation procedures described by Butler (1985) and Ravenette (1997).

Given a primary assertion of personal construct theory, that meaning is derived from contrast, individuals were asked to describe the contrast to their elicited self-descriptions. As Greg Neimeyer and colleagues (2005) have empirically demonstrated, asking for the contrast of an elicited construct is less likely to produce extreme or 'bent' constructs than asking for the 'opposite' to an elicited construct. In union with the commonality corollary, from the raft of elicited self-descriptions, themes which frequently emerged were selected as items for the profile. Despite employing the contrast in selecting items, the SIP consists of only one pole to facilitate the individual making ratings or judgements about self. The wording of items on the scale is exactly as elicited by respondents in the elicitation stage. Many self-esteem/self-concept scales are lengthy and repetitive. The child and adolescent SIPs are 25 items in length, comprised of short familiar self-descriptions, selected to ensure brevity and avoidance of repetition of synonymously equivalent items.

The SIP regards the 'raw data' – the information provided by the child – as of paramount importance. There are no attempts to convert the child's responses to fit the theoretical or mathematical constructs of those who administer the questionnaire. The SIP consists of a series of items against which the respondent is invited to rate (from 0 'not at all' to 6 'very much') according to 'how I am' (James's ratings can be seen in Figure 5.1). There is a sense of transparency in that the profile is visually available for both respondent and clinician as they complete it, enabling the person to reveal, to him/herself, as well as to the clinician, something about the way they construe themselves. Further, with no concealed lie scale (a brainchild of the suspicious or cynical) or hidden agenda, the process becomes a shared experience, with acceptance of the child's version of a sense of self and in sympathy with the model of equal expertise.

James's first rating – how I am – might be taken to represent his self-image, defined as the way an individual thinks about their self. James's ratings along the constructs represent what Bannister (1983) alluded to as the self-picture. The visual display of the profile immediately depicts how a child construes himself. This is shared knowledge, demanding no complicated scoring strategy or correlational analysis which has a tendency to quash the child's original response. James's profile at first glance depicts a reasonably positive view of self (with items 1–12 rated generally 3–6) although he rates himself reasonably highly on items such as 'mess about' and 'loud'. Constructs rated at the extreme ends (0 or 6) resemble ways in which the individual portrays a certainty about their self. James for example had a definite vision of himself as 'sporty'.

Although the SIP is 'pitched' at the psychological level of construing, with items reflecting the most frequently elicited self-descriptions, there is a theoretical acceptance of a hierarchical relationship in which psychological constructs are 'sandwiched' between core constructs at a superordinate level and behavioural constructs at a more subordinate level. Finally a unique feature of the SIP is a differentiation, both theoretically and operationally, between self-image and self-esteem, the former representing an identification about how the person thinks of their self and the latter an evaluation judgement according to the person feels about their self along dimensions considered important.

5.6 SCORING OF THE SIP

In addition to the sense of self-depicted on the visual profile, the discrepancy between ratings ('how I am' and 'how I'd like to be') hints at where the youngster feels dissatisfaction with self. The coexistence of ratings indicates James feels completely at ease with himself in terms of being 'sporty' and 'cheeky'. On the other hand a relatively wide discrepancy with 'happy' suggests discontent with self. A therapeutic agenda therefore becomes apparent and employing the SIP as a directional aid to therapy is discussed more fully in Chapter 10. During a discussion about the discrepancies James mooted the theory that his difficulty in lessons contributed to a feeling that his teachers saw him as stupid ('intelligence') thus reducing a desire to engage in school lessons and homework ('hard-working'). He enjoyed sport both for its intrinsic values but also because it enabled him to feel socially validated. Lacking such experiences with teachers, James had started to act up and be the comic ('mess about'; 'cheeky'; 'funny') in class, coupled with more recently school avoidance, providing a sense of validation from both siblings ('fun to be with') and teachers who now perceived him as a troublemaker.

For the computational or those engaged in nomothetic research projects, the SIP can be scored and related to test norms (Butler, 2001). Self-image is derived by summating ratings on 'how I am' items. It has been suggested that items 1–12 portray the desired end of self-statements, so that a cumulative high score on these 12 items gives an indication of positive self-regard. James's score of 46 is suggestive of reasonably positive self-image. Item 13 is a neutral item though does reflect a view that James tends to feel different from other people. Items 14–25 depict the more undesirable pole of self-statements, so summing these scores provides a measure of the youngster's negative sense of self – a score of 27 in James's case. This context sharpens up a working model of self-image as a non-evaluation description of how you think about yourself.

Self-esteem, being an evaluative aspect of self, can be viewed as an affective reflection of how an individual feels about the self, and operationalized as the person's estimate of where they are against where they would like to be. There is a wealth of literature based on an assumption that mental health is related to self-esteem. Reviewed excellently by Nicholas Emler (2001), self-esteem is often considered as mediating variable in a person's performance. Whereas high self-esteem is thought to be adaptive and promote academic achievement, social engagement, sporting excellence, frustration tolerance and so forth, low self-esteem is empirically associated with teenage pregnancy, eating problems and difficulties in social relationships. In short, those with low self-esteem have been found to treat themselves, not others, badly.

There is a fancy within personal construct theory that self-esteem, being an evaluative aspect of self, is characterized by the individual's perceived distance between where they are and where they would ideally wish to be. Thus a person who perceives of their ideal as achievable and within reach might be considered to have a reasonably high self-esteem whereas someone who senses a wide gulf between perceived self and how they would like to be might be considered to be experiencing low self-esteem. Interestingly it might be argued that where a person considers there is very little, if any, discrepancy between self and idealized self, they might experience a sense of complacency.

A second rating of 'how I'd like to be' on the self-image profile enables the distance between self and ideal to be observed and calculated. James's self-esteem, therefore, could be calculated by observing the size of the discrepancy between self and ideal on all items (irrespective of direction of discrepancy) and summing the discrepancies. In James's case his self-esteem score is 32. It should be noted that low scores (because they represent small discrepancies) represent high self-esteem and high scores (as they represent large discrepancies) represent low self-esteem.

Many protagonists within the field of self-concept consider the structure of self to be multidimensional. It is proposed that an individual comes to describe the self through verbalized self-representations across a series of domains such as appearance, social behaviour and sporting competence. In tune with the fragmentation corollary there is also a ready acceptance that a person can hold apparently contrasting views about self across different aspects. It then becomes troublesome theoretically to collapse scores across a number of domains into one score to represent self-concept or self-image. Whereas most scales have author-imposed domains or aspects, the SIP aspects are derived through factor analysis. The SIP-C has seven aspects of self-consisting of social, emotional, behavioural, outgoing/sporty, academic, appearance and resourcefulness. The SIP-A has ten aspects consisting of expressive, caring, outgoing, academic, emotional, hesitancy, sense of difference, activity, unease and resourcefulness.

5.7   FLEXIBILITY OF THE SIP

Although from a nomothetic perspective, items on the SIP remain unaltered, employment of the scale in the clinical context offers countless alternatives. Flexible use of the SIP is imperative clinically, as the essence and validity of any scale must equate with the apposite clinical question coupled with genuinely reflecting what is important to those completing the scale. Self-descriptions are not 'written in stone' as descriptions can be altered or removed and new constructs drafted in to meet the needs of the situation or culture. Examples of modified SIPs, with individually elicited items, are illustrated in Chapters 10 and 11.

A further illustration of flexibility arises in considering, dependent on the clinical context, adopting alternative self-presentations (rather than the customary 'ideal self'). Many different versions of self may be evaluated, through inviting the child or youngster to rate an alternative self against 'how I am' and compare the areas of discrepancy. For example, the following versions of self potentially offer appealing insights into the way a child makes sense of self:

- *'As I used to be'* – past selves fondly remembered or selves eager to forget. Of possible importance in understanding a child's account of how they were before perhaps an accident or disturbing event.

- 'As I will be ... (after the problem has resolved; after treatment; when I settle and so forth) – anticipations of possible future selves either in terms of hope or disquiet. Of particular use in understanding a child's vision of their future.

- 'How others (e.g. parent, friend, teacher) might think of me' – theories as to the expectations of significant others, particularly salient where there are apparent misunderstandings between the child and a significant other. In sympathy with the sociality corollary, this line of questioning also offers a means of understanding the child's capacity to gauge reflected appraisals. The 'theory of mind' notion suggests that some children, notably those with autistic or Asperger's syndrome-type presentations, struggle to understand the psychology of another. Thus asking about another person's view of your self tentatively offers an understanding of how other people are understood.

- 'How important is that?' – authors such as Susan Harter (1999) suggest the discrepancy between self and importance influences self-esteem. Thus a low rating for 'sporty', for example, will affect self-esteem only if the individual regards it as important.

- 'How I ought to be' – the notion of an expected self. Tory Higgins (1989) eloquently suggests the discrepancy between 'self' and 'ought to' impacts on anxiety.

- 'How I am as ... (e.g. a friend, leader, class clown) – understanding the self in different contexts offers an understanding of how children see the roles they adopt.

- 'How I am when acting as if ... (someone else) – such a version of self offers an understanding of the child's version of a role they might be encouraged to adopt experimentally.

5.8 PSYCHOMETRICS OF THE SELF-IMAGE PROFILE

What of validity, a concept embraced so endearingly by psychologists? Validity, in both its content and construct forms, respectively seeks to inquire as to the scale's potency in measuring a representative sample of the behaviour domain to be measured and to the scale's ability to test the theoretical trait under investigation. Given the child-generated nature of the self-descriptions in the SIP, seeking validity measures seems largely superfluous. Bannister and Fransella (1986) equate validity with usefulness and increased understanding. If the profile makes sense to the child, taps his vision of self and reveals patterns that the therapist can usefully harness, then it serves its purpose.

Given, however, that publication demands psychometric investigation, the SIP has been employed in large validational and reliability studies involving Stanley Coopersmith's Self-Esteem Inventory (Coopersmith, 1981), a unidimensional scale with a question format implying evaluative judgements, and Susan Harter's Self Perception Profile for Children (Harter, 1985), which has imposed multidimensional properties. Both these are American although SIP self-esteem scores equate with both Coopersmith's self-esteem and Harter's notion of self-worth, suggesting a similar thread of self-evaluation in the scores whilst many of the self-aspects correlated with Harter's imposed domains of self (Butler, 2001).

5.9   CONCLUSION

Within personal construct theory the notion of self is considered to be an act of construing like any other event. An individual is best understood as making sense of him- or herself through the same manner of construing they employ in grappling with the myriad of other events with which they are confronted. Thus if we are tempted to construe others along a dimension labelled 'stupid' versus the contrast 'bright', we are likely to align ourselves somewhere along just such a construct.

Eliciting a child's constructs therefore provides an opportunity to understand the dimensions they consider important both with respect to themselves and to others. Chapter 4 described a host of ways this might be accomplished. This chapter described a more formal means of accessing how children view themselves, utilizing the self-image profile.

George Kelly showed some hesitation about the manner in which formal assessments were designed and conducted. He was concerned that a test should address clinical issues, something David Winter (1992) has more fully elaborated in the following ways:

- Does the test or scale reflect the construing of the client or the individual who devised the test? The SIP, being composed of child-generated self-descriptions, condensed into a manageable range of items according to a commonality of themes, increases the probability of being meaningful to the youngster in question. Kelly argued that given PCT is primarily concerned with the viewpoint of its object of study – namely the young person – any measures derived from the child are objective.

- Does it elicit permeable constructs, which enable an understanding of the here and now and an anticipation of the future, rather than being concerned purely with the individual's past? Items, particularly for young people, need to be alive and relevant. A desire for flexibility – being able to modify and change according to the situation – compared to a rigid unforgiving framework customarily apparent with many scales, is built into the SIP. The format of asking the child two questions in relation to each self-description – how you are now (present) and how you would wish to be (future)

– seeks an understanding of both the child's predicament and idealized solution.

• Are items representative of events in the child's life? By eliciting items from a sample of children and locating the focus on aspects of self, their relevance and meaningfulness might be considered more appropriate than perhaps projective investigations where a youngster is faced with the challenge of construing the likes of ink blots.

• Do items strike a balance between stability and sensitivity, being concerned both with areas the child perceives as constant or core, and dimensions or avenues along which the child wishes to change? The format of the SIP highlights those aspects where the child wishes to remain stable and those regarded as problematic. Further the youngster is able to estimate the degree to which he perceives a discrepancy between his notion of self and how he would wish to be. The profile thus reveals pathways along which the child wishes to move. In Chapter 10, this notion is developed therapeutically.

• Is the outcome faithful to the data provided by the child? Unlike many other scales, the SIP has no hidden agenda. There is no intent to disguise the purpose of the scale nor is there a wish to catch the child out with lie scales. Further there are no over-complicated scoring systems, such as occur with some self-esteem scales or grid analysis, which tend to neglect the data provided by the child in favour of sophisticated correlational and cluster analyses.

• Does it reveal constructs which are communicable? By incorporating a visual profile the SIP assures the child, in addition to interested others, of the result. The child can reveal, to himself and others, something about himself. The clinician or observer might then appreciate the child's perspective on himself and begin to acknowledge the importance of balancing the child's understanding of self with the customary emphasis upon the clinician's understanding of the child.

CHAPTER 6

CORE CONSTRUING

I wonder if people judge me well.

(Thomas, an 11-year-old boy)

An intuitive sense of self is frequently evident in the way folk reflect on themselves in everyday activities. 'I'm not **my**self today'; 'I don't know why I did that'; 'I'm in two minds'; 'I don't know what's wrong with **me**'; and 'I need to clear my **mind**' are relatively commonplace utterances, particularly when people seem confounded by their own actions. Such phenomenological experiencing of 'I' and 'me' (in bold) echoes William James's notion of dualism in the concept of self. 'I' is the part of self given to pondering on the other, more public facets of self, collectively referred to as 'me'. Thomas's reflection not only classically frames the 'I – me' dualism but beds an evaluation of self in a social context, whereby a search for validation hinges on estimations other folk might have about him. Thomas's predicament hinges on never quite knowing how people might judge him.

Unless the 'I' self can also reflect upon itself, there remains a dilemma as to how the 'I' self can ever be known. William James (1892) astutely highlighted this quandary, suggesting the field lies wide open for philosophical debate. Understanding the 'I' is both theoretically and empirically problematic. However, George Kelly's (1955) proposition that core constructs govern the maintenance of a person's identity suggests we may equate the 'I' self with core construing and thus, through laddering, find a tentative route to understanding the 'I'. If, as Tom Ravenette (2003) suggests, we are typically unaware of our construing (because constructs lie at a low level of awareness) and rarely appeal to our constructs prior to acting, it seems core constructs or the 'I' self is particularly obscured from awareness. Intriguingly, however, as the organization corollary suggests, core construing directs everything we do – a central thread holding the different aspects of self, the multiple roles together. The unconscious (Freud) and natural selection (Darwin) are apposite examples of 'hidden' forces responsible for what happens in the world which remain secret, subtle and beyond our immediate awareness. Viewed in a similar vein, core construing might be thought to be fundamentally linked to each action we take although rarely, if ever, do we act with direct reference to them.

The self is an act of creation, constructed and elaborated over time. Core constructs, like other constructs, are the result of abstractions arising and evolving to assist the anticipation of our self. The youngster is in the exacting business of not only construing the 'outside' world but also of construing him- or herself. The construct 'hard-working – lazy' holds equal relevance for understanding the self as it does for understanding others. Once generated, constructs provide the basis for predicting future events, are formed into patterns of interdependence and are organized in a hierarchical manner with ordinal relationships between constructs. Those constructs relating to psychological abstractions such as friendly, moody or hard-working lie in a subordinate relationship with core constructs that fundamentally define the self. Core constructs remain relatively stable throughout life, maintaining the person as a person. It is as if, although we recognize fluctuation, shifts and transformations in the way we construe ourselves over time, the essential 'me-ness' remains the same.

Kelly considered that core constructs enable a person to maintain their identity, what may colloquially be known as their 'sense of being'. Although the sense of me-ness is often difficult to gauge, William James, early in the twentieth century, proposed a set of theoretical constructs to sketch a sense of what characterizes the core structure. Don Bannister (1983) elaborated these dimensions in a paper entitled 'self in personal construct theory', noting that superordinate constructs tend to be erected by persons in order to make sense of experiences that contribute towards the emergence of their sense of self. The dimensions include:

6.1 A SENSE OF SEPARATENESS

We each entertain a notion of our own separateness from others, and it is this detachment which enables us to formulate contrasts and distinctions between ourselves and others. Individuality provides a sense of coherence, an appreciation of being a unique bounded entity with the privacy of our own consciousness. However, the legitimacy of individuality may be affected by:

- Development – young children, in Piagetian terms, may be immersed in what observers consider to be 'egotistical' endeavours. They display their distinctiveness in terms of their name, their difference from others and the ubiquitous sense that things are 'never fair' with the child's wish for his or her needs to be recognized, despite parents testifying that they treat everyone 'equally and alike'. Adolescence is oft characterized by feverish and impatient searches for independence and individuality, which although traditionally construed as necessary and healthy in terms of a developing autonomous self, appear inevitably to stretch parental composure, patience and tolerance.

- Context – in creative ventures, such as art or writing, individualism is fostered and valued whereas other contexts such as supporting a sports team, being in a choir or entering the guides or scouts favour collective rather than individualistic construing, where commonality of construing is paramount. Ironing out individuality is a stated aim.

- Culture – Western societies tend to highly value the sense of individuality, separateness and distinctiveness, whereas in more Eastern cultures such individuality may seem egotistical, indulgent and narcissistic.

6.2 A SENSE OF CONTINUITY

Don Bannister (1983) elaborated the notion of continuity, that sense of being essentially the 'same person' you were yesterday, or last year, or in distant memories, despite encountering many significant and varied life experiences. Children reflect a continuity of self through identification with their name, family membership, possessions (e.g. I still have the teddy bear I had as a baby), activities and hobbies (e.g. I've played piano since I was seven years old; I've always liked reading). Later continuity is understood through a sense of permanence in personal characteristics of the self (e.g. I've always been shy), then with an ongoing recognition of self by others (e.g. My friends have always known how moody I can be) and finally at a high developmental level with reference to more abstract understandings of self (e.g. I've always been unlucky; I've always believed in hard work).

By employing one's biography as a thread, a narrative elaborated over a timeline, the individual is able to vividly link the past to the present self. Whilst some youngsters reflect on the dynamics of their continuation, discovering their competency, talents, weaknesses and vulnerabilities, others, perhaps of a more impulsive and aggressive ilk (in the Kellyan sense), live more in the here and now. As Don Bannister, poetically suggests, for such youngsters, the past represents a 'limited catalogue of events which are seen dimly and as of little present relevance'.

The stories individuals have regarding their psychological growth rarely fit the developmental stages outlined in the many texts and tomes on child development that clutter the creaking library bookshelves. Phil Salmon (1970) fully debated this issue, highlighting how the experience of development does not accord with identified stages or points. More usually children reflect on their own development by noting 'watershed points'. Perhaps events perceived as trivial to others may have an enormously significant and lasting influence in creating a notion of self. Although there may be a tendency to look towards the trauma of family disruption or upheaval as potentially influential in development given life event theory, personal construct theory values the individual's construing of an event, not the event itself, with greater importance. What is often significant in moulding a view of self are not events anticipated by an interested 'other' as significant, but what the youngster construes as significant. Potentially influential are events that pose a threat to the child's core construing, not the severity of the event itself.

The experience corollary, which states that a person's construction system varies as they successively construe the replication of events, might help to further this point. We change our view of self in relation to the accuracy of our anticipations. Thus we might, as a youngster, consider our self to be mature, self-assured and reasonably streetwise, until perhaps innocently but disparagingly, another child on a school trip points out how neatly our lunch box is packed. Suddenly the child's constructions about self, regarding maturity and independence, are found wanting. Kellyan hostility might help preserve the child's sense of maturity – he may resort to bullying and taunting the child who made the comment in order to reduce the potency of the remark. Alternatively the child, in accounting for how he has acquired such a well-presented lunch with all its trimmings, might revise his self-construing and begin to entertain the notion that he really is something of a 'mummy's boy'. Thus what may appear 'trivial' to others may have prodigious personal significance.

6.3 A NOTION OF PERSONAL CHANGE

Change, particularly of self-construing, is demanding, particularly in light of Bannister and Agnew's (1977) astute observation that permanence is a central characteristic of the self. The perception of self as unchanging is deterministic and often thought to be genetically loaded. It generates statements such as 'I am not one for going around making friends', 'I'm just like my dad in his love of music', 'I was brought up to respect other people's property', 'I keep out of trouble. I keep quiet. In that way I don't get noticed' and 'I'm no good at maths'. The choice corollary highlights how individuals seek to elaborate their self-construing. One option is preservation of the self through repeated experiments, something Kelly thought of as definition. A youngster might choose to continually define the self in a particular fashion with well-rehearsed methodology and known results. Such choices may resemble perfectionism, a desire for control, a need to avoid chaos and striving for security and safety. The known self is repeatedly played out. Repetitive the actions may seem, but they remain personal choices.

At a fundamental level, individuals are aware that they are the initiator of any action relevant to themselves. They are aware of their sense of agency or 'free will'. The choice corollary, in depicting a person's search for elaboration of self identifies an alternative strategy to definition – that of extension. With this choice, the youngster moves in the direction of experiments where the answers may be unknown. Extension is marked by risk-taking, accepting challenges and trying fresh approaches in trying to make sense of their world. Placing the self in new and unusual settings enables a youngster to entertain views about the robustness of self. They may discover their core construing is validated from new sources. Thus a child may seek to extend their sense of achievement through taking up a new venture such as playing the guitar and notice either they 'can do it' or find it 'too difficult'. Either way, core construing relating to achievement has been extended. The outcome is dependent on validational experiences, with the youngster evolving a sense of self as either musical or tone-deaf.

6.4   A NOTION OF PRESENTATION

Although, being social creatures, individuals are enmeshed in the social fabric of others, there remains an issue as to how the self is presented to others. This representation of self appears to hinge on the eagerness a person has to communicate the vision of the public self versus the desire to remain mysterious to others (the private or hidden self). This construct has been elaborated by social psychologists interested in the authentic versus false selves we present to others.

A public self is marked by a desire for recognition, belonging, being genuine, avoiding rejection, pleasing others, avoiding criticism, meeting others' approval and being understood, whereas retaining a private self is characterized by being difficult to know, being unpredictable, being reserved over talking about themselves, protective over who knows what about them and only occasionally, if at all, letting their 'guard down'.

Such modes of presentation are far from fixed. Youngsters may eagerly show something of their 'real self' to some and remain protective of other aspects of their self with other people. Ross, for example, felt easily able to share something of his desire for achievement with adults. His public self – that of being intelligent, someone who reads a lot and able to hold scientific debate – was presented successfully in his relationships with adults but failed miserably in his attempts to get on with children. In his words he speculated that 'Kids don't understand me'. Ross therefore manufactured another public self for when he was with children, a major experiment in self-creation, where aspects of self were generated anew. Ross told the tale: 'I've made a character up at school. Stupid. Dummy. I act like I'm stupid. Others understand me easier. I make jokes up. They think I'm stupid. At least they don't pick on me or beat me up. They leave me alone. Then I'm all right'.

Ross's experience fits well with Miller Mair's (1977a) contention that we often construct our selves as 'fortresses set up against a hostile world and assume, on the psychological plane, that the Englishman's home is still his castle'. Ross was able, it seemed, to construe himself as both bright and stupid depending upon the context in which he was functioning at any one time. In formulating a protective public persona concerned with being stupid, Ross was in effect developing a 'splinter self'. He appeared easily to be able to step in and out of a new 'stupid' self at will.

Miller Mair (1997b) developed an idea around the self as a community. He postulated that individuals may adopt very different, often contrasting, roles in different contexts, each role with its own self-history, anticipatory nature and validational history. The common phenomenon of a child behaving very differently at home from at school is a broad illustrative example. Of importance, in personal construct theory terms, is whether the child perceives of himself differently in these two contexts. Only if he does so, might he be conceived as having two selves. Ross's description of himself as behaving as if he were in two minds – the private adult self and the dummy child self – is a lived experience of this notion of a community of selves.

The idea of the person living through different selves is not to regard the individual as pathological. It is an invitation to consider youngsters as if they were able to take on different selves in making sense of the different and varied situations which confront them. Rather than being pathological, a community of selves may, instead, enable the person to actively experience and explore the world from numerous perspectives. Having many vantage points from which to act might indeed enhance the individual's pursuit of making sense. To paraphrase Robert Bolt, could it be that Ross is 'a child for all seasons'?

6.5 STRUCTURE OF SELF

As with all means of making sense, the organizational corollary suggests the self has a hierarchical structure. The properties of an object lead us to categorize it in more abstract, universal forms. Thus the specifics of a wooden object with four legs, a seat and a back lead to the categorization of 'chair' whereas four legs, a seat and no back leaves us with 'stool'. Both chairs and stools are types of furniture, a higher order construct. Figure 6.1 diagrammatically presents the hierarchical structure of self.

At the most subordinate level, constructs consist of physical characteristics (e.g. size, height, hair colour), social roles (e.g. mother, teacher, friend) and of a behavioural nature (e.g. plays the piano). Such constructs are predominantly produced by young children when asked to elicit constructs relating to themselves or others. They may also be elicited by pyramiding from higher order constructs by inviting youngsters to describe the detail of what a construct means to them, or how they see the construct operating with someone else. Performance profiles (see Chapter 7) are maps of elicited behaviours or characteristics that an individual considers are important in being 'expert'. They have importance in providing a display of how the youngster sees his performance against how he would wish to be (Butler and Hardy, 1992; Butler, Smith and Irwin, 1993).

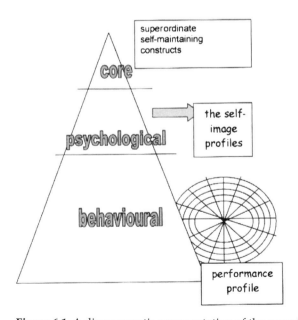

Figure 6.1 A diagrammatic representation of the organization corollary.

Inviting slightly older children and youngsters to describe themselves tends to reveal descriptions of a more psychological nature. Laddering from behavioural constructs also tends to elicit constructs of a more psychological nature. Those most commonly employed by children and adolescents are highlighted on the self-image profiles (Butler, 2001)

Core constructs lie at the pinnacle of the hierarchy. They are the self-maintaining notions that fundamentally underpin all self-descriptions and behaviours and may be characterized as:

- *Fundamental* – Kelly (1955) proposed that core constructs govern the maintenance of a person's identity and as such lie fundamentally at the heart of the individual's sense of self.

- *Executive* – Core constructs guide each anticipatory choice, action and stance an individual takes. The core is the banner under which a person fights; the person's guide to living. Dorothy Rowe (2003) suggests core constructs are concerned with survival as a person.

- *Superordinate* – Core constructs, sited at the pinnacle of a hierarchy, have a wide range of convenience, encapsulating the raft of self-descriptions and actions a person characteristically accounts for in terms of their self (Stefan, 1977; Butt, Burr and Epting, 1997).

- *Resistant to change* – Compared to constructs at a lower level, core constructs remain invariably stable. Interestingly it is in the area of core construing that we may not always act as if we are good scientists, strongly holding on to a core belief about our self, even in the face of invalidating evidence. The possibility of change in core construing leads to Kellyan hostility and threat with the determined desire of preserving the self rather than re-construe.

- *Being at a low level of awareness* – Core constructs are not readily accessible yet we come to understand the world through the lens of our core constructs with little conscious awareness (McWilliams, 2004). We rarely appeal to core constructs, yet our actions ultimately seek to validate or avoid invalidation of a core construct. Larry Leitner and Jill Thomas (2003) suggest core constructs exist at a low level of awareness because of the possibility of profound threat if invalidated.

- *Finite and few in number* – Almost by definition core constructs, being at the pinnacle of a hierarchy, are limited in number.

- *Universality* – Interestingly Dorothy Rowe (2003) found, to her surprise, that not only is there a limited number of core constructs, but they also tend to have a degree of universality.

6.6 ELICITATION

Revealing core constructs requires reflection. Laddering offers a befitting means of tapping into the hierarchical structure of self and eliciting core constructs. Fay Fransella (2003) suggests successful laddering requires the listener to suspend their own construing (tempering their own assumptions) and seek to subsume the youngster's construing (accepting their construing), not a particularly easy venture. It is in the process of laddering that one gets closest to an experience of being almost a part of the other person.

As every act is a presentation of self, the starting point for laddering is immaterial. It may be a behaviour, preference (appearance, music, activity), possession or self-description. They are all social questions in the sense that they express a youngster's identity. Laddering promotes the elicitation of higher order constructs. It begins with asking the youngster to either select a preferred pole of a bipolar construct or inquire as to whether the behaviour, possession or event is important for them.

The apposite question then transpires. Fay Fransella and Peggy Dalton (1990) have suggested that laddering is 'no more and no less than asking the question "why?"'. However, with youngsters such questions can be experienced as intimidating and accusatory as they seem inevitably confronted with questions of 'Why?' in the context of wrongdoing. With children therefore, an alternative laddering question takes the form of: 'How come this is important for you?' As each construct is elicited, the questioning continues in the same vein, moving up the hierarchy, through psychological constructs to core constructs. For the youngster the task appears increasingly difficult, if only in finding appropriate words to express notions emerging into awareness. When youngsters can no longer find a means of expressing 'importance' or where responses appear repetitive, the hierarchical summit is, for all practical purposes, reached. Eliciting core constructs is a powerful endeavour, with youngsters maybe experiencing and revealing for the first time something of their 'true self'. Being a collaborative venture such discovery may helpfully lay the foundations of a beneficial therapeutic alliance with the youngster sensing that their view is being seriously listened to and assimilated.

6.7 CONTENT OF CORE CONSTRUCTS

There is a view that core constructs are uniquely individual. However Dorothy Rowe (2003) suggests otherwise, proposing that individuals have a limited number of universal core constructs, although the content of such constructs remains open to conjecture. Rowe contends that the person either experiences a sense of existence in terms of relationship to others with an accompanying fear of abandonment and rejection, or experiences existence in terms of a sense of order, achievement, clarity and control with the accompanying fear of chaos. Psychologists with alternative theoretical perspectives, such as Roman Tafarodi and William Swann (1995), echo this stance, suggesting two core dimensions or axes – self-liking and self-competence. Self-liking, which is socially dependent, draws on Cooley's proposition, and is formed through a process whereby one comes to view oneself as represented in the evaluative reactions of others. This internalization of the other's perspective gives rise to constructs relating to social approval and fear of rejection. Self-competence, on the other hand, relates to the sense of oneself as capable, effective and in control, judged against some internal standard.

Early psychological texts might have framed these two strands in terms of affiliation and achievement, both with their 'motivational' nuances. From a Kellyan perspective, core constructs maintain the individual's identity not so much by motivational force but by anticipatory actions. Behaviours are forms of questions through which the youngster seeks validation. Thus core constructs may be viewed as the person's needs.

However, a survey in adults has revealed not two but four clusters of core constructs (Butler, 2006). Given the idea that core constructs are characterized by a sense of permanence and continuity, it is reasonable to propose such core needs have their origins in childhood. The four types of core constructs are shown in Table 6.1 and have been conceptualized as follows:

1. *Making sense* – here core construing rotates around a youngster's sense of their capacity to impose meaning and establish coherence leading to a sense of *self-competence*. The question faced by a youngster's is, 'Am I capable?' Where a sense of competence is important for young people they eagerly choose activities they anticipate will validate this sense of self, showing a ready appetite to understand and engage in tasks. Only when a child seeks information and feedback (as opposed to appraisal) for their work and effort, are they testing out issues of competency. Taking the perspective of William James and, more latterly, Susan Harter (1999), a person's accomplishments are largely evaluated in relation to an internal frame of reference or personal standard. Thus youngsters might be observed deeply focused on a task they wish to master. Jacob Bronowski (1973) compellingly reflected that 'the most powerful drive in the ascent of man is the pleasure of his own skill. He loves to do what he does well and, having done it well, he loves to do it better'. What applies to 'man' applies equally as well for children.

Alternatively youngsters may avoid experiences that could invalidate a sense of competence, opting out of ventures that might not fit with a view of self. Core construing around self-competence embodies Kelly's fundamental postulate, whereby a person strives for personal meaning. Although all actions,

Table 6.1 The four types of core constructs in relation to youngster's self-construing

Cluster	Fundamental question	Core constructs
1. *Self-competence* based on *a need to make sense*	'How capable am I?'	Understanding Competence Master situations Being understood Need for fairness Authenticity
2. *Self-respect* based on *relatedness*	'How well liked am I?'	Meet others' approval Avoid criticism Attempt to please others Avoid rejection Conforming
3. *Self-determination* based on *achievement*	'Will I succeed?'	Looking for challenges Being competitive Achieving success Avoiding failure Achieving recognition Seeking control Seeking power
4. *Self-reliance* based on *individuality*	'Am I being myself?'	Individuality Being different Not conforming Anti-authoritarian Independence

according to Kelly, are scientific in the sense of enabling the person to check their theories, where a youngster's core construing resonates with notions of competence, that person's actions also test their sense of self as a good scientist.

2. *Relatedness* – here a person's sense of self, as contended by Rowe (2003) is embedded in the notion of relationships with others, particularly in terms of the search for approval, the desire to draw favour, acceptance or recognition from others and avoidance of criticism, displeasure or rejection, leading to social conformity and *self-respect*. Recognition of the way we would wish to be seen, by others who independently and freely give it, validates the view we have of ourselves. Susan Stager and Richard Young (1982) sought to study self-construing in young children by applying a semantic differential model (evaluation, potency and activity) to represent the theoretical heterogeneity of self-concept. They invited children as young as four years to rate themselves on a number

of supplied pictorial/verbal scales (e.g. happy – sad; strong – weak; fast – slow) and found through factor analysis that the most important factor was defined by relatedness – specifically how well the young child felt they were liked or disliked by other people.

The youngster, for whom this core sense of self is important, trades as it were in the sociality corollary, seeking to detect the opinions of others about themself and incorporate these into the sense of self. A youngster's theory of self is thus tested through actions that anticipate favourable reactions from the other, either real or imagined. This idea is elaborated by Larry Leitner and Jill Thomas (2003), in which they suggest it makes little sense to consider the self apart from the social milieu in which the individual operates, thus contending that the self is best understood as a social construction. Through employing the core construct of *self-respect*, youngsters make choices dependent on the imagined effect their actions may have upon another's mind. They are likely to seek out the company of other people, build friendships, enjoy social engagements, value trustworthiness, support and help others, try and please others through humour, and show their accomplishments to others for approval.

Youngsters seeking validation for their self-respect are likely to construe themselves psychologically as friendly, outgoing, having a sense of humour, caring, being helpful and trustworthy. They seek appraisal for their school work, acknowledgement for their appearance and recognition for their successes. They may also look to avoid potentially invalidating experiences by, for example, shyness. Lonely it may be, but evading social engagements at least means avoiding possible invalidation. There are of course youngsters who seek affirmation from their peer group at the expense of wider disapproval. Thus whilst risk-taking, destructiveness, being loud, sarcastic, bitchy and bullying may validate a sense of self and indeed self-respect within a group of immediate friends, parental or societal disapproval is effectively devalued through Kellyan hostility.

3. *Achievement* – the third strand of core construing meshes with Rowe's sense of existence in terms of achievement. Through the challenges and competitiveness of sport, academic pursuit, projects, video games and so forth youngsters seek validation of self by striving for success and avoidance of failure. This cluster of core constructs has been framed as sense of *self-determination*. Validation usually arises through other people's acknowledgement of performance, sometimes roused by a child's insistence that others note their accomplishment. Thus newly acquired skills are readily 'shown off' in the hope that others will recognize their ability. Many structures within school are designed around validating a child's sense of self-determination through recognition and emphasis

on both the process (effort and hard work) and outcome (awards, passing tests, projects and exams, winning a merit, achieving a promotion into a higher class or stream and so forth).

4. *Individuality* – a fourth cluster, framed in terms of *self-reliance*, suggests a youngster's sense of self is bound up with notions of nonconformity, freedom of choice, independence and individuality. Here the person chooses, in a Kellyan sense, to act with creativity, rebellion, impartiality, unconventionality, dissent, maverick intent and possibly eccentricity in anticipating the greatest possibility for elaboration of their sense of individuality. As adolescence flourishes, a sense of difference often assumes importance. Against a background of perceived control, rules and authority, some youngsters choose to elaborate their individuality and autonomy through anti-authoritarian and rebellious acts. They detach themselves from conventional settings through mischievousness, creativity, humour, risk-taking and acting weird, wacky or strange. The fundamental endeavour is to create a sense of being 'myself' and avoiding conformity or situations that may promote a sense of 'falseness'.

6.8   CONCLUSIONS

The organization corollary suggests a person's construct system is composed of constructs relating with each other in an ordinal manner. Thus any behaviour or act may be seen as ultimately resulting from core construct needs. Behaviour poses a question relevant to the needs of core constructs. Thus laddering from any construct, no matter how subordinate, should reveal higher order configurations, ultimately leading to those which maintain the person's identity – the core constructs. Thomas, whose quote 'I wonder if people judge me well' which kicked off the chapter, appears to have evolved a core construct concerning the need for approval from other people. Thus it might be anticipated that Thomas would act so as to facilitate good reactions from other folk. He may endeavour to tidy his room, avoid teasing his brother and give his best effort to homework tasks. It is of course possible that acts do not produce the anticipated reactions from other people and it is in such circumstances, where ultimately core construing is threatened, that youngsters act with Kellyan hostility in seeking to extort, perhaps through extra effort or earnest claims for acknowledgement, validational evidence in favour of being judged in a good light.

Embracing the principle that all behaviour ultimately makes sense to the protagonist, within the context of the organizational corollary, implies that whatever stance an individual adopts, it serves to validate the person's core construing. Thus, destructive behaviour, stealing, mutism, impulsivity, cruelty to animals and so forth remain choices that serve to validate core construing. Those who consider themselves as lonely or alienated adopt behaviours that validate such a stance. They may choose to play on their own, refuse invites to parties and absorb themselves in isolating activities. Roy Baumeister (2005), a social psychologist interested in the core construct of approval and acceptance and the contrast of exclusion and rejection, has taken an empirical approach by manipulating experimenter-determined social invalidation. He has found compelling evidence that when individuals experience rejection they act in socially undesirable ways, with aggression, impulsivity, cheating on tests, selfishness and being less likely to help others. The person's stance is a means of validating a sense of rejection and thus it is maintained. Thus individuals may develop a view of self at a core level which stands in contrast to how they would wish to be. They may seek approval but begin to see self as excluded and rejected.

As core constructs are concerned with survival as a person and as they remain at a low level of awareness, bringing them into the open can cause the person to feel vulnerable. Thus laddering has to be undertaken with care. Revealing core constructs can, however, enable a youngster to begin, for the first time, to understand how his or her acts are linked to deeper needs and notions about the self.

Any behaviour may serve to validate more than one core construct at any one time. Thus a youngster might best anticipate the greatest possibility for the elaboration of both their self-respect and self-determination by choosing to work diligently and revise for a test in the anticipated hope that the outcome will be successful and bring approval from teachers and parents

It is likely that a youngster's notion of self is maintained through a range of core constructs and the variety of roles they adopt may serve to validate different core constructs. Thus a youngster may primarily seek validation for a sense of self-determination whilst at school, self-respect when out with friends and self-connectedness when on the terraces supporting the local sports team. Mair (1977b) suggested the metaphor of a 'community of selves' to account for this experience and to help articulate the complicated nature of our role relationships. Core constructs may also serve to moderate a youngster's actions or, in Kellyan terms, aggression. Jim seeks self-respect so readily he accepts invites from his friends to join them in late-night activities, ensuring he avoids rejection. However, Jim has a second core construct concerning the need for competence. When the need to be competent overrides pleasing others he has to turn down his friends occasionally to concentrate on homework.

Without a moderator, an individual's acts serve only one need. The desire for achievement may lead to a preoccupation with academic tasks, the need for self-reliance may create eccentricity and the need for approval may lead to a chameleon-like acceptance of doing what others wish. It is interesting to postulate that a reliance on the validation of only one core construct may create

psychological vulnerability for the individual. Where a youngster is dependent on one core construct to maintain their sense of identity, they may appear
especially distressed should they experience invalidation. Thus should a child
for whom self-respect dominates their sense of identity, experience criticism,
they might endure an acute sense of isolation. A youngster for whom being
in control dominates their anticipatory validation (as someone with compul-
sive nature might), it is likely they will experience acute distress should they
experience a situation that prevents them asserting control.

Sometimes there may be a compromise amongst core needs, and effective
adaptation requires a balance to be maintained between them. Failure to
maintain the balance creates dilemmas and conflict in core constructs which
can form the basis of distress. For example, a need to avoid parental disapproval may generate a desire to tidy up a bedroom, yet an emerging need
to be anti-authoritarian may require an adolescent to live in the messiest of
bedrooms. Thus conflict between core constructs may result in annoyance
(at parental invalidation of untidiness) and hostility. Academic pursuit (the
need for competence)] may conflict with peer popularity (need for approval)
or being anti-authoritarian. In validating the need for self-reliance and self-
respect, an adolescent girl is fine having fun with friends in her bedroom yet
when one suggests going out to hang about on the street, she senses anxiety as this brings into play a conflicting construct – that of being in control.
She anticipates suddenly losing control and being unsure she is able to fully
understand the implications of hanging around on the street.

CHAPTER 7

PERFORMANCE AND COMPETENCE

I want to be an astronaut.

Substitute train driver, doctor, cowboy, pop singer, dancer, footballer or bank robber for astronaut. Such ubiquitous assertions from young children reveal something of their anticipations of future selves. And such hoped for identities, given George Kelly's claim that 'a person's behaviour is determined by the nature of their construct system' (Kelly, 1955), guide action. Youngsters seek to adopt behaviours that align them with a desired identity. Dance moves choreographed in front of a mirror, playfully operating on the cat, teaching a teddy bear to eat greens and practising ball control in the mode of a professional footballer are a sundry collection of identities tried on for size. The behavioural expression of a role or identity may be seen as a performance.

A performance may be understood as the delivery of a prepared set of behaviours. They take many forms. Acting a role in the school play (even just a sheep or stable door in the nativity), a sporting performance, building a brick tower, making a model with a construction toy, doing a drawing, playing the violin, playing competitive games on the computer, playing chess, mending a bicycle, setting up the video for an incompetent parent, mowing the lawn for an elderly aunt, doing an audition or writing a story are a few of the myriad of daily examples. A performance may of course represent a perfected set of behaviours that draws disapproval from others yet endorses the child's stance and identity. Thus youngsters can perfect dawdling, silly or argumentative stances, for example. Interestingly such renditions are often disparagingly considered to represent the child 'putting on' a performance or 'showing off'.

As with all behaviours, performances represent questions. Questions relating to a youngster's desired identity, their vision of self, and ultimately their core construing. In the playground, classroom, music lesson, sports field and swimming pool, children put on performances. Feedback, either asked for (e.g. 'Look what I've done') or sensed, either validates or potentially invalidates core needs. Thus an accomplished performance may satisfy a need for approval, a sense of mastery, a feeling of independence or a desire for control. In contrast, a poor performance, depending on the youngster's core construing, might lead respectively to a sense of disapproval, failure, rejection or chaos. Three particular aspects of performance – competence, confidence and connoisseurship – will be the focus of this chapter.

7.1   COMPETENCE

An individual's estimate of their ability to undertake a task might aptly describe the notion of competence. Children might perceive themselves as good at certain tasks yet perhaps simultaneously claim their incompetence in other areas. The appetite children have for what is construed to be within their capabilities with accompanying claims of 'Watch me!' and 'Easy-peasy!' contrasts markedly with a tendency to avoid ventures considered to be beyond them.

Children of course cope with perceived incompetence in many ways. A child, for example, may opt out of activities such as sport, music, languages and art, thus avoiding further instances of incompetence, although the notion of self as incompetent is validated by the very experience of avoidance. The commonplace and recurring affirmations we hear from adults as to their inability to play music or reflections about how bad they were at school with languages appear confirmation of their preparedness to construe themselves as incapable.

A mark of performing is the desire to accomplish the task with some sense of expertise. The performance marks the child out as approved of, competent and/or independent depending on their core construing. In fashioning their expertise, youngsters are the focus of much unprovoked and unsolicited advice as well as being recipients of needed support, inspiration and consolation. However, the influence of a 'mentor' is not contained by the role they play, be it parent, teacher, coach, older sibling or private tutor, but by their relationship with the youngster. Kelly's initial thoughts when asked about how his theory applied to a child who failed to learn to read, were 'Find out if the child likes the teacher!' It is this sense of respect that a child has for their mentor which determines the extent of their engagement with a task. Children invariably turn their back on 'areas of learning' where instructors and teachers fail to acknowledge the child's stance. It would indeed seem important to like one's mentor if you are to trust him or her to guide you through a venture so fraught with potential embarrassments and humiliations. A teacher's role from a construct theory perspective might best be conceptualized as one who encourages, with support, a child's tentative steps towards the unknown, always with vigilant recognition of his experiments and elaborations. Perhaps the most creative and inventive learning occurs when we aspire to teach in ways that a child learns best.

Wherever a child turns, he or she is faced with validational experiences regarding their performance. At home there is compelling evidence linking parental attributions and feelings towards a child with how the child construes him- or herself (Rowe, 1983; Butler, Redfern and Holland, 1994). Parental annoyance, anger and intolerance towards a child's mistakes, misdeeds and fallibilities in the guise of such negative comments as 'You're useless, give it here', firmly places the youngster in a position of internalizing the feeling. Hence children blame themselves. Indeed they may readily come to feel useless, incompetent and unworthy.

At school, a child is potentially further at risk of construing self as incompetent. Teachers who customarily focus their concerns and efforts on the child's ability and effort will inevitably at times evaluate the child as lacking in either ability or effort, or sometimes both. As far as homework and test marks are perceived in comparative terms by the child, there is an inherent vulnerability to construe themselves as incompetent compared to others in their class. However, more subtle dynamics are also apparent in the teaching process. With regards to art for example, Betty Edwards (1988) has discussed the joy many young children experience in their early doodlings with pencil and paper and how they construct and share with delight their first drawings. She has eloquently argued that children, who are then subsequently corrected in their art, as if there were a prescribed way of doing it, come to construe themselves as not very good. They advance the notion, both to themselves and to others, that they can't draw. Thus in middle childhood we see many children give up on drawing. They lay their frustrated and meddled experiences of drawing to rest. What they maintain is a sketchy but readily volunteered construction of themselves as pretty lousy in that department.

The playing field, often the source of success and nourishment of achievement and competence may, for some, become a further arena in which incompetence is promoted. Error correction is indubitably a kernel of traditional coaching. However, a ceaseless focus on what a child is doing wrong generates the notion, and one often expressed, that 'I'm no good at that'. It is not surprising then that many children opt out of sporting, music and artistic endeavours at the earliest possible opportunity.

Peers, it might seem, offer a safer haven. The compelling security of friend-ship may defuse much unwanted criticism and nurture the child's sense of competence. Those very acts of bravado and daring many children pursue in the company of other children may be seen as means of gaining credibility and 'currying favour' with their peers. However, peers are also the source of much threat. Sometimes their actions undermine the child's notion of self as competent and raise the child's awareness, in a Kellyan sense, that sweeping changes in core construing may be imminent. The widespread taunts and jibes many children bear may focus the child's own attention on his or her incompetence. The dread of social exclusion, by peers not allowing the child to join in shared activities, may leave a child feeling isolated, unusual and lacking in social competence. Flippant quips, jokes and banter along with more critical remarks about a child that he is no good, has to seek help, or has to have special needs, also severely endanger the child's notion of self as competent.

Although avoidance of tasks with which the youngster feels incompetent is a means of coping, it narrows the child's perceptual field. Lost are the var-ied validational experiences, the desire to test out new experiments and the sense of elaborating fresh facets of the self. However, some areas of perceived incompetence cannot be so easily avoided. They have to be continually en-dured. Literacy, the agony of those with unrecognized dyslexia, and numer-acy are two such areas. A child's struggle with the experience of dyslexia is discussed further in Chapter 9. As for the acquisition of mathematical con-cepts, interestingly, Piaget regarded the teacher's role as being intellectually non-interventionist and relatively unimportant; with mathematics being es-sentially 'constructed by children themselves'. The teacher who intervenes, he argued, may foster the child's sense of incompetence.

Margaret Donaldson (1984) predicted that children have considerable dif-ficulty in learning mathematics because much of what is taught in school is relatively 'dis-embedded' from the immediate context. Martin Hughes (1986) has elaborated on this, regarding mathematics as a secret code, a code which contains a number of features that distinguish it from the in-formal mathematics children acquire before school. He argued that the diffi-culty for children in acquiring mathematical concepts lies in their difficulty translating from one form of representation to another – from recognizing that $6 - 2 = 4$ is a representation of 'me only having four sweets left if I give my sister two of them'. Written arithmetic problems serve no obvi-ous purpose for the child first entering school. Hughes argued that in order for maths to prove meaningful, the child has to translate the problem into everyday usage. The teacher's role might be best utilized in helping chil-dren translate – to see the advantages that grasping mathematical concepts might have for the child in his contact with the world. Hughes discussed how children who struggle with maths may not have been convinced that the journey of understanding is worth taking. Children need help in decid-ing that a journey is indeed worth exploration. As Bannister and Fransella (1986) vividly surmised in relation to change, 'No one voluntarily walks the plank into the unknown depths of the ocean.' The teacher is of course piv-otal in encouraging the child to walk that metaphorical plank and take the plunge.

7.2   CONFIDENCE

Confidence might be conceptualized as related to the 'goodness of fit' be-tween how an individual expects to perform, based in part on their sense of competence, and how they actually perform. There may be an anticipatory sense of confidence (or lack of confidence) in the person's predictive assess-ment of whether they will (or will not) meet their expectation in addition to a reflected feeling of confidence depending on how well the performance 'fits' with their expectation. Such a model of confidence adopts Mildred McCoy's (1977) notion of goodness of fit, as discussed in Chapter 3. Where there is a discrepancy between expectation and performance, the person experiences guilt (behaving in a way they would not have anticipated of themselves). Such a model equally describes a person's lack of confidence in 'goodness of fit' terms as it does a person's sense of confidence.

Butler (1996) extended McCoy's notion of goodness of fit, originally within the sporting context. What follows an estimate of efficacy or competence appears crucial. Should the youngster's estimate be validated, there is goodness of fit. Thus when the competent piano player gives a virtuoso performance their expectation is confirmed and they are likely to experience confidence. A child who perceives herself as good at maths experiences a goodness of fit and sense of confidence if she happens to do well in the maths test.

There is a similarity of goodness of fit where a child's sense of ineptness is confirmed. A child's early attempt at perhaps learning to catch a ball is heralded with cries of 'It's too hard; I can't do it'. Their expectation seems well-founded when a succession of catches fails to be held. The child's expectation is confirmed, leaving him reasonably confident that he is indeed pretty lousy when it comes to catching.

Perfect performances are noticeably rare events. Errors and mistakes creep into the performances of even the most adept and competent. In contrast, successes, perhaps infrequent, but successes nevertheless, emerge and litter the efforts of novice performers. When our predictions are temporarily or briefly invalidated there is a fleeting incongruity of goodness of fit and a flicker of hostility. Hostility in personal construct theory terms is the indi-vidual's effort to protect the view they have of themselves despite evidence to the contrary. They tamper with the evidence by rationalizing, excusing or blaming. Hostility thus preserves the individual's sense of competence (or lack of competence). Thus the pianist who plays a wrong note or two maybe denies it, blames the conditions (e.g. 'My hands were cold') or attributes it to tiredness. In contrast, a child who in endeavouring to catch the ball surprises himself or herself by clutching feverishly to prevent the ball falling to the ground yells in amazement 'Did you see that?' The tendency is to construe success as if it were beginner's luck, thus again confirming the sense that ball-catching is not as yet an expected or familiar experience and one the child cannot as yet feel confident about.

When an individual's estimate is consistently invalidated, guilt is experienced. Thus were the pianist to unremittingly hit the wrong notes, the experience might undermine the individual's view of self as competent. The consistent lack of a goodness of fit generates an acceptance that they are not perhaps as good as they thought, culminating in a loss of confidence. Yet again, conversely, a child's construction of self as incompetent in terms of ball-catching will begin a re-construing of self when his emerging skills bring him further success and enable him to predict his success. He too experiences guilt in accomplishing a task he imagined he was incapable of. Perhaps the child will then begin to revise the view of self from someone who can't catch balls to someone who is reasonably competent in such an activity.

7.3   CONNOISSEURSHIP

Individuals might be regarded as connoisseurs of any endeavour, undertaking or activity over which they actively elaborate. Just as the artist is a dab hand with colour, perspective and contrast, the taxi driver has 'the knowledge' of street plans, the tennis player has an intricate understanding of the top spin lob, so too children might be considered expert in computer games, music, fashion, fishing or whatever they actively engage in. Engagement here refers to an appetite to enhance an understanding through imposing an increasing raft of constructs on the particular event. Table 7.1 illustrates the depth of expertise one 10-year-old boy demonstrated in his construing of football shirts.

Youngsters who exhibit problems invariably become connoisseurs of the predicament. Fay Fransella (1972) presented an in-depth discussion of how youngsters who stutter invariably become expert at that experience. They have elaborate notions of themselves as stutterers and little idea of what it would be like to be fluent. The implications of stuttering are known. In contrast, the implications of being fluent are ill understood. Through various interventions focused on developing speech, Fransella was able to help such individuals develop fluency, but they found it extremely difficult to be fluent. The final hurdle – seeing themselves as fluent – was the most difficult. Youngsters previously incapacitated by their stuttering would, following treatment,

Table 7.1 A connoisseur of football shirts: the elaborated constructs of a 10-year-old

Colour of the shirt
Different tones of colour
Whether a pattern was sewn into the shirt
Complicated or simple design
Stripes, hoops of full colour
Stripes, fuzzy or clear
Old-fashioned or modern design
Colour of trim
Elasticated trim
Texture of material
Sleeves different or same colour as shirt
Stripes down sleeve
Details on cuffs
Presence of collar
Colour of collar
Details on collar – striped or not
Buttons on collar or elasticated
Colour of buttons
Triangle on collar
Polo neck or 'v' shape
Whether sponsor's name is displayed
Type of sponsor (e.g. beer, computers)
Sponsor's colour
Whether sponsor's colour contrasts or blends with shirt colour
Sponsor's shape
Badge central or to the side
Shield around the badge
Badge size
Manufacturer's name displayed
Position of manufacturer's name (to the side or central)

demonstrate a high level of fluency but, as if loathe to leave the known self behind – that of being a stutterer – they would occasionally revert to stuttering.

The difficulty in changing is often embodied in a lack of understanding of what the change will imply. A change in behaviour might occur, perhaps as an experiment on the child's behalf, but if the notion about self is not revised, the individual is apt to resort to what is familiar. Thus a child fearful of school, who entertains notions about themselves as likely to panic if asked a question in class, is sorely tempted to avoid school. Such a child may develop a reasonably comprehensive view of life without school, and take to sleeping in on a morning, honing their knowledge of daytime television and developing an expertise in deceiving parents. Although such a child, refusing to attend school, may be enticed back into school under threat or graduated exposure and support, the youngster may still retain a view of self as incompetent if asked questions in class. The anxiety faced by such a child, unsure of the possible implications regarding himself were he to have to answer questions, might maintain a sense of self as inept. In Kellyan terms, such a child experiences anxiety because the possible implications of failure – such as embarrassment, being thought of as foolish and so forth – are difficult to anticipate (lie outside the range of construing) as aspects of self-construing. Therefore despite attending school, such a child, with unresolved notions about publicly answering questions, is perhaps likely to revert to avoidance again.

Nine-year-old Frances, referred for, amongst other problems, her very fussy eating, demonstrated elaborate notions about food. Despite an avoidance of all but a few foods (fishcakes and cheese spread sandwiches being the notable exceptions), she was able to describe a reasonably elaborate set of constructs which she employed to evaluate any food she was faced with:

Crisp _____ Soft
Warm _____ Cold
Sweet _____ Not much taste
Don't need to be cooked _____ Food which is cooked
Smooth _____ Has bits/lumps in it
Gooey _____ Rock hard
Looks horrible _____ Yummy

The construct concerning consistency (smooth – has bits/lumps in it) seemed to predominate. Frances would not sample even the smallest morsel of food if she considered it to be lumpy. Such food 'felt horrible' and made her 'feel sick'. Concentrating therefore on the smooth end of the construct, Frances was invited to explore, and hopefully sample, food which she knew would not have lumps in. Apart from the sweet – not much taste construct, Frances could determine the qualities of food along all other her constructs by merely looking at the food sample. Appearance greatly influenced her choices.

Frances threw herself into this experiment, deciding that even food which looked horrible (e.g. baked potato), provided it was smooth, was worth a try. Interestingly she discovered that she actually liked the taste of baked potato. Frances's very cautious sampling of smooth food led her to the discovery that whether food was crisp or soft, warm or cold, sweet or without much taste, cooked or not cooked, looking horrible or yummy, did not influence her sampling. Only rock-hard food was avoided. Frances was then invited to consider both taste and smell in addition to appearance in her sampling of smooth and non-rock-hard food. She again tackled this with some enthusiasm and discovered a range of foods including seedless jam, cheese toasties, milk shakes and pancakes that she began to acquire a taste for.

Children who construe themselves as socially 'incompetent' may regard themselves as experts in aspects of social isolation. They construct well-validated notions of self as a loner and develop avenues of exploration based on this version of self. The implications of being socially inept might include not being able to get along with others, finding other people's behaviour difficult to fathom, and whenever one tries to make a friend one gets rebuffed. When such experiences occur, the child's construing of social self as incompetent is confirmed. The child opts to prefer his own company. He might go so far as to avoid all social contact, preferring to engage in the physical world, rather than the psychological world of people and having to comprehend the confusing rules that govern social behaviour.

Such extremes of social avoidance are seen with children who have Asperger's syndrome. Lorna Wing (1981) encapsulated the specific expertise such children often develop. They become intensely interested in one or two subjects such as steam trains, bus timetables, prehistoric monsters or fossils, to the exclusion of all else. They, as it were, become connoisseurs of asocial and idiosyncratic events. Being unable to anticipate the social reactions of others, such children seem unable to interact appropriately and may talk incessantly about something that holds their special interest despite other people's obvious boredom, or tend to make obscure, irrelevant or tactless remarks in company.

7.4   PERFORMANCE PROFILING

Developing a youngster's expertise is no matter of rote learning and absorption of facts. It requires personally grappling with subtler ways of construing events, a venture often facilitated by a mentor liked by the child and who is sympathetic with trying to understand the child's stance. An alternative to the 'teaching' relationship between a youngster and mentor, one that Kelly advocated for therapeutic encounters, is that of a supervisor – PhD student where a model of equal expertise forms the foundation of the relationship (Butler, 1997). Here youngster and 'teacher' are both acknowledged as experts in their particular fields and share each other's knowledge in constructing the best way forward. This of course fits with the sociality corollary where the social role of 'teaching' is enhanced when that mentor sees fit to construe the child's perspective.

Capturing a sense of the child's expertise has led to a methodology, consistent with the principles of personal construct theory, called performance profiling (Butler and Hardy, 1992; Butler, Smith and Irwin, 1993; Butler, 1999). Performance profiling facilitates both the youngster and mentor's (parent, teacher, coach) awareness with regard to performance. In its traditional format it consists of a visual display of those areas perceived by the youngster to be important in achieving the best performance they can envisage, onto which their current assessment of behaviour is mapped. It takes seriously the notion that the youngster is in the business of constructing often quite elaborate theories of their performance and that interventions might best be focused on the child's perceived needs.

Christopher was 14 years old and keen to know whether he might pursue science subjects at school, and indeed whether he might ultimately seek a career as a scientist. He enjoyed the science lessons, engaged with the teachers and felt reasonably competent about the subjects yet wondered about 'fitting' with the identity of a scientist as it is often portrayed. Christopher felt scientists tended to be viewed as boring, nerdy, quiet, lacking friends, geeky and scatty, a raft of constructs which certainly did not mesh with how he wanted to consider himself. We explored the idea, originated in Kelly's metaphor, that all our actions might be seen as scientific exploits in that they test the hypotheses we construct in order to develop a better understanding of the world. Indeed the question he posed, that of 'Can I see myself as a scientist?' was a scientific pursuit. Christopher liked the idea and, in the spirit of developing a performance profile, agreed to reflect on the qualities that he felt were important about being a good scientist.

Performance profiling begins with inviting the youngster to reflect on those qualities perceived as important in those who excel in the field they wish to perform, a process not unfamiliar to construct elicitation. This might be in social, artistic, scholastic or sporting endeavours. In Christopher's case this was being a good scientist. The emergent qualities, representing the child's view of an idealized performance, are written onto the base of the profile. Christopher produced a list of 19 qualities and reduced this to the 12 most important for him, as shown in Figure 7.1. Although not displayed, a contrast is implied and can be elicited by asking the youngster where the personal meaning of the construct is necessary.

The youngster is subsequently invited to rate their current standing on each quality, using a 1–10 scale where a score of 10 suggests an ideal state, and shade the profile accordingly. Christopher was then asked to mark with a dotted line, also using the 1–10 scale, how he would like to be on each quality. As with the self-image profile (see Chapter 5), performance profiles honour the raw data, posing no predicament in terms of analysis for the characters involved. Protagonists in the exercise may then digest an individualized visual sketch of the youngster's perceived strengths and weaknesses on meaningful constructs. Christopher was immediately able to see from his performance profile that on many qualities he was acting in ways a good scientist might and was also close to where he would ideally like to be. In McCoy's (1997)

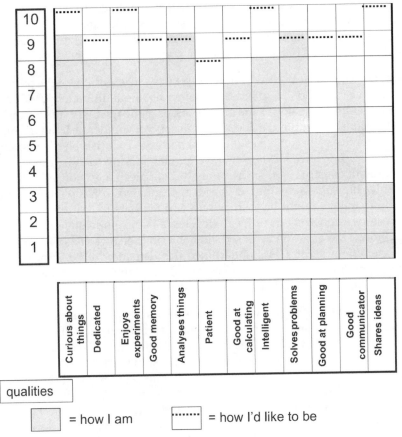

Figure 7.1 Christopher's performance profile in relation to being a good scientist.

terminology there was a goodness of fit, and one that Christopher was able to gain a ready sense of confidence from.

On three qualities – 'patience', 'good planning' and 'shares ideas' – it was effortlessly noticeable to Christopher that there was a discrepancy between where he was and how he would like to be as a good scientist. He proposed that due to his eagerness to succeed, he probably rushed into engaging in tasks before working through the planning stages and, by rushing onto the next intended project, he gave little priority to sharing results and ideas with others. Christopher could sense what he now needed to work on in order to develop the identity of a good scientist he wished to become. As David Winter

(1992) advocates, instruction and support is at its best where constructive social interaction enables interventions to meet the child's needs.

Performance profiling offers a methodology that fosters a sensitive and idiographic approach to performance enhancement. Flexibility is a fundamental characteristic of the performance profile, and to this end Butler (1997) has described further developments in the way they may be employed. They may, for example, be used to

- monitor progress through repeated administration, so that Christopher, were he so inclined, might repeat his ratings at a later date to check out his movement towards becoming the type of scientist he wished to be;

- detect mismatch between ratings of a youngster and that of a mentor, teacher or coach (who may also rate the youngster's performance on the selected qualities), leading to jointly agreed targets and mutually acceptable intervention schedules.

CHAPTER 8

THE GROWTH OF SOCIALITY

This chapter considers some of the developmental implications of Kelly's sociality corollary. Personal construct theory emphasizes that the quality of our social relationships is governed by 'the extent that one person can construe the construction processes of another'. While there is a strong argument that humankind's cooperative capacities have conferred a major evolutionary advantage on our species, the ability to understand our fellow humans and be understood by them in return does not emerge in a universal or inevitable manner. Some individuals find it very hard to put themselves metaphorically in others' shoes. Some social groups struggle to achieve a sense of mutual appreciation. When young people fail to develop their potential to relate to their peers the consequences at both a personal and societal level can be costly.

8.1 INDIVIDUAL DIFFERENCES – THE CASE OF AUTISM

Autism is classically understood as a pervasive developmental disorder characterized by severe difficulties in social interaction and communication and a limited capacity to adjust to change. More than 75 % of sufferers also have a significant learning disability. Current diagnostic practice tends to refer to a spectrum of disorders that encompasses a range of handicap including classic autism as described by Kanner and less debilitating variants such as Asperger's syndrome. Recent population estimates (National Autistic Society, 2005) consider that 91 out of every 10 000 UK citizens (including both adults and children) fall somewhere on the autistic spectrum – which sums to a total of over half a million people.

While there is a growing body of evidence implicating the causes of autism to atypical neurological development there remains some uncertainty as to the specific site and nature of the responsible abnormality (Volkmar et al., 2004). However the typical developmental picture suggests that whereas human infants usually demonstrate a biologically primed 'preparedness' to form relationships, particularly with their primary caretaker (Berger, 2006), those destined to be diagnosed as autistic do not. They tend to avoid eye contact and do not respond in the expected fashion to changes in their mothers' facial expression. As a consequence, research suggests it is harder to establish a convincing emotional bond between parent and child as gauged by various attachment measures (Rutgers et al., 2004). Hard but not impossible, as we shall see shortly.

By the age of about four or five, children start to acquire what has come to be known as 'theory of mind' (Baron-Cohen, Tager-Flusberg and Cohen 2000). This means they are able to infer another person's inner mental state from cues provided by their external behaviour. This sophisticated capacity to read others' intentions is generally tested by the use of scenarios in which children are asked to anticipate what certain characters in a story might be thinking in particular circumstances. For example, the tale might unfold along the following lines. A child finds what he thinks is a tube of Smarties. He picks it up and shakes the contents. Then he opens the tube to discover that it is in fact full of stones not chocolates. He replaces the top on the tube and puts it back down again. Along comes another child who sees the same Smartie tube. What might he be thinking? Most, but not all, youngsters on the autistic spectrum fail to separate out what they know about the contents of the tube from the information available to the naïve second child. They assume the second character will ignore the tube because he realizes that it's full of stones rather than chocolates. This specific somewhat artificially devised example of an inability to 'construe the construction processes of the other' is replicated in the real-life social experiences of autistic youngsters for whom friendships rarely come easily (Badanes, Estevan and Bacetc, 2000).

It seems therefore that autistic children carry the dual handicap of struggling to appreciate the experience of others and not being able to naturally convey their own state of mind to those that care for them. This represents a formidable challenge to their parents. A recent meta-analysis of research conducted into the quality of the attachments demonstrated between mothers and their autistic children found that, as expected, secure attachments were less frequent in this group when compared to a 'normal' control group (Rutgers *et al.*, 2004). Furthermore these secure bonds were harder to establish when the child concerned had more pronounced autistic features. However, the statistical differences between the groups were not as marked as one might theoretically have suspected. The average percentage of secure attachments (as assessed by the Strange Situations test) for the autistic families was 53 %. The comparable figure for typically developing children is 60 %. So despite the evident social and communicative limitations of youngsters on the autistic spectrum, the majority manages somehow to build a secure attachment to their primary caretaker – usually their mother. What's going on?

Perhaps the particular characteristics of individual infants are not as important to their mothers as common sense might suggest. The process of attachment begins while the baby is in the womb so mothers are already connected to a representation of their baby well before he or she sees the light of day. There is also no reason to doubt that babies destined to be diagnosed as autistic in later life will share the appealing physical characteristics of newborn creatures (such as big heads and big eyes) that trigger instinctive protective reactions in their caretakers. Maybe the nature of the mother's own relationship with her parents is a better predictor of her ability to connect with her new baby than any particular quality of the child him- or herself.

There is, however, a thread of evidence that links this phenomenon with Kelly's sociality corollary. Generally speaking those parents who make secure attachments with their offspring possess the capacity for what has been described as 'reflective functioning' (Slade, 2005), defined as the ability to hold in mind and carefully appraise the internal state of their infant. This psychological position enables mothers, in particular, to interact in a way that is attuned to the child's moment-by-moment experiences. It is not so easy to convey that sense of emotional availability to a youngster whose distress levels are hard to gauge and whose response to comforting is unpredictable. However, it appears that some mothers are able to consciously develop communication skills that are uniquely attuned to the nuances of their autistic child's signalling system (Biringen *et al.*, 2005). Quite how they (and their children) achieve this surprising sense of connection is not well understood. However, a study started in 2006 by Claudia Dickinson is following the old personal constructivist principle that 'If you don't know, why not ask them?' and interviewing a small group of mothers who have made strong attachments to their autistic children to invite them to reflect on how they might have managed it. Her thesis should prove interesting reading (Dickinson, 2007).

8.2   GETTING TO KNOW YOU

With the notable exception of those on the autistic spectrum, most youngsters appear to have a genetic propensity to establish mutually satisfying relationships with others. However, this capacity does not suddenly reveal itself in fully fledged form like the butterfly from the chrysalis. The sociocultural view of theory of mind development (Dunn, 1993) argues that appropriate life experiences are also necessary if children are to achieve their social potential. Peer friendships provide these opportunities to discover what makes others tick from an early age when, for example, toddlers play alongside each other at a preschool nursery. At this age children don't appear to mind very much whether their play partner is a boy or a girl. The pattern changes dramatically around the age of three to four when a definite preference for same sex playmates develops. This phenomenon has been found to recur across a wide range of cultures and settings (Maccoby, 1998). Furthermore a policy of strict social segregation appears to be strongly sanctioned by the peer group (especially by boys) throughout the pre-adolescent years. It is intriguing to reflect on why this tendency emerges and persists and also to consider its longer-term social consequences.

One credible cause of this spectacular parting of the ways is the characteristically different play styles that boys and girls seem to prefer. Boys are drawn to the all action 'rough and tumble' excitement of war games and noisily racing around the playground together. Girls' play by contrast is a much quieter more conversational affair characterized by a more sensitive emotional appreciation of shared experiences. Of course this picture represents a broad stereotype. Boys can comfort one another when distressed and girls can sometimes be cuttingly cruel to their alleged friends. But the trend towards typically different gender-specific play styles is a robust research finding. It has been suggested that boys are biologically primed to enjoy the stimulation of roughhouse play whereas that kind of activity just does not appeal to the less excitable feminine temperament. The argument is essentially one of mutual incompatibility.

A more psychological take on why children might begin to prefer to play with same sex friends considers what the implications of defining yourself as male or female might be. The capacity to discriminate between the genders is established very early on in a child's life. They subsequently learn to identify themselves as boys or girls. The next developmental level of understanding is held to be an emerging appreciation of what it means to be a boy or a girl in a specific cultural context. Kelly described this attribution of a cluster of qualities to a particular element as 'constellatory construing'. This dawning awareness of 'so that's what boys/girls are supposed to be like' could inform subsequent decisions regarding which play activities children consider fit their evolving view of themselves. Our four-year-olds would then be seen as opting to elaborate their ideas about the implications of belonging to their own gender rather than being inquisitive about what members of the other lot get up to. Their curiosity about the opposite sex will likely be rekindled in adolescence when mixed gender peer groups come back into vogue.

Opinions vary as to whether this early social segregation of the sexes is inevitable or desirable. Perhaps we should assume that a pattern that has proved so widespread and enduring probably confers some evolutionary benefit. Could the separate peer cultures in which girls and boys grow result in their acquiring different sets of social skills that equip them to play complementary roles in adult life? However, that scenario presumes a traditional consensus on the parts men and women are expected to play in society. With greater contemporary flexibility in adult roles, today's children might be better served if their early choice of companions allowed them to develop both 'masculine' and 'feminine' competences as well as expanding their opportunities to learn to construe the construction processes of members of the opposite sex.

The 'like plays with like' rule governing children's friendships does not of course absolutely preclude any social contact between boys and girls. Brothers and sisters will probably spend more time in the company of their siblings than they do with even their 'best' friends. The title of a provocative paper published by Josef Perner and colleagues (Perner, Ruffman and Leekam, 1994) – Theory of mind is contagious: You catch it from your sibs – suggests that the intimacy of these close family relationships might have a peculiar power to promote children's capacity to appreciate another person's perspective. The study found that three- and four-year-old children with several siblings performed better on the false belief story tasks described earlier than did youngsters who had grown up in smaller families. The investigators interpreted this finding as suggesting that sibling interaction provides 'a rich database for building a theory of mind'. That outcome probably depends somewhat on the nature of the relationship between the siblings concerned. Siblings compete as well as cooperate. The constructions of brothers and sisters will differ from each other and be continually revised in the light of experience.

Judy Dunn (1993) cites two contrasting accounts of a sibling relationship to illustrate the point. Ten-year-old Nancy described her six-year-old brother Carl thus:

> Well, he's nice to me. And he sneaks into my bed at night time from Mummy. I think I'd be very lonely without Carl. I play with him a lot and he thinks up lots of ideas and it's very exciting. He comes and meets me at the gate after school and I think that's very friendly . . . He's very kind . . . Don't really know what I'd do without a brother.

Carl saw his relationship with his sister somewhat differently:

> She's pretty disgusting and we don't talk to each other very much. I don't really know much about her ... Sometimes when I do something wrong she tells me off quite cruelly.

No evident signs of mutual understanding there it appears. Or contagion.

As Kelly argued, it is not contact with others that of itself prompts the development of mutual understanding. Siblings can get stuck in unproductive rivalry. Pupils in multicultural schools will frequently choose to associate exclusively with those they classify as their 'own' (Graham and Cohen, 1997). A culture of teasing may inhibit any penchant children have for making cross-gender friendships. Opportunities for construing the constructions of others need to be maximized. Later we shall consider a number of therapeutic and educational interventions that have been designed to assist in that process.

8.3   BULLYING

One evident way in which the adult world attempts to manage young people's relationships with each other is the introduction of explicit anti-bullying policies in schools. These well-intended interventions tend to emphasize the protective and indeed punitive role that teachers and other staff can play in trying to make the school environment a safer place in which to learn. Helpful though these systemic measures may be, they do not tend to focus on the relationship between bully and victim. How effectively do the parties in these exchanges 'read' each other?

There is an ongoing lively debate between child development theorists about whether school bullies should be best understood as oafish thugs with minimal social skills or Machiavellian psychopaths with an exquisite understanding of their victims' weaknesses (Arsenio and Lemerise, 2001; Sutton, Smith and Swettenham, 2001). It makes sense to differentiate between those whose aggression is reactive and defensive (e.g. when responding to some imagined slight or threat) and those who 'plan-fully' use violence for the material rewards it delivers. The former group of bullies probably misunderstand others' intentions and may not be fully aware of the hurt their actions cause to fellow pupils. Essentially they are making mistakes in what might be termed their social cognitions. The latter group can be characterized as being well able to appreciate the suffering their victims experience but doing it anyway. Maybe they have found that crime pays and exercising power over those whom they frighten brings a range of social and economic benefits. More worryingly some might discover they actively enjoy inflicting pain on their fellow humans. The bullying then becomes an end in itself rather than a means to an end. Either way these characters don't seem to lack an intellectual appreciation of the hurt they cause but they fail to make an empathic emotional connection with their victims.

At first glance it looks as though it is the first 'incompetent' class of bullies that fits more straightforwardly into the personal construct framework. Their misinterpretations of others' intentions suggest an underdeveloped theory of mind. What about what might be termed the instrumental bullies? Attentive readers will recall that the sociality corollary refers to our evolving capacity to play a role in a 'social process', not a prosocial process. So the ability to construe the constructions of another can be used for selfish rather than mutually satisfying ends. A military general might successfully anticipate the strategy of an enemy commander and so inflict a bloody defeat with great loss of life. A chess champion might become so expert at reading her opponent's plays that she wins effortlessly. By this reading of the sociality corollary, war, sport and bullying are all social processes in which successful participants need to be competent mind-readers. This argument recognizes that it is not only psychopaths who will from time to time employ their interpersonal acumen to take advantage of others. Not all our social exchanges can be reconfigured as win–win situations.

However, were we to adopt this callously strategic approach to all our relationships our crucial capacity to find fellow feeling with other humans would wither on the vine. Herein lies an important conceptual difference between theory of mind and personal construct theory. Theory of mind is defined in exclusively cognitive terms as an inability to represent mental states. The autistic child is seen to struggle to work out how other people's thinking differs from his own. In contrast Kelly was adamant that construing is more than a merely intellectual act. He saw emotion and cognition as indivisible. So construing the construction processes of another requires that we appreciate how they feel as much as we understand how they think. So the apparently socially skilled bully is also handicapped in the range of social roles that he can play with other young people by the limited 'extent' to which he is able to empathize with the emotional experiences of his peers. To use a currently fashionable psychological term he lacks 'emotional intelligence'. The use of the male pronoun here is not intended to imply that it is only boys who display this kind of insensitivity to others' discomfort. The indirect forms of bullying such as social exclusion commonly displayed in girls' peer groups are just as heartless (Hay, Payne and Chadwick, 2004).

The emphasis of the discussion thus far has been on the construing of the bully. What of the experience of the victim? Many parents will have been confronted by tearful tales of their child having been mistreated by a fellow school pupil. It may prove instructive to reflect on the sort of advice we find ourselves offering to our beleaguered offspring in these circumstances. 'Don't react.' 'Don't give them the satisfaction of seeing you're upset.' And of course,

'Tell the teacher.' It seems that whereas there are evident disadvantages that accrue from the 'inscrutable' nature of an autistic toddler, we consider that the victims of bullying may be too scrutable for their own good.

In the film *The Shawshank Redemption* the main character Andy Dufresne played by Tim Robbins manages to escape the threat of a sadistic homosexual assault from a thuggish fellow prisoner by inducing doubt in his tormentor's mind. Is he lying to save his own skin or might he just be telling the truth? The strategy relies not only on retaining something of a mystery about yourself but also having a timely sense of your would-be assailant's Achilles heel. This fictional spot of quick-thinking does not immediately sound transferable to real life, but Sharon Jackson and Don Bannister (1985) identified an intriguing subgroup of adolescents who were eminently capable construers of the construction processes of others while remaining an unfathomable enigma to the outside world. So perhaps a fatherly recommendation to 'try and not let them know what you're feeling' is not so impractical after all. In *The Shawshank Redemption*, Andy Dufresne was never going to be so foolish as to turn to the corrupt prison governor for protection. Victimized children too are frequently sceptical about the benefits of turning to the authorities for support. In response to a sketchy playground drawing a 13-year-old girl identified a girl who was being teased by other pupils in the scene. She described how upset the girl was becoming and the danger that would follow if she finally lost emotional control as she could 'end up doing something really stupid like telling her teacher!'

8.4   THERAPEUTIC INTERVENTIONS

Why does it matter that young people should become competent at comprehending the psychological processes of their peers? In the short term, children who lack this understanding are likely to struggle to establish secure friendships (Badanes, Estevan and Bacete, 2000). In adolescence an absence of more suitable companionship can pitch these vulnerable young people into consorting with a more deviant peer group *faute de mieux* (Hay, Payne and Chadwick, 2004). In adult life, individuals who have experienced difficulties in making and keeping friends seem more vulnerable to a range of mental health problems, perhaps because they cannot rely on the web of social supports that keeps others afloat at times of crisis (Sarason, Sarason and Gurung, 2001). So if children fail to acquire this necessary interpersonal sensitivity spontaneously there are good reasons for seeking to devise therapeutic interventions that will increase their future social viability.

8.5   INTENSIVE INTERACTION

Most psychotherapeutic interventions rely on our capacity to put our thoughts and feelings into words. However, children with profound learning disabilities have to negotiate their social worlds without that opportunity to exchange meanings with other people. In the UK the intensive interaction movement (Kellett and Nind, 2003) has sought to transfer the non-verbal communication styles that characterize mother and baby interaction to the relationship between young people with major learning difficulties and the adults who care for them such as teachers and classroom assistants. Staff are trained to 'mirror' the sounds and movements of the children and to strike up the kind of conversations that mothers have with their infants. For example, they might attribute communicative intention to a facial expression such as 'Oh you are pleased to see me, are you?' The young person hence receives a high dose of consistent, playful and intimate attention from a sympathetic adult who is determined to find a way of entering their world. This innovative approach has yet to be extensively evaluated but early qualitative studies report that staff can develop a fresh sense of connection with those in their care at a much more personal level.

Experiencing such level of empathic understanding tends to bring out our more altruistic instincts (Batson *et al.*, 2002), which offers the promise of greater job satisfaction for the adult and a better quality of life for the child. The most satisfying outcome of these exchanges is when the learning-disabled young person herself initiates some form of contact by, for example, reaching out to touch her teacher and a pattern of two-way communication begins to be established. Intensive interaction probably has its intellectual origins in attachment theory but sits very comfortably alongside the sociality corollary for two reasons. Firstly Kelly well understood the importance of preverbal and non-verbal construing in human relationships. Secondly he appreciated the reciprocal nature of our most satisfying social exchanges. While there may be some occasions when it is adaptive to remain mysterious, the goal of most of our therapeutic interventions will be to enable young people to understand others and be understood themselves in return.

8.6   INTERVIEWING THE INTERNALIZED OTHER

The Canadian family therapist Karl Tomm shares Ravenette's interest in the power of the well-phrased question (Tomm, 1988) and has devised an innovative way of inviting family members to try and see the world through each other's eyes that he called the internalized other interview or IOI (Burnham, 2000). The format is engagingly simple. Two people who are struggling in their relationship – say a mother and her teenage daughter – are invited to swap identities for the course of a brief conversation lasting perhaps 20 minutes. The therapist checks that each party understands the rationale of the exercise and proceeds to interview each person as if she were the other (i.e. mum becomes daughter and vice versa). So the mum-as-daughter might be quizzed about her taste in clothes or boys; her hopes for the future; or whether there is anything bothering her at the moment. Meanwhile the daughter herself listens in on the conversation (usually intently) but makes no comment. Once the initial interview is completed the therapist might ask the daughter what she thought of her mum's guesses. What answers were spot on? Where was she off-beam and how?

Then the roles are reversed and the daughter-as-mother is put in the hot seat. The questioning might turn its focus towards the pair's own relationship. What makes you feel most proud of your daughter? Did the two of you used to get on better than you do now? Again the mum listens attentively until the conversation closes, and she is invited to comment. Although IOI can sound like a psychological parlour game it has the potential to open up some highly fruitful discussion. Because the conversations are neither planned nor scripted, participants have to rely entirely on their ability to construe the construction processes of the other. What they don't know, they are obliged to imagine, and guessing wrong may ultimately prove more helpful than guessing right. Tomm locates his ideas within the social constructionist tradition but the internalized other interview could also have been designed following personal construct principles.

8.7   CBT AND SEXUAL OFFENDERS

Adolescents who have committed sexual offences can talk very dismissively of their victims' experiences. This has led some commentators to propose that they might suffer from a generalized failure to establish empathic connections with their fellow human beings. In the case of the sadistic psychopath this may be true but the picture for the vast majority of juvenile sexual offenders is likely to be more complicated (Marshall, Anderson and Fernandez, 1999). When faced with tests that require them to put themselves in the shoes of say a facially disfigured person being mistreated in a public place, these young men are perfectly capable of appreciating how painful it is to be on the wrong end of wilfully antisocial behaviour. However, when it comes to acknowledging the emotional impact of their own conduct on their victims, they are likely to engage in a number of self-serving 'cognitive distortions' such as 'She was asking for it dressed like that' or 'She enjoyed it as much as I did'.

Cognitive behaviour therapy (CBT) psychologists argue that this post hoc justification of what are essentially indefensible actions serves as a way not just to excuse or minimize the severity of the perpetrator's crimes but also to protect the individual's positive view of himself. He can then continue to construe himself as not the sort of person who would ever terrify and injure a woman for his own sexual gratification – hence avoiding feelings of guilt in both a Kellyan and everyday sense of the word. CBT therapy challenges these convenient misattributions. Using a range of psychological exercises such as written reflections or dramatic role-plays the young offenders are required to contemplate carefully what the experience of their victims must have been. No avoidance. No explaining away. The treatment process is described as an intense and serious undertaking in which these young men have to construe the construction processes of those they have assaulted at both an intellectual and emotional level. There is some limited evidence to suggest that this crash course in empathic awareness contributes to reduced rates of reoffending. Again the proponents of CBT rarely cite Kelly as an influence but the intervention described fits well within the theoretical framework of personal constructs.

8.8   CIRCLE TIME

The interventions described thus far have been therapeutic ventures; that is to say they were targeted at specific individuals who were judged to need some form of special assistance. The circle time approach is different. Pioneered by the UK educationalist Jenny Mosley (2002), quality circle time provides an opportunity for all pupils in a class to learn social and problem-solving skills in a shared forum. It therefore represents education for all as opposed to treatment for the few. Large teacher-led group meetings aim to include every pupil in the class sitting in a circle formation in which everyone can see and hear everyone else. So the segregated smaller groups of the playground are balanced by a safe and structured opportunity for all pupils to get to know one another better. Groups operate according to a few basic ground rules and adherence to a simple core philosophy. Do listen – don't interrupt. Everyone's views are of equal value in an explicitly democratic setting. Regular weekly meetings allow children to develop a culture in which they listen appreciatively to the thoughts and feelings of their fellow pupils with the shared intention of resolving interpersonal difficulties as and when they arise – with a few fun exercises thrown in for good measure. A framework of conversational rules allows a quite sophisticated process of mutual negotiation to develop. 'I need help because ... ' elicits a 'Would it help if I ... ?' reply. Mosley (2002) cites the following heart-warming report from a class teacher of the transformational power of circle time conversations to help a boy who was rejected by his classmates:

> He had a bed-wetting problem and smelled. His home life was fairly inconsistent and generally his life at school was miserable. Most of the class picked on him and consequently he became a victim who also instigated trouble. I started doing Circle Time with the class. At first they interrupted each other and did not take anything seriously. Slowly that changed. Children began to come up with problems of their own that they wanted to develop strategies for. Other children would share feelings or ideas and most importantly come up with solutions. The bullied child found Circle Time very difficult to deal with and initially he would

leave the circle or the room because he could not cope. However, slowly he began to stop and share his feelings with the others. After a time he plucked up the courage to explain to them how they made him feel when they treated him badly. I remember listening to this and becoming aware that the whole class was hanging on his every word. I looked up and noticed that almost every child, both boys and girls, was crying. After that his class life changed. He was accepted and although there were still flare ups it was never so bad ...

In this instance letting others in, rather than keeping them out, paid a spectacular dividend.

The circle time philosophy is an eclectic pragmatic mix of approaches including, for example, a complex system of individual and group incentives. Mosley acknowledges how much her methods resonate with the ideas of Rogers and Moreno among others. She does not cite Kelly – but she could have done!

8.9   CONCLUSION

The discerning reader will have noted how many of the theoretical notions and therapeutic interventions mentioned in this chapter did not originate in personal construct psychology. Our experience of trying to help troubled children is that we are generally prepared to use any trick in the book! Kelly too advocated both technical diversity and a continuing openness to new ideas – provided this eclecticism was not bought at the cost of theoretical coherence. That is precisely the balance we have aimed to strike here.

CHAPTER 9

TROUBLESOME BEHAVIOUR

A person's behaviour is determined by the nature of their construct system.

(George Kelly, 1970)

In putting forward such an idea, it might be considered that George Kelly's construing of behaviour was somewhat pre-emptive. If, however, it is thought that people do not appeal to their constructs in order to act, but rather they are their constructs, as Tom Ravenette (1977) suggests, then Kelly's declaration makes convincing sense. Should this hypothesis be widened and amplified so that problems are also deemed to arise from a person's construction of events, then we are faced with what Ravenette (1980) suggested is a 'tricky dilemma' when we seek to understand the behaviour problems of children.

Personal construct theory fundamentally proposes that individuals derive meaning through the way they construe the events they encounter. When a person cannot make sense of an event but feels he should, then he has a problem. Thus a child who wishes to have friends but who finds her approaches to others are unceasingly rebuffed, has a problem. Her attempts to socialize, actions that reflect the child's notion of self as friendly, are exposed to serious invalidation. To avoid invalidation, a child might experience Kellyan hostility by denying there is any trouble with friendships and persistently seek out new relationships in ways that have already proved unfruitful. Alternatively, invalidation might generate Kellyan threat in that the child may begin to anticipate a revision or 'comprehensive change' of self-construing, leading the child to feel ultimately disagreeable, disliked and unsociable. Youngsters who appear puzzling both to themselves and others, and may be thought of as *troubled*, have been discussed in Chapter 5.

9.1 CHILDREN WHO ARE COMPLAINED ABOUT

In contrast, children with so-called behaviour or conduct problems very rarely bemoan they have a problem. Generally they are complained about. They are primarily problems to others, not to themselves, and because their behaviour typically impacts on other people – parents, teachers, neighbours, other children and so forth – they are routinely thought to be *troublesome*.

Ravenette (1988) sketched some customary gripes that adults have concerning children. They generally complain when they fail to understand the child and the child's way of conducting himself. Metaphorically they are ready to pull their hair out. Typically adults' efforts to anticipate the child's actions are met with disappointment, their attempts to unravel the puzzle create frustration and their expectations are defeated. Thus a child becomes a threat to the adults' sense of 'knowingness'. Seeking to grapple with events that lie outside a construct's range of convenience, as involved adults are in such circumstances, generates anxiety in the Kellyan sense. Adults are assuredly faced with circumstances that are difficult to construe.

A second issue relates to the adult's sense of helplessness or incompetence. They complain when their efforts to alter the way the child is behaving fail to make any difference. Nothing they do seems able to influence what the child does. From a personal construct theory perspective it might be suggested that since the relationship between child and adult is proceeding far from smoothly, there is a failure in the adult's construction of the child's construing. As the sociality corollary predicts, when adults are faced with a child they find difficult to understand they may end up reacting, often in an authoritarian and intolerant manner, but primarily fail to relate to them. Behaviour perceived as problematic and unresponsive to the adult's best efforts to foster change represents an invalidation of the parent or teacher's construing, and ultimately of their core role construing – that of a good parent or concerned teacher.

A complaint reveals who has the problem. Who is grappling to understand, striving and agonizing over how to lessen the impact of the behaviour? For youngsters their actions in all likelihood make perfect sense. What perplexes us about a behaviour may be completely understandable to the child. Sharon Jackson and Don Bannister's (1985) intriguing study, briefly described in earlier chapters, emphasizes this point. A group of children seen by their teachers as problematic and difficult were invited to discuss themselves, their troubles and relationships with the team of researchers. Fascinatingly Jackson and Bannister broadly discovered that most of the children perceived as difficult and incomprehensible made perfect sense of their own behaviour.

9.2   TAKING DIFFERENT PERSPECTIVES

The notion that youngsters have a grasp of the meaning of their behaviour exposes a dilemma for clinicians who invest heavily in rating scales to assess the degree of abnormality of a child's behaviour. Almost without exception, such scales seek an opinion of the complainant, not the child complained about. Parents and teachers are invited to assess the child's behaviour as they perceive it. Such scales illuminate nothing of the meaning of the behaviour. Thus a child might be classified as disturbed, maladjusted or unbalanced because of how his actions are perceived, yet this same child might perceive his own behaviour to be no more out of the ordinary than would the classically obedient child. As yet, few, if any, scales have been developed which tap the child's perception of their own behaviour. Personal construct theory, however, offers the possibility of understanding what sense a child makes of his or her actions.

Elaborating Kelly's theme that all actions are purposeful, Ravenette (1988) has compellingly offered an alternative to the conventional view of a behaviour being problematic. From the child's standpoint he suggests we might persuasively ask for what problem is the behaviour a solution. Thus the child might be perceived as acting in a certain way because in doing so he resolves some other predicament.

It is difficult to imagine that any child might find bed-wetting a solution. Nevertheless studies which invite children to discuss what sense they make of their bed-wetting have found, for a small number of children who wet the bed, this seems to be the case. Through employing Finn Tschudi's (1977) method of asking for the advantages and disadvantages of both the problem and perceived contrast, a few children volunteer advantages in continuing to remain wet at night. These were the very children who failed to respond to traditional interventions, indicating that indeed they may have found the enuresis to be a solution, rather than a problem. Some of the perceived advantages of wetting included retaining a bedroom for themselves, avoiding having to sleep over at relatives, having the effect of stopping parents coming into the bedroom and 'telling me to tidy up', stopping the dog sleeping on the bed and considering that the smell 'stops burglars breaking in' (Butler, 1994; Butler, Redfern and Forsythe, 1990). For such children, bed-wetting would appear to be not so much a problem but a means to avoid facing perhaps a more difficult issue such as sharing a bedroom, staying over at a relative's house, facing a nagging mother and so forth.

9.3   THE MEANING OF BEHAVIOUR

A list of childhood behaviours that adults complain about would be mind-bogglingly long. It may contain such acts as lying, being cheeky, swearing, disrupting other children, calling names, graffiti, being cruel to animals, threatening others, stealing, fighting, breaking into other people's property, fire-setting and vandalism. Personal construct theory postulates that such behaviour is an expression of how the child construes himself and his world. Tom Ravenette (2003) indeed posed the question as to how much of a child's disturbing behaviour is an assertion that 'I do exist'.

Were a youngster to construe himself as a bully, given the notion that behaviour is considered a question, it is likely he will endeavour to find opportunities to taunt other children. In such scenarios the youngster is able to test out his predictions. Teasing another child to the point where they recoil in tears would serve to confirm or define the protagonist's notion of self as indeed a feared tormentor. Such a child may subsequently seek to extend a notion of himself as powerful, dominant and forceful by acting in an intimidating manner towards other children or in other situations. Kelly (1955) described such active elaboration as aggression, being keen to define aggressiveness as what was happening for the protagonist, not in terms of other people's reaction to the individual. Thus aggression is understood both as an individual's active search to check out their construing and their desire to widen the range of their understanding. The bully who seeks to extend his range of construing by taunting others on the rugby field might well come a cropper. He might give up on that experiment and alternatively test out being hard, disciplined or the perfect gentleman – all acts of Kellyan aggressiveness. Then again he might just decide to give rugby up altogether.

Behaviour, however, is not always a question of observable movement. It may represent a particular stance, a viewpoint from which a lack of movement makes perfect sense to a child. A refusal to eat, listen, sleep, speak or go to school illustrates some examples of determined inaction. In a similar vein to how children's behaviour is conceptualized, declining to act may also be seen as an experimental question, with a search for validation of self-construing. Butler (1985) described, for example, how a 12-year-old girl's refusal to attend school was best understood as a frantic attempt to avoid separation from her parents, with a father about to embark on employment overseas and her mother recently starting work as a county councillor. The girl's school refusal appeared experimentally to be testing the parents' decisions about their employment and ultimately to protect (or solve for her) a sense of vulnerability.

9.4 UNDERSTANDING BEHAVIOUR PROBLEMS

The following case might further elaborate some of the issues concerning children who are complained about because of behavioural problems. Gary, the middle of three children, was 11 years old when referred by his GP. His elder sister was described as very bright intellectually and thriving at school whilst his brother, just a year younger, was excelling at sport, both at school and at a local club. Gary's mother was white and his father was a black South African, and they were bringing the children up within a nuclear family unit.

Gary's mother frankly but compassionately expressed her concerns. Gary was involved in a wide range of behaviours that she found baffling and she felt despondently incapable and powerless to change his conduct. Gary was sniffing petrol, aerosols, deodorants and butane gas, smoking regularly, breaking into premises such as shops and houses, stealing (for which he was already on conditional discharge) and taking vehicles.

Gary's parents had tried in vain to intervene, usually through grounding him and recently, being at their wits' end, had stopped him from going on a rugby tour with a local club he played for. Predictably this served only to escalate the tension between Gary and his parents. In seeking to understand the mordancy, Gary described how he felt his mother lacked trust in him and that she was ashamed of him. Further, Gary surmised that when his mother quizzed him about his behaviour, this afforded more evidence that he was not to be trusted and validated her opinion that he had let her down. Sport seemed to be one area where Gary shone. Being stocky and well built, he was ideally suited for rugby, and his other passion, boxing. Gary eagerly completed the self-image profile, although he wished to adapt the conventional scale slightly by omitting some items and adding others he felt more apposite. The profile (Figure 9.1) endorses the importance sport played for Gary and overall indicates a sense of positive regard. Gary construes himself as helpful, sporting and pleased with his appearance. His sociability is manifest by high ratings on making friends easily, helpfulness and being good fun coupled with low ratings on loneliness and shyness. Gary reveals a sense of feeling different from others, which he considered was the upshot of his colour and the consequent gibes and provocation from others.

The profile also highlights where Gary construed himself more 'negatively'. He regarded himself as inclined to argue (with his sister, mother and teacher) be stubborn, cheeky, bad-tempered, easily bored (especially at school) and always in trouble. A hint of Gary's predicament was revealed in his account of why he seemed always in trouble, when he described an inability to say 'no' when egged on by others.

Gary was further invited to make a rating of how he would ideally like to be on each item, which, as Figure 9.1 indicates, was invariably placed at the extreme

		0	1	2	3	4	5	6
1	kind					■		✦
2	makes friends easily					■		✦
3	well-liked				■			✦
4	good fun				■			✦
5	lots of energy					■		✦
6	helpful						■	✦
7	honest			■				✦
8	good at sport						■	✦
9	intelligent						■	✦
10	like the way I look						■	✦
11	feel different from others	✦				■		
12	lazy	✦					■	
13	lonely	✦						■
14	stubborn	✦						■
15	moody			✦		■		
16	always in trouble	✦					■	
17	shy	✦						■
18	cheeky	✦				■		
19	argue a lot	✦						■
20	bad-tempered	✦						■
21	get bored easily	✦						■

■ 'as I am'   ✦ 'as I'd like to be'

The Self Image Profile is published by Butler (2001) and reproduced with permission from Harcourt Assessment

Figure 9.1 Gary's adapted Self-Image Profile. Source: The Self-Image Profile is published by Butler (2001) and reproduced with permission from Harcourt Assessment.

end of each construct, thereby possibly representing something of a fantasy. As Kelly (1955) indicated, an alternative to the problem, although available, may be unrealistically drawn and oversimplified. How Gary imagined he would like to be seemed a distant, almost unobtainable vision; a vision which may have, by its contrast, corroborated Gary's perception of self as 'antisocial'.

Having recently moved to high school Gary was undeniably struggling to settle. He was described as disruptive and willingly volunteered his resistance to doing any homework. His explanations hinged around a conviction that other children on his table prevented him from working, an acute nervousness about having to read in class and his experiences of finding written work laborious, uninviting and difficult. An assessment of Gary's level of cognitive functioning subsequently revealed no obvious areas of anomalous or unusual performance other than a slight difficulty with spelling.

Out of school, partly because of his thickset appearance, Gary chose to spend time with boys older than himself. From a list of peers, from both within and outside of school, Gary described how he was both similar and different from these friends. By seeking contrasts of the elicited descriptions, a series of constructs were derived, as arranged below. Gary perceived himself to be on the left-hand side of each of these constructs:

Likes to go out _____ Boring

Likes sport _____ Boring

Bad-tempered _____ Kind of shy

Shows off when with friends _____ Shy

Can't say no _____ Can say no

Messes about _____ Does work/listens to teacher

If dared, he'd do it _____ Too serious

Has fun _____ Serious

Once written down like this, Gary was quickly able to appreciate not just how notions about himself led to him being persistently in trouble, but also how the implication of the contrast states made change a potentially hazardous undertaking. Not to be in trouble crucially implied seriousness and boredom. In his customary perceptive way, Kelly (1955) had discussed how clients' and parents' complaints are usually 'poorly formulated' in the sense that they rarely open up avenues to a happy solution. He was, however, a keen advocate of listening to the complaint, and of seeking to understand it, which he argued helped establish rapport through attending to areas which the complainant considered important.

Gary further elaborated this notion of himself as always being in trouble, being unable to say 'no' and eager to accept a dare by reflecting on the advantages such behaviour accrued. Asking for advantages of the present state and disadvantages of a contrast state, according to Finn Tschudi (1977) highlights the dilemma facing an individual wishing to change. Without hesitation, Gary intimated that the advantage of showing off, undertaking dares and so on, was the attention he received. He described how you get a 'name', become known as someone not to be messed with, and avoid being called a 'chicken' or 'wimp'. The disadvantages of refusing a dare were that 'You might not be part of the group', face being called chicken and get called 'paki'. Such powerful implications of the contrast tend to maintain the individual's course of action. Change, for Gary, would indeed be perceived as hazardous at best. Gary appeared to seek validation from his peers. He successfully experienced acceptance and recognition through his behaviour. Most individuals strive to be recognized rather than remain anonymous. Gary would rather have a 'name' than be a 'nobody' or worse still, be known as a 'paki'. Personal construct theory, as we have advanced a few times, suggests that all behaviour is legitimate and meaningful, a principle clearly in operation here, once an understanding of Gary's perspective is elucidated.

9.5   AVENUES OF CHANGE

Another well-established maxim within personal construct theory is the notion that behaviour might best be understood as an experiment. This subtle invitation dramatically presents a positive reframing to what others might perceive as a problem. Kelly (1970) suggested that behaviour is a human being's principal instrument of inquiry. Our actions invariably test out our hypotheses. We examine predictions against how things turn out. We strive to create meaning and certainty. Ultimately actions validate aspects of the way we construe ourselves. Gary's behaviour was undoubtedly persistent. It had brought him face to face with the police on at least two occasions, dogged complaints from school and enduring appeals from his parents for help. Whilst his actions made perfect sense to Gary, validating his notion of self, he was in danger of serious trouble and exclusion from school should they persist.

What then were the avenues of change? The contrast to his construing looked a bleak and uninviting option for Gary. However Kelly (1970), in his inimitable style, offered a teasing possibility. He suggested that if a person endlessly repeats the same behaviour then 'I suspect he is still looking for the answer to a question he knows no better way of asking'. In seeking fresh options for Gary, Kelly, as so often, provides a starting point. In much of what he discussed about individuals being experimenters and creators of their own worlds, he invites us to extend this capacity to invent ourselves anew and change what we do not like about ourselves. Therapy might thus be construed as self-creation, not self-correction (Neimeyer and Harter, 1988). Peggy Dalton and Gavin Dunnett (1992) suggest that if all our present interpretations of the universe are subject to revision or replacement then this must include our interpretations of ourselves. Laudable intentions no doubt, but what of an individual like Gary, who didn't reckon much to the idea of change?

Perhaps therapy, as Franz Epting (1984) suggested, has to become something of a 'playful enterprise'. Gary may need to be coaxed into considering change. If we search sweepingly, avenues of possible change can surprisingly appear and the self-image profile is often an enticing start. A survey of Gary's SIP (Figure 9.1) shows the extent of the discrepancy between self and ideal. Such discrepancies have customarily, within personal construct theory, been employed as a measure of self-esteem, as discussed in Chapter 5. A small discrepancy suggests high self-esteem whereas a large discrepancy suggests low self-esteem. Reducing the discrepancy between self and ideal has therefore been suggested as a means of increasing self-esteem. At the very birth of modern psychology, William James (1892) suggested that a re-examination or re-construing of the ideal self may be as appropriate a therapeutic goal as a re-construing of the actual self. However, such 'downgrading' of the ideal self from fantasy to reality has the danger of reducing the child's aspirations. Do we really want to shatter children's dreams of inventing a time machine, scoring the winner in the cup final or being a Hollywood star?

Rather than focus on those aspects of the self-image profile where there were large discrepancies between Gary's vision of self and ideal, he was cautiously asked to mull over two aspects where the discrepancy was not so great – 'kind' and 'always in trouble'. His profile suggested there were times when he was kind and not in trouble. He was thus asked to describe such times, to illustrate with examples what he would be engaged in when he was kind and not in trouble. Seeking behavioural descriptors of constructs in this way, as described in earlier chapters, is a form of pyramiding (Fransella and Dalton, 1990).

Gary said he was kind when he cleaned up at home. As for when he was not in trouble, he elaborated this in three ways. He was not in trouble when

1. Playing sport – boxing, running, rugby and athletics;

2. Doing practical work such as fixing things like his bike, which also relieved boredom; and

3. When he tackled an interesting project at school and the teacher told him he had done well.

David Winter (1992) has suggested that only those interventions which offer the child the possibility of further extension or definition of the construct system can be expected to lead to reconstruction. In asking Gary to reflect on times when he was kind and not in trouble, possible avenues of change are hinted at. Further, in inviting Gary to describe his feelings (good) and implications (achievement) at such times, the intention was to both elaborate these experiences and foster a definition of himself as someone 'not always in trouble'. Seeking such exceptions and harnessing an understanding of what might account for the exceptions can be a powerful means of re-creation. When undertaken in the presence of a complainant – parent or teacher – at the very least it enables them to consider the problem as transient and the child as possibly responsive. Hopefully it may also secure a shift in their perception of the youngster, and thus enhance the opportunity of them recognizing the changed behaviour, which in turn validates the child's reformulated vision of self.

In seeking to enhance Gary's vision of himself as kind and not always in trouble there was an intention, as eloquently expressed by Fay Fransella (1972) to 'locate the self in the contrast'. To, as it were, dismantle Gary's way of life (as always in trouble) and seek to increase or develop the implications for constructs which form a new way of life. In her work with stutterers, Fransella (1972) found that unless she developed the individual's vision of self as fluent (the contrast to stuttering) through encouraging experimentation with fluency then the child was forever locked into a vulnerability towards stuttering.

Facilitating a change in behaviour may be reasonably straightforward, but securing a more permanent change only occurs once the individual comes to see the new behaviour as representative of him- or herself. Thus so long as stutterers perceive themselves as stutterers, no matter how fluent they become, they will inevitably revert, on occasions, to stuttering. The hazardous task in the process of change is not so much supporting the individual in making changes but in fostering a revision of self, so the person feels the new behaviour fits with their vision of self.

Phil Salmon (1995) made a similar point in her description of the learning process. She contends that as all learning carries implications, there is a Kellyan choice in whether an individual will embark on learning anything new. If it defines or extends the vision of self the person may embark willingly on new ventures. Connoisseurs have a healthy appetite to learn new skills in areas in which they are expert. Thus Gary might willingly venture into antisocial behaviours which extend his notion of troublesome behaviour and hone a definition of 'always in trouble'. Salmon further argued that as knowledge is not 'free-standing or disembodied', particular spheres of knowing 'belong' to particular concerns and particular lifestyles. Thus learning a musical instrument or understanding opera might not be an option to someone who conceives of himself as 'tone-deaf', not because he hasn't the capacity to learn, but because the individual perceives himself as unmusical in these very areas.

Such ideas alert us to the importance of working within the child's construct system. Only through understanding the child's sense of self, his mode of construing and the implications of change for the child can he be encouraged to explore different behaviour. Too often, in our eagerness to help, we fail to respect the constraints imposed by the structures in which the child currently lives (Neimeyer and Harter, 1988), which further serves to emphasize the futility and impotence of 'off the shelf' solutions, standard advice or glib reassurance.

9.6   DRAWING ON NEW EVIDENCE

Staying with the thesis of considering change from the client's perspective, another powerful means of controlled elaboration is asking the child to, as it were, become an observer. Gary was asked about other children who sometimes got into trouble, who were dared to do things they knew were troublesome and invited to observe how they dealt with such situations differently from how he might typically act. Here 'sometimes' is the operative word. David Winter (1992) has suggested that by engaging clients in this way they may come to consider the complaint within socially shared rather than purely personal dimensions, and that if they are able to view the complaint as if it were someone else's, then reconstruction might appear less threatening.

Gary identified one boy in his school class who generally kept himself out of trouble. He described him as 'in control'. Through pyramiding (asking Gary to describe what this boy did when he showed he was in control), he said the boy would do what he wanted, not what other kids dared him to do; he would laugh off any taunts; walk away from any jibes; listen in class; and he would ask teachers for help when he got stuck. This was a fairly thorough elaboration of the contrast. Asking Gary to describe how he felt this boy was able to conduct himself in this way, he reckoned the boy would be cool and he would think others who called him a wimp would be thick and stupid. A follow-up question sought to understand how Gary might feel if he were able to be like this boy. Without a hint of hesitation he said that for him to act like this boy would mean he would 'feel like I've turned a corner'.

9.7   INVITING FRESH EXPERIMENTATION

Gary was subsequently asked if he could imagine himself undertaking any of these alternative courses of action. He reckoned he could laugh off the taunts and dares of others and in class he felt able to ask the teacher when he got stuck. Here the aim was to attempt to design an experiment for Gary to test outside the therapy room. Gary was being invited to approach familiar situations as if some new construction reflected his vision of self.

The invite to act *as if* is an especially valued approach in personal construct theory. In its most formal state it has been scripted into fixed role therapy (to be discussed in Chapter 10). More usually it takes the form of an invitation to the child to enact an experiment, to act in a planned alternative way. Winter (1992) has argued that such experimentation enables the child to 'disengage core constructs from the experimentation by seeing it as only acting a point'. Any threat which the 'new' behaviour might normally evoke by virtue of its inconsistency with core structures is therefore minimized.

However, it is wise to anticipate the emotional implications of change. Kelly defined emotional experiences as the consequence of constructs in transition. Thus any change in construing might therefore be expected to result in some degree of anxiety, threat or guilt. The adoption of a changed way of acting or reconstruction might only occur if the anticipated change or change itself does not confront the child with too high a degree of such emotional experience. Where a 'new' behaviour results in awareness of stark unpredictability so that current construing is found wanting, then anxiety is provoked. If change results in the person becoming aware of an impending change in their sense of self that is inconsistent with their core role structures (their vision of self) then threat is experienced. Finally where a person recognizes they are acting or likely to act in ways they would not have predicted in themselves then they experience guilt. Guilt might be construed as the awareness of specific dislodgement.

Having explored some alternatives for Gary, he was asked to try to imagine himself in various scenarios – being dared to do things that he knew would lead him into trouble; struggling with some work at school – and to picture in 'his mind's eye' his new, alternative ways of responding. Once able to do this Gary was asked to try it out, to act as if he were the sort of person who took control by laughing off ridicule, provocation and baiting, and seeking help with class projects when stuck. He was asked to try this out over a two-week period. Imagination and enactment facilitate re-construing by tempering the emergence of emotional responses. A playful enterprise indeed.

However, before embarking upon the new role, Gary's mother, who had been present throughout, was invited to contribute to Gary's new venture. In facilitating the mother's understanding of Gary's viewpoint and his imminent experiment it was hoped that both the mother's sense of 'knowingness' would increase (thus reducing her complaints of an inability to comprehend) and that there would be an increased chance that Gary's new ventures and adopted construing would be validated outside the therapy room. In tightening up her responses to Gary she agreed:

1. Not to shout, but listen to Gary's version of events.

2. To be clear with Gary about what was expected of him, so that any reversion to former behaviour would be met with a reminder of what it was he had agreed to try out.

3. To be positive, not looking for when things went wrong but searching out and recognizing the efforts Gary made to maintain his experimental behaviours.

Gary returned two weeks later in jubilant mood. He described some successes in laughing off the exhortations to mess about in class, although the baiting by his peers he sensed, if anything, had increased. He was able to construe his persistent experimenting in the face of such pressures to succumb, as further evidence of his resilience to persist and 'take control'. Gary was most eager to tell of his success in class where his endeavours to listen and seek help had resulted in the achievement of a merit. Interestingly, Gary had also begun to make some decisions about developing his sporting talent to a greater extent. He had been to rugby training sessions regularly, begun to mix more with other players and had been picked for the first time to captain the team in a competitive match the next weekend. It was tempting to ask if Gary had endeavoured to elaborate his new construing in a different context – rugby – from that which we had originally set out. However, instead, his enthusiasm for this new venture was harnessed by seeking to discover what it was that he had changed about his approach to rugby, with a view of possibly engaging this construing in other aspects of his life.

Gary eagerly talked of how he approached his game and what was expected of him. He described the need for discipline, the need to follow the coach's instructions, the need to support others on the field, the need for nerves of steel in tackling and so forth. All of these attributes Gary noticed were possible to apply to other settings, both when out with his friends and within school. A second experiment was suggested, whereby Gary would endeavour to apply his sporting self to the rigours of school and the harassment of peers; a further version of the *as if* approach. Miller Mair (1977a) has noted how the use of a metaphor like this can facilitate an elaboration of construing and experimentation. Gary was undoubtedly ready to have a go with this further experiment.

9.8 CONCLUSION

Children's behaviour is often a source of concern. There is a growing sense, within society, that children's behaviour is becoming worse. Most referrals to general child psychology and psychiatry services consist of complaints about behaviour, framed in terms of disturbance, non-compliance, aggressiveness and being 'out of control'. When it comes to their behaviour, it seems children are typically complained about, but rarely complain themselves.

A personal construct perspective implies that the child's behaviour, however perplexing to the complainant, makes sense to the child. The child's actions are experiments, ways of testing out their construct system. As the example of Gary illustrates, the changes other people – parents, teachers and society in general – might expect or wish for, in a young person's behaviour, will only occur if the change makes sense to the individual. The task for those who wish to foster change in youngster's behaviour is to find ways of engaging and guiding them towards more 'socially appropriate' experiments, but ones that do not pose a threat to the child.

CHAPTER 10

EXPLORING AVENUES OF CHANGE

I would be inclined to argue that all of us would be better off if we set out to be something other than what we are.

(George Kelly)

Kelly's statement here appears to meld the idea of people being unremittingly a form of motion with the notion that determinedly harnessing such flux towards a desire to be different would prove beneficial. A sentiment presumably as applicable for those folk content with their lot as those who are burdened with personal troubles and difficulties. The statement further implies that any valuable movement ought to encompass changes in what is our current view of self. Thus although youngsters may be 'taught', 'coached' or 'treated' to act differently, unless such behaviours are incorporated into the individual's view of self, they remain just that – acts.

The many taught lessons at school proffer knowledge and techniques that youngsters fail to connect with. The information just passes them by. Others, of a more conscientious nature, may labour over homework, memorize facts and incidents and cram to pass exams yet think no more of their efforts when they move to the next phase of the curriculum. Learning is not a matter of acquiring 'nuggets of truth'. Only when a youngster connects the gained wisdom with an emerging construction of self – the budding scientist; proficient piano player; emerging linguist, dab hand with IT, competent painter – will they begin to understand their behaviour as meaningful. Where before children might interpret only dimly, there is sudden understanding in which acquired notions begin to connect up in exciting ways.

In the clinical context there is a laudable estimate that behavioural change instigated through techniques that fail to incorporate a change in self-construing is unlikely to endure. As discussed in the previous chapter, youngsters considered troublesome to others are unlikely to adopt less antisocial behaviours, even those robustly reinforced by powerful others, unless the new acts are incorporated into a fresh construction of self. Even children dissatisfied with their predicament, perhaps being overweight, bullied, fearful of school, or in conflict with parental attitudes, are unlikely to make changes if it implies stepping psychologically into the unknown. Fay Fransella found that for children who stuttered, the self at present is known, whereas other states (such as being fluent), perhaps more desired, are unfamiliar and only sketchily, if at all, construed. Interestingly she discovered that despite lengthy technique-driven interventions to improve fluency, such children remained with the known (stuttering) until they were able to construct a robust view of self as fluent.

The philosophical heart of PCT is constructive alternativism. Kelly pyramided this lofty idea into its more playful and behavioural constituents, describing how the 'events we face today are subject to as great variety of constructions as our wits will enable us to contrive'. This reminds us that all our present perceptions are open to question and reconsideration, broadly implying that even the most obvious occurrences of everyday life might appear utterly transformed if we were inventive enough to construe them differently (Kelly, 1970).

Such a philosophical assumption suggests optimism about the potential for change. Individuals have endless capacity for altering the way they behave and construe themselves. The key notion in Kelly's abstraction is arguably that of the individuals 'inventiveness' to construe events and themselves differently. Without intervention, creativity and imagination, the individual remains stuck.

10.1   SOME THERAPEUTIC PRINCIPLES

Kelly's early realization was that the only criterion for useful therapy was that it should be relevant to the client's needs and carry novel implications for a possible solution (Kelly, 1969a; Fransella and Neimeyer, 2003). Here the client's needs derive from understanding the problem from the youngster's perspective, where their stance may be seen as a means of constructing and preserving meaning. Behaviours, if viewed as questions, are the youngster's means of testing the social environment for predictability. Given the thrust of the organizational corollary those behaviours also reflect some more superordinate notion of self. Youngsters often ask the same repeated questions (behaviours) resulting in similar answers that validate the child's notion of self. Thus an adolescent may provoke an argument which frustrates the parent, thus validating their rebellious stance. As Kelly intimated, therapeutic interventions need to invite innovative questions and fresh experiments which conjure imaginative solutions that hopefully sustain a new conception of self.

Therapy pivots on the type of relationship between child and clinician. Kelly was keen to consider the idea of intervention in terms of person-in-relation-to-person rather than as specialist-in-relation-to-illness. He proposed a supervisory model to best represent what he had in mind. More recently this framework, driven by the sociality corollary, has been described as the model of equal expertise which has been alluded to in earlier chapters. It seeks to acknowledge the validity of each participant's (child, parent/s and therapist) story. Youngsters are well versed in many facets of their stance and the impact of their behaviour on their lives and their carers. They have, in Kelly's supervisory metaphor, a specific understanding of the research area, rather like a PhD student. Therapists on the other hand have a broad understanding of theoretical models, assessment techniques and interventions to assist the youngster in trying alternative questions, analysing outcomes and examining implications. Therapists, according to Kelly's template, are akin to a PhD supervisor. According to the sociality corollary, the appreciation and construction of each other's expertise fosters the therapeutic role where youngsters feel safe to test new ventures.

Kelly chose to express his ideas somewhat abstractly, so his writings contain plenty of implications for clinical practice but precious few fully operationalized applications which might be straightforwardly transferred into work with children. This appears to have been no accident because Kelly point-blank refused to provide sure-fire psychological remedies which might lure therapists into energetically treating their patients without going into the 'messy business' of understanding them first (Kelly, 1969a). The therapist, teacher, coach or parent wishing to help a child change or discover new ways of construing and behaving might therefore valuably assist by fostering and supporting the child's inventiveness, finding creative ways to encourage the child to experiment, to discover the outcome of such testing and hopefully re-construe. Kelly viewed therapy as effective when it enabled an individual to undergo psychological reconstruction, so that he 'feels he has come alive' (Kelly, 1980).

Adopting appropriate questioning with youngsters has been a strong theme throughout this book. With many constructs being held at a low level of awareness, some of our questioning encourages children and parents to see themselves for the first time. Vertical elaboration (Butler, 2006) acknowledges the ordinal nature of the organizational corollary and takes the form of either pyramiding or laddering items on which a youngster feels a sense of dissatisfaction. Pyramiding enables behaviours that underpin the psychological construct to be discovered. It involves inviting the child to describe what they or others typically 'do' when they are being described by the construct (Winter, 1992). Thus a youngster may be asked what they or others are doing when they are described as 'helpful', 'fun' or 'moody'.

Laddering enables the construct system to be 'ascended' to identify more superordinate constructs and ultimately to reveal those core constructs that fundamentally determine a youngster's sense of self. Such superordinate constructs are often at a low level of awareness and laddering can reveal to the client, often for the first time, which core constructs are implicated by items on which there is a sense of dissatisfaction in self. Laddering requires inviting the person to describe why they prefer to be at one pole of a construct. Thus in asking an adolescent, who wished to be more organized, 'How come it is important to be like that?', she suggested 'It helps me do my homework better'. Continuing the laddering process may indicate that it is important to do homework well because it 'avoids disapproval', thus revealing a core construct concerning how other people may judge the self.

Tom Ravenette (2003) was actively interested not only in furthering an understanding of the youngster's construing and the sense they made of their problem, but also in how questions can be employed to help make a difference. In the context of accepting Kelly's suggestion of first enquiring why an individual wishes to change, before launching into techniques to promote change, three avenues of change, concerned with horizontal elaboration – exception, elaboration and experimentation – are described.

10.2   EXCEPTIONS

To paraphrase Kelly's first principle, exploring exceptions is fundamentally based on the idea that if you wish to know what's right, then why not ask. Although a problem may appear overwhelming and unrelenting, a child may be invited to reflect on times when things are not quite so bad. The universal law of variability implies there are moments when phenomena change and events are different. We might listen for key phrases that hint of better times when the youngster grappled with solutions (e.g. 'except', 'it was different', 'until recently'). Exceptions may be seen as self-initiated experiments where youngsters, perhaps in a Kellyan aggressive fashion, seek to check their validity. Youngsters may be asked to think about when the problem/issue does not exist; about times that the story unfolds differently, about when a 'desired' behaviour happens and about when things are as they'd like them to be. Alternatively a youngster may be invited to consider how it would be if they woke up one morning without the problem. Searching for such exceptions raises an awareness of the possibility of change.

A next step is to elaborate the meaning of the exception. The youngster may be invited to explore eventualities, particularly what it is they do that increases the likelihood of the exceptionable behaviour happening. It makes sense to encourage thoughtful reflection as to the youngster's role in the change or solution. Taking credit, or 'internalizing the success', imparts ownership to the youngster. Inquiry in the form of 'What might you do, in order to experience that again?' or 'What is it about you that helped you do what you did?' enhances the child's sense of control over the actions.

Though many youngsters allude to exceptions and entertain behaviours that represent a solution to their problem, they may nevertheless resist fully subscribing to them. What may appear a solution to the clinician or parent may of course represent no such notion for the youngster. For exceptional acts to be fully endorsed they have to mesh with the child's construing of self. Occasional acts of benevolence for a youngster bent on being unsociable are unlikely to unite with their conception of self. For exceptions to prove therapeutically valuable, the search for noteworthy exceptions inevitably requires marrying with the youngster's self-construing. Thus children might be invited to consider any potential change in terms of what the changes say about them, what difference it will make to them; what it might imply in terms of other changes they may need to adopt; and how the change might effect how the youngsters think of themselves.

10.3   ELABORATION

Our personal construct system fundamentally allows us to read the world. It locates us from moment to moment and defines the stance we take to others, events and learning opportunities. Further, our construct system represents the possibilities for action and the choices made. Horizontal elaboration entails exploring the implications of potential change along a construct where the client has identified dissatisfaction with an aspect of self. This may arise from a discrepancy on the self-image profile for example (see Chapter 5). Elaboration may take a number of forms:

Clarification of meaning invites the youngster to explore the personal significance of being different from the current 'self' by describing in detail what it might be like to operate at the 'ideal', the preferred pole of a construct or indeed what would it be like to be just one point different along a construct rated from 0 to 6. The youngster might be asked to write a self-characterization as the ideal. Alternatively the elaboration may be facilitated by observing someone who displays such qualities as the ideal and noting what it is they do; what the world would look like to metaphorically stand in their shoes and what the possible impact on others might be. For some children, the ideal or the anticipated self without the 'problem' may be only hazily sketched or perhaps unknown, whereas the self with the 'problem', in contrast, is well understood.

Employing another construct to the matter at hand requires exploring how change can be anticipated by adopting the threads of a familiar construct to the problem area. This type of reconstructive process might involve, for example, encouraging a child who struggles to write to explore how he might undertake such a task were he to postulate writing a story by adopting the determination he employs in the sporting arena. Thus the youngster might creatively open up ways of re-construing writing. He might consider what his determination in the sporting context implies and then be invited to 'tackle' a piece of writing with the same enthusiasm and commitment.

Increasing the range of convenience of certain constructs Staying with a youngster's aversion to writing, the range of convenience of such a construct may be explored by testing the permeability of the contrast pole. Thus enquiries about activities involving writing that the youngster already undertakes, such as writing his Christmas list, might increase his awareness that writing is not necessarily tedious and followed by failure. Further, the child might be introduced to new activities involving the written word such as word search puzzles, writing jokes, keeping a diary of his best sporting moments or designing a new game, including instructions, as a means of increasing the implication that writing is fun, possible and an activity that can be completed successfully.

10.4 EXPERIMENTATION

Kelly proposed the metaphor of 'man the scientist' to represent his considerations about how individuals sought to make their world meaningful. Such an analogy naturally gives rise to the notion of experimentation as a means of promoting change. Key to such a concept is that authentic experiments are conducted without preconceived ideas about outcome. Answers to experiments are unknown. Rather than propose ready-made solutions for the youngster to embrace, as might be envisaged with more behaviourally or cognitively orientated therapies, personal construct theory encourages scientific enquiry where youngsters explore hypotheses and test out their theories for predictive validity. Kelly (1970) suggested that there is no such thing as adventure with safety guaranteed in advance.

Let's be a scientist is a task suited to children who appear troubled or perplexed by their own behaviour and builds from the idea of finding exceptions towards constructing a framework of understanding. At the outset, the therapist shares with the youngster the view that here lies a puzzle. By observing and carefully monitoring certain eventualities, the youngster is informed, the mystery may come close to being solved.

At 14 years old Lucy continued to wet the bed frequently. She remained frustrated and perplexed as to why on some nights she would be dry and on other nights the bed would be soaked. There were no obvious or apparent differences between the nights and it was threatening to severely curtail Lucy's friendships on account of her avoiding regular sleepovers and overnight school trips. Lucy elected to keep a diary of possible reasons for wet nights and over the following four weeks she recorded the reasons for the five wet nights as follows:

- 'had to [sic] much to drink, two blackcurrants and three waters.'

- 'I had a lot of homework that night and got stressed about it.'

- 'I went to see a play that my dad was in. After the play we helped clear up so buy [sic] the time I got to bed it was 11.30.'

- 'I got my brace that day. The brace was really hurting and I was worried about what people at school would say.'

- 'I went out for a meal with my family and my auntie, uncle and cousin. And I had two cokes and a lemonade.'

Through encouraging Lucy to be scientific she was beginning to develop some theories as to the reasons for wet nights. Both the volume and/or type of evening drink emerged as distinct possibilities, which Lucy was keen to further test out with a more rigorous experiment, setting aside a week each to check on four drinks (water, lemonade, coke and blackcurrant), having just one glass in the evening. Tiredness and her emotional state also appeared to increase Lucy's vulnerability to bed-wetting, which she continued to monitor on 0–6 scales prior to going to sleep. Embracing the idea of being a scientist had captured Lucy's imagination. She remained eager over the following weeks to share her data and theories, ultimately being able to predict she would remain dry at night by drinking either water or lemonade in the evening and going to sleep as if (see below) she was her pet cat.

Acting as if... is authentic Kellyan experimentation in action (Kelly, 1955). Perhaps considered a more utilitarian version of fixed role therapy, the propositional nature of the 'act as if ...' venture invites youngsters to try on for size alternative actions involving different constructions and roles for a limited period. Such a venture typically complements Kelly's seminal notion of constructive alternativism, which holds that there is an infinite number of ways to construe the world. In order to gain a fresh and potentially transforming perspective, youngsters may be invited to entertain novel and inspired possibilities for construing in a different way, commit themselves to undertake the task and test out new possibilities by acting 'as if' these new constructions were true. After a short trial the youngster is asked to reflect on the playful exploration. Successful experiments may be analysed to determine just which personal constructs were validated and which the youngster might wish to test further. Where constructions prove less than useful the youngster may be encouraged to formulate further alternative constructions of the same events and act 'as if' these apply instead.

A remarkable illustration of the potency of 'as if' experimentation is found in a study undertaken by Robert Hartley (1986). He asked a group of seven- and eight-year-old children to undertake a matching task and then asked them to complete the tasks again, first as if they were 'clever' and then as if they were 'not very clever'. Hartley found children were able to easily adopt the different roles. Children who 'as themselves' had completed the task impulsively or inaccurately (with an average 13 errors), engaged in the task much more vigilantly, accurately and diligently when they responded as if they were clever (average four errors) and far more inaccurately when responding as someone who is not very clever (average 38 errors). Hartley suggests that for a child to achieve this, he or she had to seek the right answer before they could 'successfully' offer the wrong answer.

Such results indicate that even such supposedly inflexible and rigid attributes as cognitive functioning may be the product of roles we inhabit. With some creativity these children showed the potential for changing the way they were, by reinventing themselves (although only for the duration of the ex- periment), and what's more they devised some appropriate behaviours to bring it about. Hartley summarizes that the perspective a child takes towards problem-solving, necessarily involves aspects of the way the child identifies him- or herself. His work appears to emphasize that for youngsters, alter- native selves may well be understood but they choose to enact behaviours which seek to validate their self.

After being knocked down by a car in the city centre a nine-year-old boy, Mark, became tearful and clingy, suffered nightmares and tried determinedly to avoid traffic to the point of refusing to cross even the quietest of roads. This severely affected his socialization; he became increasingly dependent on his parents for even the most mundane routines such as going to school. Mark understood the advantages of crossing roads by himself in that he would feel better, not get muddy going over fields and be able to go to fish and chip shop, though constantly he anticipated he was 'going to get knocked down again'. After little success with traditional behavioural techniques he was invited to think about how his favourite rugby player might address the situation. Mark suggested the rugby player would tackle it with confidence, wouldn't give in and would keep focused on what he was trying to do. Mark then became enthusiastic about the idea of trying to cross roads as if he were the rugby player and discovered he was immediately able to deal with the situation.

Acting as if a different self provides a platform for trying out alternatives and generally elicits less Kellyan guilt as the process inspires experimentation rather than supporting acts that are out of kilter with expectations of the self. The intention is not to impose a form of construing on the child but rather to provide a platform for experimentation. Successful experiments foster new observations, explore the implications of a new venture and encourage fresh theories. Finally the success of any such intervention should be judged by how able it is to facilitate the youngster's awareness that they have the potential for change. To appreciate, in Kelly's terminology, they have the capacity for constructive alternativism.

10.5 EMPLOYING THE SIP

A 10-year-old boy, Liam, entered clinic somewhat indifferent to the concerns parents and school were expressing about him. He was frequently in trouble at school for bullying other children, which many unproductive meetings at school had failed to resolve. He reportedly had no friends either in school where he was a victim of bullying (with the school mentor suggesting it's like 'he has a sign above his head saying "bully me"') or at home where he was effectively isolated by other boys in the street by being excluded from a neighbourhood gang. Mum feared that Liam lied to her and couldn't be trusted whereas Dad's theory amounted to Liam being an attention seeker.

In clinic Liam slouched in the chair, fiddled with the upholstery and customarily responded to questioning with a 'Don't know'. In the hope of opening up a reasoned dialogue and furthering an understanding of Liam's self-construing, the self-image profile was suggested. On hearing the clinician say 'I wonder if we could try something which will help me get to know you a little better', Liam immediately became attentive and interested. He was shown the profile with items depicting how other children had described themselves and invited, for each item, to shade the number along the scale according to how he would describe himself. After the first couple of items with the clinician shading in Liam's ratings, he completed the rest of the profile unaided. With no trouble Liam then completed the profile again, placing a star to represent where he would ideally like to be. Figure 10.1 depicts Liam's completed self-image profile.

Although there are various ways of scoring the SIP (Chapter 5), the visual representation of self readily evoked a number of notions and areas for discussion with Liam:

		not at all					very much	
		0	1	2	3	4	5	6
1	kind						☆	
2	happy					☆		
3	friendly		☆					
4	funny						☆	
5	helpful					☆		
6	hard-working					☆		
7	lively							☆
8	honest							☆
9	like sport							☆
10	brainy						☆	
11	sensitive		☆					
12	like the way I look		☆					
13	feel different from others					☆		
14	lazy				☆			
15	get picked on	☆						
16	moody							☆
17	mess about in class	☆						
18	shy	☆						
19	always in trouble		☆					
20	cheeky	☆						
21	teases others	☆						
22	easily upset		☆					
23	bossy	☆						
24	bad-tempered							☆
25	get bored easily					☆		

[ ] = how I am   ☆ = how I'd like to be

The Self Image Profile is published by Butler (2001) and reproduced with permission from Harcourt Assessment

Figure 10.1 The Self-Image Profile of Liam. Source: The Self-Image Profile is published by Butler (2001) and reproduced with permission from Harcourt Assessment.

- There was generally a less than positive sense of self with many low ratings on the more 'positive' items (1–12) and a large degree of discrepancy overall between how Liam thought of himself and how he would like to be.

- 'Extreme' ratings (either 0 or 6) suggested Liam was particularly convinced of his unhappiness, lack of being funny, dissatisfaction with his appearance, laziness, vulnerability to upset and susceptibility to boredom.

- A correspondence of 'self' and 'ideal' ratings implied a contentment with self in terms of sport and moodiness.

- A sense of accord between Liam's view of self and the concerns of teachers and parents in terms of invariably being in trouble and being picked on.

- A discrepancy between how teachers and Liam construed himself, notably in the area of teasing others.

Appreciating Liam's standpoint through exploring such issues helps foster a shared understanding, a notion heralded by the sociality corollary as fundamental in constructing a beneficial therapeutic relationship. As Ravenette (1988) has been at pains to point out, the pivotal trigger to therapeutic change is grasping an understanding of the youngster's understanding.

The SIP further hints at where therapeutic intervention might be most usefully focused. Items where there is a perceived discrepancy between 'self' and 'ideal' suggest the child is some distance psychologically from where he or she would like to be. With Liam there are many points of such discrepancy. Although initially it is tempting to select items of greatest discrepancy (e.g. 'get picked on'), the 'ideal', being such a distance from where the youngster currently sees their self, may arguably be regarded as a fantasy rather than a reality. Usually it is therefore appropriate at first to identify items with less exacting discrepancy which may then be elaborated both horizontally and vertically through interested inquiry.

Liam considered himself as 'always in trouble' (rating 5) and wished to become less so (rating 1), an apposite item for initial consideration. Finding the contrast helps clarify meaning. Liam thought hesitatingly about this and suggested 'acting your own age' as a contrast. The construct was then fleshed out through pyramiding, whereby Liam was invited to describe what it is he does when he finds he is in trouble/acting his age and through identifying the context in which the behaviours occur. For Liam being in trouble occurred when he acted silly, when he acted younger than his age and when he was being stupid. A behaviour he claimed as typical of this was calling other children rude names, which was most likely to happen when others were having fun. Liam recognized his actions in turn led to him being teased and told off, thus validating a 'rejected' notion of self.

The contrast 'acting your age' meant, for Liam, being clever, and consisted of listening to teachers and joining in with other children's fun. This was most likely to happen when he was feeling good. The implications of such actions were that it would stop him being bullied (and thus hopefully and indirectly also reduce the extent to which he was 'picked on') and help him acquire more friends. Tapping into more superordinate constructs through laddering (by asking 'How come it's important to act your own age?') proved a demanding task for Liam but nevertheless he indicated it would mean that friends might like him more, suggesting the importance of relatedness in his core construing. Exploring exceptions by asking Liam when other children might appear to like him, he eagerly suggested when he played sport. This was also when he 'acted his age'. It happened, he thought, because he was a good player, others wanted him on their side and he enjoyed himself. After wondering how things might be if he were able to act as if he was a sportsman where usually he found himself vulnerable to being in trouble, Liam swiftly elaborated the connection. He recognized there certainly might be times he could try his best, support other children rather than call them names and have fun with others, all aspects of his 'sporting' self, during non-sporting contexts. Liam was the scientist Kelly might have anticipated, his experimentation with the role-play proving so successful that Liam returned to clinic four weeks later enthusiastic about how he was now included, rather than rejected, by other children, had been praised by the teachers and as his dad said 'It's difficult to believe the change in him'.

10.6   A MORE FORMAL APPROACH

A procedure which incorporates many of Kelly's ideas about change and one which he most explicitly described is fixed role therapy. This is a brief intervention where both therapist and client jointly construct a specially tailored part for the client to play. The role is intended to lead the client into a novel behavioural experiment, but not impel them to act out in a fashion that is either in total contradiction to their usual self or represents a brief excursion into their ideal way of functioning. The case of Arthur describes how children may be encouraged to sample a different version of self and judge the implications of different actions (Green, 1997).

Arthur was an 11-year-old boy. His mother, a single parent, had frequent contact with the health service for managing the severe behavioural problems presented by her youngest five-year-old son Ben, who suffered from a range of developmental delays. She expressed a legitimate concern that Arthur would be adversely affected by being constantly asked to tolerate Ben's angry outbursts. Arthur, although much older than his brother, was described as being terrorized by his younger sibling and, in his mother's eyes, failing to assert himself appropriately in the relationship. Although Arthur appeared to function reasonably well outside the family (e.g. with friends and at school), his mother feared his personality development might be impaired if he continued to be ruled by his handicapped brother.

Arthur acknowledged that he would like Ben to stop hitting him but did not share his mother's concern that being subjected to this regular pummelling would cause him long-term psychological harm. He impressed as a gentle young man eager to please his mother and sensitive to the pressures under which she was struggling to bring up a family. The clinical challenge was to enable Arthur to try out new ways of coping with Ben's difficult conduct without instructing him to adopt a style grossly incongruent with his prevailing positive view of himself as a tolerant, considerate, kindly young man. Arthur was asked to produce a self-characterization in which he wrote a brief pen-picture of himself described as if a character in a play. The account is written in the third person but is nonetheless an intimate and sympathetic portrayal of the important facets of the individual's personality. Arthur sketched himself thus:

> Arthur is an artistic boy. He likes PE and maths, but his favourite subject is art and craft. He is very trustworthy and gets along with people too. He wouldn't hurt a human or an animal, but he would try to defend himself if someone attacked him first. If he worked on a farm and had to kill a chicken or turkey for Christmas, he would probably refuse.
>
> He loves his family very much and knows what is right and wrong.
>
> Arthur is a bit shy when he talks to adults, because he thinks he might say something that the adult might not like.
>
> It is very important that his family is around him or near him.
>
> He used to have a Granny and Grandad but they died. They were nice people. They were his mother's parents.
>
> He enjoys going to his best friend's house. They go to the library and get some books out on things he is interested in. His friend is going to grammar school in September.
>
> It bothers him a little bit, but he hopes they still will be best friends.

In conversation, Arthur confirmed his view of himself as more of an Athenian than a Spartan who prided himself on his artistic gifts and sympathetic nature and had a strong aversion to violence no matter whether he was cast as the victim or aggressor. His sense of moral integrity and strong affection for his family also shone through. The overall tone of the self-characterization is hopeful rather than self-critical and begins to explain why dealing with Ben's troublesome behaviour placed Arthur in something of a dilemma. How could he be true to himself and his values but nonetheless adopt a more determined and effective attitude towards his younger brother?

Arthur's mother also recognized that she wouldn't want him to change because 'He is a lovely lad who has a stream of nice qualities any mum would be proud to see in her son'. With Arthur's problems stemming from his tricky relationship with Ben the fixed role sketch was designed around a tight domestic 'mini-script' (Epting, 1984). The new identity Arthur was invited to adopt was that of Adam, whose character was typified as follows:

> Adam is the sort of chap who likes to try and find solutions to problems. Sometimes answers come easily and it's good to know you've definitely got something right, but Adam also likes a challenge, and you can certainly call Ben a challenge.
>
> It's quite a trick to see some of Ben's antics as puzzles to be worked out but Adam is starting to get into the habit. Not that Adam always knows what to do

– even Ben's mum is stumped by him sometimes. However, when there isn't a right thing to do, Adam just experiments and tries something new.

Sometimes he's kind and understanding. Other times he takes no notice at all. Sometimes he gets upset and concerned. Other times he just doesn't give a damn. Sometimes he imagines he and his brother are two dinosaurs battling for survival. Other times he thinks of them as two co-stars in some epic film. He's decided that it is a good idea for now to keep Ben guessing and to become a bit more unpredictable.

One of the things that allows Adam to take this relaxed 'suck it and see' approach is that he is very confident of his family's backing. Nobody is going to get seriously hurt so they trust his judgement. It's no big deal if things don't work out, and it's nice to get a bit of fun out of a situation that could get Adam down a bit if he let it.

Above all, Adam likes to enjoy life and when he's happy he usually finds people around him are happy too. He finds he is at his most creative when he just follows his instincts and does what comes naturally. He likes to go his own way.

The new part aimed to introduce Arthur to novel ways of reacting to Ben without asking him to adopt ways of construing himself that were in complete opposition to his prevailing self schema. Rather the introduction of the notion of Adam as a relaxed problem-solver tried to bring an unexpected and interesting fresh perspective to bear. In his role as Adam, Arthur might be freer to experiment in his dealings with Ben.

Arthur found Adam's character both acceptable and understandable and required little amendment. When asked how Adam's characteristics compared with his own personality, Arthur replied, after some reflection 'about half and half'. Such a common-sense appraisal fits well with Kelly's more complex direction that the fixed role sketch should take an 'orthogonal' path in relation to the individual's dominant constructs regarding self.

As Kelly suggested, prior to enacting the new role, Arthur was asked to familiarize himself with the sketch, anticipate how Adam might react to Ben in various circumstances and briefly rehearse the role-play with his mother. He proved a convincing improviser and an inventive and plausible actor. The enactment proper lasted two weeks and applied only to Arthur's conduct within his home. He opted not to receive intensive support during the two weeks but asked that the therapist send him a postcard addressed to his alter ego, Adam. Following the enactment, Arthur attended the clinic with his mother to discuss how the experiment had gone and reflect on lessons learned.

Both Arthur's own report (through a diary log of his experiences) and his mother's contemporaneous observations confirmed that he enacted the Adam role faithfully and with an intriguing effect on Ben's conduct. While Adam was acting in a more relaxed unpredictable fashion, Ben was reported to have become less aggressive and more respectful of his brother's wishes. An adapted and brief version of the self-image profile was employed, which enabled Arthur to describe himself on a limited number of personally important characteristics. Arthur rated himself on nine constructs drawn from both his own self-characterization and Adam's fixed role sketch using a six-point scale. The constructs were:

- Gets along with people
- Relaxed
- Knows what's right and wrong
- Likes to enjoy himself
- Trustworthy
- Likes solving problems
- Would not hurt anyone
- Tries something new
- Loves his family.

Arthur's profile whilst undertaking the role of Adam (Figure 10.2b) indicated he had a conceptual understanding of how the character differed from himself (Figure 10.2a). As Adam he was more likely to try something new and be more relaxed. It might have seemed the lessons to be drawn from the fixed role experiment were self-evident. Of course, Arthur would conclude that his new repertoire of ways to manage Ben's difficult behaviour was both effective and personally comfortable and he would change accordingly. Arthur thought otherwise. He had listened closely to the terms of the experiment and understood correctly that he was to act 'as if' he were Adam for two weeks while his usual self was on a sort of brief holiday. Following the enactment phase the old Arthur returned. He concluded that the fixed role had been very diverting but, upon reflection, had not led him to wish to redefine himself. He was quite happy with himself as he was.

Arthur's calm insistence on opting to retain his established version of himself is clearly portrayed in the post-enactment profile (Figure 10.2c) which closely resembles his baseline image. Not perhaps the 'good, rousing, construct-shaking experience' Kelly claimed fixed role therapy should provide, or so it appeared. Arthur's mother feared he was putting a brave, public face on his private suffering and restated her continued concern that 'underneath' he was a sad and troubled young man. Arthur heard all this with a calm and un-

a. baseline	1	2	3	4	5	6
gets along with people						
relaxed						
knows what's right and wrong						
likes to enjoy himself						
trustworthy						
likes problem-solving						
would not hurt anyone						
tries something new						
loves his family						

b. fixed role therapy	1	2	3	4	5	6
gets along with people						
relaxed						
knows what's right and wrong						
likes to enjoy himself						
trustworthy						
likes problem-solving						
would not hurt anyone						
tries something new						
loves his family						

c. post enactment	1	2	3	4	5	6
gets along with people						
relaxed						
knows what's right and wrong						
likes to enjoy himself						
trustworthy						
likes problem-solving						
would not hurt anyone						
tries something new						
loves his family						

d. 3-month follow-up	1	2	3	4	5	6
gets along with people						
relaxed						
knows what's right and wrong						
likes to enjoy himself						
trustworthy						
likes problem-solving						
would not hurt anyone						
tries something new						
loves his family						

Figure 10.2 Adapted Self-Image Profiles for Arthur.

ruffled dignity, appreciated his mother's viewpoint but sought to reassure her that he did truly hold a positive view of himself, his future and his capacity to deal constructively with Ben.

Three months later, during which time Arthur moved from a small junior school to a large senior comprehensive school, a follow-up meeting brought evidence of a stunningly positive consensus. Arthur had coped with the school transfer in assured fashion and felt that, as he had predicted, he was managing Ben's behaviour to his satisfaction. Arthur's mother endorsed this change, describing his sense of buoyant self-worth and how, during the school holiday, she had noticed Arthur reassuming some of the ways of coping with Ben that he had previously only employed in his fixed role persona of Adam. This was further highlighted by the adapted self-image profile (Figure 10.2d) with Arthur describing himself as much more relaxed and likely to try something new.

As much of the improvement appeared to lag behind the fixed role experience, coupled with the many other plausible and intervening positive influences in Arthur's life at the time, it would seem hazardous to claim that fixed role played a significant part in Arthur's increased confidence. On completion of the enactment phase of fixed role therapy, Arthur elected to reassume his former identity and run his life on familiar lines – as if nothing had happened. In personal construct terms choosing to define rather than extend one's construct system (to opt for an established way of viewing oneself rather than elaborating a new but risky perspective) is the preference of a person who feels better able to anticipate events from this position at this particular time. Arthur's candid resistance to further exploration of the implications of acting as if he were Adam can be seen as a healthy recognition that some of his core constructs of himself were under threat of imminent change, a process he was not about to rush into.

Kelly viewed creative problem-solving as an unending cycle of experiment and analysis, which he termed the loosening and tightening of the personal construct system. If fixed role therapy represents a carefully designed project to loosen existing constructs, then Arthur's immediately consequent choices can be seen as a timely tightening exercise. It is important, however, for this cycle to continue if the opportunity for change offered by the fixed role sketch is to be maintained. In terms of renewed behavioural experiment, Arthur's mother described how Arthur had acted in a more assertive manner towards Ben during the school holiday, feeling herself more relaxed about these brotherly changes and not impelled to intervene to protect Arthur. This picture resembled very similarly that reported during the fixed role enactment, only now it was Arthur, not Adam, who was centre stage.

The adapted self-image profiles also provide evidence of continued reconstruing. The final profile (Figure 10.2d) shows significant shifts from all three previous profiles. Arthur did not see himself as just like the Adam character he adopted during the fixed role enactment. It seems he found his own way of incorporating the qualities of being more relaxed and open to trying something new into his view of himself, whilst retaining those caring characteristics (such as being trustworthy and knowing what's right and wrong) that remained core to his identity. This appears to confirm Kelly's prediction that 'fixed role therapy is . . . not a panacea but an experiment. In fact we have learned that if it is presented as a panacea it fails its purpose and the client does not get on with the process of finding out for himself' (Kelly, 1969c).

10.7 CONCLUSION

Although movement is the nub of psychotherapeutic endeavour, not least the removal of some problematic action, change is far from automatic or straightforward. Through discerning questioning, framed around the disadvantages of the proposed solution or ideal, or in contrast, the advantages of the current (problem) situation, Tschudi (1977) observed just how intractable and complex change might be. Sometimes what appears problematic to others (e.g. behaviour, anorexia, nocturnal enuresis) is a stance that acts as a solution for the youngster. Thus defiance or stubbornness, as perceived by a parent, may be a valid stance on behalf of the child, with their actions ensuring for example independence or autonomy. Although bed-wetting is a distressing condition for most youngsters Butler (1994) found a few who put forward theories as to why it remained advantageous to wet and thus resist change. For such youngsters, bed-wetting is not perceived as a problem, but a solution to some other problem. Bed-wetting may be advantageous because it preserves a particular relationship with parents or carers (contact); it enables the youngster to resist the responsibility of adulthood; it achieves special status in the family (e.g. bedroom to self); it enables avoidance of unwanted social engagements such as a stay over with grandparents; it may control other people's actions (e.g. 'It stops Mum coming into my room to tidy up); or it may avoid other unpleasant eventualities (e.g. 'It stops the dog sleeping on the bed').

Change carries with it many implications. Firstly, there is the potential step into the unknown. The self without the 'problem' may be only hazily sketched or ill-constructed, whereas the self with the 'problem', in contrast, is well understood.

Secondly although change brings about anticipated gains, there is also inevitably a sense of loss. The notion of 'how I am' is depleted, if only in terms of the original 'problem'. There can never be a turning back. Change means we are never the same again. Like the child who discovers Santa to be an illusion, he or she must give up a delightful part of early childhood. Thus a reluctance to change may arise through an avoidance of anticipated loss.

Change inescapably reverberates around the construct system. Change is rarely the acquisition of a single, isolated behaviour. Altering one behaviour tends to bring about change in other areas, including closely associated constructs. Dennis Hinkle (1965) devised a neat procedure for anticipating this by asking clients to predict that if they were to change on one construct, on which other constructs are they likely to change. The SIP is ideally formatted to entertain such enquiry. Clearly change becomes that much more hazardous the more a youngster predicts extensive change on implied constructs. Change, in all its ramifications, also tends to involve implications for more superordinate construing. Unless the youngster's 'new' behaviour aligns with their core construing, it is unlikely to make much sense and will quickly be discarded, revealing the comprehensiveness and intricacy that change may imply for any youngster.

Finally, as Kelly intimated, change of construing also involves emotional ramifications. Guilt may be an expected consequence of change because the individual, by behaving in new ways, is acting in ways they might not have expected of themselves. Thus despite Kelly's laudable assertion that we would be better off if we set out to be something other than what we are, change is far from straightforward. But the experiment is worth undertaking.

CHAPTER 11

BEING IN TROUBLE WITH THE LAW

It just seemed like a bit of fun.

It was August bank holiday Monday and the drought of that summer stretched on. Three boys woke to a cloudless, sun-baked morning. Another sweltering long day stretched in front of them. A day, they anticipated, for amusement, recreation, horseplay and the customary dash of devilment. Time indeed to relish. No different to the start of many other days that had characterized the extended school holiday. Except that this would end with the death of an elderly lady and one of the boys – a mere 10 years old – charged with murder. What had seemed like just a bit of fun had dramatically veered alarmingly, in seconds, into a nightmare.

Police records provide a summary of that fateful day. John, along with Alan and Carl, had 'tricked' their way into a high-rise block of flats as they had done on a number of previous occasions. Once inside the building they made their way onto the roof, through a vandalized door. The flat roof provided a spectacular view across the busy city but the 10-year-old boys were not necessarily taken in by the panorama. Besides they had been there before. They were experimenters, curious about their world, interested in action and thrills. Before long the boys found an orange and then a piece of wood, which were both propelled excitedly over the 5-foot parapet to the ground below.

Escalation seems a fundamental characteristic of play; amplifying, intensifying and expanding a theme as the child's involvement grows. In such vein a discarded block of concrete weighing almost 20 lbs was heaved up and placed on the parapet, a ledge some 2 inches higher than John's own height. As John admitted later to the police, he was responsible for then pushing the concrete block over the edge. Directly below, unseen by John, stood a group of people returning from the shop, via the back entrance, to the block of flats. The concrete block hit and instantly killed one of them, an elderly lady. Unhesitatingly the boys fled the scene though, within an hour, all three were picked up by the police.

11.1   LEGAL FRAMEWORK

After admitting responsibility, John was legally described under the terms of the Child and Young Persons Act 1953 as *doli incapax*. This Act states that children under 10 years cannot be found guilty of an offence, and that children between 10 and 14 years are presumed to be incapable of forming criminal intent. In order that John might therefore be tried, the Crown Prosecution Service had to counter the presumption of *doli incapax*. It had to seek to demonstrate that John knew or understood the difference between right and wrong, and was aware at the time that he was acting in a way that was seriously wrong, in contrast to what might otherwise be construed as naughty or mischievous.

Determining a child's awareness of the 'wrongness' of an act he is engaged in has proved to be a hazardous business. The behaviour itself cannot be presented as evidence to provide a child knows right from wrong because the immediate repercussions of the behaviour (such as arrest) may affect the child's judgement retrospectively about the seriousness of the act. Neither can the child's reactions following the behaviour be used to demonstrate that, at the time, he knew he was engaged in behaviour which was seriously wrong. For example, running away from the scene cannot be used to judge the wrongness of the act, because children customarily tend to escape from commonplace and petty acts of mischievousness.

The legal question of ascertaining whether John knew, at the time of pushing the block off the roof, that he was engaged in an act that could be considered seriously wrong, is identical to that placed before Bobby Thompson and Jon Venables, the boys found guilty of abducting two-year-old James Bulger and killing him on a railway line in 1993. In that case the Crown Prosecution

Service requested a psychiatric opinion to determine if there was a case of 'diminished responsibility' and a clinical psychologist to assist in the assessment of moral understanding. Only Jon Venables agreed to be seen, although at a very late stage with the weight of forensic evidence against him, Bobby Thompson agreed to see a child-and-adolescent psychiatrist appointed by the defence, but refused to see the psychiatrist for the Crown.

11.2   ASSESSMENT

John was seen within six weeks of the fateful day. It was explained that the purpose of seeing a psychologist was to seek to understand how it was that he had arrived in this predicament and that a report of the interview and assessments would subsequently be written for the Court. There was undoubtedly some anticipated unease concerning the troublesome task of harmonizing psychological information with what can appear to be a rigid legal framework.

On first meeting John, Kelly's first principle of finding out – that of asking the client – was considered perhaps not to be the most apposite strategy in ascertaining his version of the event. After all John was not seeking the resolution to a problem in the way Kelly had in mind in his appeal for personal inquiry. John had not been brought kicking and screaming, but because the system so demanded. It was therefore considered more appropriate to ask about the events on the roof at the very end of our two sessions. Even though John would communicate about many things during the sessions, often with a flash of humour, he resurrected a tight-lipped, avoidant posture to any 'awkward' questions. Interestingly this bears a resemblance to Jon Venables, who also reportedly became subdued and uncommunicative when asked about the charges by the psychologist (Smith, 1994).

'Mental normality' has in practice often been accepted as proof of a child's ability to distinguish right from wrong. The contrast suggests that a child who demonstrates bizarre or 'abnormal' development cannot be held accountable for his behaviour and would therefore be described as *doli incapax* on the grounds of diminished responsibility. There seemed little evidence to suggest John's mental development was abnormal. His mother described him as a normal cheeky boy 'in common with others of his age', with a tendency to resort to swearing and an inclination to play with mischievous boys, sometimes younger than himself. John's mother blamed her partner, whom she described as 'a really foul-mouthed person when drunk'. John's favourite TV programmes were World Wrestling, *The Simpsons* and the *Power Rangers*. If he were a Power Ranger he said he would be able to fly and do somersaults in the air. John fully recognized this made them different from himself, and as some might argue, demonstrated a differentiation of reality from fantasy. Interestingly he struggled to find any difference between himself and Bart

Simpson, primarily, indeed exclusively, because the character was construed in terms of always being in trouble. John perceived an affinity with Bart Simpson through their shared infringements of parental and societal expectations.

A youngster's level of intellectual capacity has traditionally been linked, perhaps understandably although not always logically, with the child's capacity to distinguish right from wrong. There was little doubt that John's level of cognitive development, assessed on the British Ability Scale (BAS), was within a 'normal range', although at the lower end of this range. Interestingly this placed John's intellectual capacity on the very boundary where the law absolves the child of responsibility. Thus the Children and Young Person's Act 1953 regards children under 10 years (chronological not intellectual) as *doli incapax* and unable to be found guilty of an offence.

However, what emerged from the assessment of cognitive functioning and attainment tasks was clear evidence of a specific learning difficulty. John, it turned out, was profoundly affected by dyslexia. Both his decoding (reading) skills and encoding (spelling) ability were estimated to be around the 6–6.6-year level, so ill-developed that his scores lay beyond the range of the centile scales. For example, John read 'here' for her, 'can' for cup, 'did' for bird and 'pig' for dig. He attempted only eight words on the BAS spelling test, with 'mi' being his attempt at 'my', and 'yu' for 'up'.

A delineation of dyslexia demands primarily that there is a significant discrepancy between the level of intellectual functioning and level of reading (Rutter and Yule, 1975). Tables in which reading achievement is predicted on the basis of the observed correlations between educational attainment, age and intellectual level in the general population offer the most appropriate means of understanding the degree of underachievement (Rutter and Yule, 1979). According to tables published by the BAS (Elliott, 1983), only 1 % of children would have a discrepancy as large as John's between reading level and what would be expected given his level of intellectual functioning. The experience of struggling with dyslexia can be undoubtedly traumatic. Of relevance here, however, is how such a specific difficulty might have played a part in John's plight. Noticeably, perhaps significantly, John's dyslexia had gone unnoticed at school. A Statement of Special Educational Needs, designed chiefly to emphasize John's behavioural difficulties, made reference to literacy difficulties in passing, but no specific or focused help for John's dyslexia had ever been envisaged.

Run-of-the-mill implications for those with dyslexia include a difficulty in assimilating and processing information in both the verbal and visual modalities, and an inability to think through or analyse all the possible consequences of any behaviour (Rutter and Yule, 1979). Youngsters with dyslexia may therefore neglect to take things into account before acting. Kelly might have considered this as a shortening of the circumspection-pre-emption-control (CPC) cycle where the child omits to consider all the information (lacking circumspection), but elects to act pre-emptively and perhaps impulsively in relating to events before him.

The very nature of John's dyslexia may thus counter the notion that he knew at the time of the incident that he was engaged in a behaviour which was seriously wrong. It could be argued that he would have struggled to weigh up or predict the ramifications and thus the entire risk of his action, particularly as he was prevented, by the height of the parapet, from gathering information about what was below. Nevertheless the prosecution would argue that John's two companions, keeping an eye out for what was happening below, shouted to him not to do it. What the boys actually shouted, the intentions behind their cries and John's possible interpretation of this remains open to question. What seems crucial is not what was said, but what meaning John attached to what was said. It is of course commonplace that we read other people's intentions wrongly. We can easily misinterpret other people's meaning. When a mother eventually gives in to the toddler's request for a biscuit, do all her earlier 'nos', from the child's perspective, really mean 'yes'?

The issue of misinterpretation has perhaps never been more powerfully exhibited, in British criminal circles, than in the case of Derek Bentley. In 1952, Bentley, along with another youth, Christopher Craig, set out one November evening looking for excitement. Their thoughts turned to the possibility of robbing a store in Croydon, and with this in mind they climbed on the roof of a warehouse building. Soon they were confronted by the police. Bentley, aged 19, and who suffered with a 'low IQ', a reading age of between 4 and 5 years and a history of epilepsy, was quickly apprehended. Craig, aged 16, then pulled a gun. It is alleged Bentley, who was already under arrest, shouted 'Let him have it, Chris' to the other boy, who then shot and killed one of the policemen. Bentley said he meant it as an instruction to surrender the gun. However, the prosecution at his trial argued that Craig had interpreted the comment as an instruction to shoot. Both were found guilty of murder under the ancient doctrine of 'constructive malice'. Because of his age, Craig was sentenced to be detained at Her Majesty's pleasure and served his time in Wakefield Jail. Bentley, being of an age of criminal responsibility, went to the gallows. He remains the only accomplice to a capital crime ever to be executed when the principal had, for reasons of youth or insanity, escaped the death penalty.

11.3   UNDERSTANDING JOHN'S DILEMMA

Rutter and Yule (1975, 1979), amongst others, have described how dyslexia can have a profound effect on a child's behaviour, self-worth and social development. These three phenomena play a vital part in understanding John's dilemma.

11.3.1 Behaviour

John's behaviour, particularly at school, had been in the spotlight for some time. Following the Bulger case where the boys' school teachers gave evidence both on the school's philosophy – the importance of teaching children to behave responsibly towards one another – and specific teaching of right and wrong, it was natural that John's teachers would be asked to comment. The evidence of two of John's most recent teachers outlined a weighty history of wrongdoing and their sustained efforts to teach the difference between right and wrong.

The teachers' endeavours in seeking to raise an awareness of what was acceptable and unacceptable behaviour led to an assertion that John had indeed been taught to understand what was wrong. However, a complication arises when a child who has been taught to understand wrongness continues to act in ways that are seen to be wrong, as John had done. It might be considered that the moral teaching failed to be absorbed by the child. A difficulty in assimilating information, a root attribute of dyslexia, might plausibly have impeded John's access to such teaching. What is under question here is the degree to which what is taught is correlated with what is learnt. Alternatively a child might continue to act in inappropriate ways despite moral teaching because the child chooses to, as it were, to ignore what is taught. Thus a child may have a fair grasp of the concept of wrongness, but still choose to act in ways that are considered wrong. Knowledge and action might therefore fail to be correlated. This issue is at the core of countering the presumption of *doli incapax*.

Herein lies the problem for teachers. They typically tend to construe children from, as it were, the outside, looking in. They adopt an observer's perspective. However comprehensive and accurate that perception is, it is nevertheless a view, a construction of the child, based on a framework that makes sense to them. An observer's attribution of a problem is generally marked by a constitutional belief. We reason that a child behaves as they do because of something (wrong) about them. This generally contrasts with the actor's perspective, the person engaged in the behaviour. They tend to attribute the reason for their behaviour in situational terms. The particular circumstances at the time are seen to be contributory. In seeking the 'inside version', the child's perception of events, a teacher might take the opportunity to try Kelly's first principle on for size. This suggests that if we wish to know why a child persists in behaving in troublesome ways, it might prove fruitful to ask about their version of events. As Ravenette (1977) proposed so clearly, gathering an awareness of the child's troubles can be assisted greatly by going beyond the traditional grasp of understanding (the observer's perspective) and seeking to understand the child's understanding.

An extensive 'behavioural log' was kept by the teachers for a 12-week period in the autumn of the school year which saw John first excluded from the

Table 11.1 A summary of teacher's construing of John, from the behaviour log

A	B
1. Concentrates	Bored
2. Sit quietly	Singing; muttering; talk loudly; noisy making silly baby noises loudly; swearing; banging legs on desk
3. Sit in own place	Moved around carpet; leaving seat; fidgeted around classroom
4. Settle	Disruptive; telling tales; show off
5. Ask for advice; listen to my opinion	Ignore me; cheeky parrot towards me; mimic me
6. Cooperate (do what I ask)	Flat refused; ignored
7. Worked well, worked hard	Wouldn't work; refused to do work
8. Work with others (collaborate)	Prevented others working
9. Join in; offer suggestions; take turns	Sit on own; standing out; refuse to join in
10. Worked with a partner; worked well together	Chatting loudly to them; mocked others; hit others; teasing; taunting; incited; saying unkind things to others; tried to annoy others; punched; insulted; threw conkers at others

school, then enter a special school, and concluded with a charge of murder against him. Table 11.1 is a summarized representation of that behaviour log. It represents the contrasting statements made by John's teacher and presents a framework to resemble a series of constructs. The fascinating insights generated by this are manifold, but the broad outcome reflects Kelly's view that explanations offered about children's actions often tell us more about the construct system of the adult than the child. The more 'acceptable' end of the construct is arranged on the left side, under A, and the unwelcome or undesirable pole on the right side, under B.

The constructs have a time-honoured pedagogic flavour. John was expected to conform to traditional educational values: concentrating on task, constrained to his seat, showing respect and submissiveness to authority, putting effort into his work and working constructively alongside or with other children. The agenda was fixed. John was to be moulded into what school expected of him. There was little leeway. Sadly missing was any consideration of John's perceived needs.

Tellingly, the behavioural log indicated that John was at various times located at both poles of every construct. Sometimes he worked well and at other times he refused to work. Occasionally he joined in with others and offered helpful suggestions, yet at other times he sat on his own away from the group. From time to time he would listen to the teacher and then he would mimic and 'parrot' her. From the teacher's perspective John would seem to slot rattle – vacillate rapidly between the two opposing poles of a construct. Kelly argued that shifting between poles of a construct in this way represents the least stable form of change (Winter, 1992). The behaviour log reported that John 'can only be good for so long'. Essentially John perplexed the teachers. They could not readily predict his behaviour.

From John's perspective he might have felt misunderstood. He might be seen as actively testing out, like the scientist Kelly postulated, the strangulating system within which he was being expected to function. Kelly considered this might be viewed as aggressiveness – the vigorous elaboration of one's perceptual field. Kelly aspired to be non-judgemental about such experimenting, seeing it as the individual's search for validity, although from an observer's point of view suffering the effects, John's spirited elaboration might well have felt like a disturbing experience.

Of further note, Table 11.1 illustrates that John was mostly located at the troublesome end of the constructs (B). He was construed, mostly, as contravening appropriate school behaviour, to the point whereby transgressions might have been predicted as the norm for John. He was expected to misbehave, and any such acts would serve to validate the teachers' view of John. From the behaviour log the teachers' reasons for John's behaviour can also be discerned. There is a tendency amongst teachers, caught up in the pressures and maelstrom of large classes, to construe children with dyslexia in terms of laziness and lack of intelligence. They attribute the problem to constitutional (within the child) factors. In John's case, explanations for his behaviour seemed much broader and damning. He was considered to be behaving in such ways 'out of mischief', because he was 'obviously showing off' in 'an awkward frame of mind' and because he was 'obviously trying to make me cross'. One statement even suggested that John punched another child 'for no reason at all!'. Kelly would have keeled over sideways. Behaviour, however perplexing to us, Kelly argued, must make sense to the child. Youngsters do not act in a vacuum. By considering this in regard to the sociality corollary it might be inferred that the relationship between John and his teachers was bereft of mutual understanding. Neither seemed able to construe the other's construction process, leaving their relationship lacking in rapport. As Bannister and Fransella (1986) suggested, if we cannot understand a child, that is we cannot construe his constructions, then we may indeed *do* things to him, but it cannot be presumed that we *relate* to him.

The behaviour log was also awash with predictions. Almost invariably, however, John's teachers appeared to have their predictions invalidated. They couldn't quite anticipate how their own attempts to relate to John would be received. Here are a few examples. Asking John to do his work led to point-blank refusal, stomping across the classroom, but also to occasions of sustained compliance. Telling John to do his work led to point-blank refusal but also disruptiveness. Confrontation made things worse but, just occasionally, John did alter his behaviour after a stern word. Finally, acknowledging his efforts positively 'obviously provided comfort' but then again praising his efforts sometimes led John to feel embarrassed and deface his own composition. Many of the teachers' predictions about John were therefore at sea. Kelly might have understood the teachers' predicament in terms of both anxiety (John became increasingly more difficult for them to understand in their pedagogic system of constructs) and hostility. Although recognizing that John was become increasingly difficult to anticipate and manage, the teachers persisted in their efforts (Kellyan hostility) to construe John in ways they were familiar with. Whilst John rattled around an increasingly untenable system of constructs his teachers found themselves, rather than modifying their way of viewing John, encapsulating him within a series of pre-emptive and negative characteristics.

The police had a much more direct way of discovering if John understood the difference between right and wrong. In true Kellyan spirit they asked him. Following the charge of murder it was fairly predictable that John might respond to questions concerning wrongness with 'Don't go on high stuff and don't chuck stuff off'. What was perhaps less predictable was John's silence when asked if there was anything else wrong. To further direct prompts about whether stealing and telling lies were wrong, John said 'Yeah'. The paucity of John's replies reflect not an intention to obstruct but a staggering indication of the improbability that he construed events in terms of their rightness and wrongness. Here was a matter of imposing legal construing on to a child's version of events.

In listening to John talk about his and other children's behaviour, his construing seemed free of terms such as right and wrong. Rather, John described behaviours in terms of being fun, good, bad and those 'you get done for'. He had mentioned to the police that it was fun being bad and not fun being good. Fun for John was equated with playing, messing about, being cheeky, fighting, getting into trouble and being bad. He had a reasonably encyclopaedic view of being bad, but apart from being boring, good was very poorly elaborated. Fransella (1972) has argued that individuals resist behaving in ways (being good for John) when their construing about that behaviour is only partially elaborated. In contrast behaving badly for John served to validate his version of himself. As Kelly intimated the way we construe determines the way we act.

In order that a comprehensive understanding of John's construing of behaviour might be gathered, he was asked to sort a set of behaviours under

Table 11.2 Categorization of behaviour

Behaviour	Fun	Wrong	Get done for
Being cheeky			✓
Calling names		✓	
Showing off		✓	
Telling lies		✓	
Fighting			✓
Messing about	✓		
Getting others into trouble		✓	
Talking in class		✓	
Stealing			✓
Bunking off school		✓	
Swearing		✓	
Damaging other people's things			✓
Hurting others			✓
Playing tricks on others		✓	
Breaking into places			✓
Throwing stones at others		✓	
Joyriding			✓
Housebreaking			✓
Vandalism			✓
Throwing stones off motorway bridges		✓	
Shoplifting		✓	

three categories: fun (in contrast to good), wrong (in contrast to right) and ones you get done for (a phrase John had used in reference to law-breaking behaviour). Table 11.2 presents the results of this exercise which John completed without difficulty. He employed the wrong – right construct with discrimination, allocating 11 behaviours to this category. The closest behaviours to the one John had been charged with – throwing stones and throwing stuff off motorway bridges – were placed in this category of wrong. They were, however, not seen to be activities like joyriding and vandalism, which John saw as breaking the law. It might therefore be contended that John was able to make a distinction between right and wrong, and indeed between wrong and seriously wrong (things you get done for) but that his actions of the roof that day (given he was unaware of the possible consequences) was not construed by John to be seriously wrong.

Intriguingly this inference bears a close correspondence to Gitta Sereny's (1995) conclusion about Mary Bell, the 10-year-old girl found guilty in 1968 for the murder of two young boys in Newcastle. Because there seemed no reason for her to commit such iniquitous deeds, she was construed as an evil, freakish and monstrous child. However, Sereny's careful study of the events concludes with the possibility that 'death', 'murder' and 'killing' had a different connotation for the girl than it had for other people. Basically for Mary, 'all of it had been a game – in the sense that an experiment can be a game for children – a grisly game, but a game nevertheless'.

11.3.2 Self-Image

John, it seemed, construed much of what he did in terms of being fun and bad. Kelly would contend that his actions were an expression of his construing and that they were essentially means of testing out his predictions and ultimately of how he saw himself. With this in mind, John was invited to complete two scales which would hopefully tap his sense of self – a modified self-image profile (Butler, 2001) and the Harter (1985) self-perception profile for children (SPPC). The attraction of employing both scales is that different aspects of self can be discerned. Figure 11.1 illustrates John's completed SIP and Table 11.3 presents a summary of the SPPC.

John had an extremely positive view of himself as a sportsperson. He was also very content with his appearance, apart from not liking curls in his hair.

	not at all				very much		
	0	1	2	3	4	5	6
kind						▓	
make friends easily			▓				
well-liked	▓						
good fun							▓
lots of energy							▓
helpful							▓
honest					▓		
good at sport							▓
dress smartly							▓
like the way I look	▓						
feel different from others		▓					
lazy	▓						
lonely							▓
stubborn	▓						
moody			▓				
always in trouble	▓						
shy	▓						
cheeky	▓						
argue a lot	▓						
bad tempered		▓					
get bored easily		▓					
good at school work	▓						

Figure 11.1 John's self-image profile. The self-image profile is published by Butler (2001) and reproduced with permission from Harcourt Assessment.

Table 11.3 Results of the Harter self-perception profile for John

Schoolwork	Appearance
Worry about whether I can do it	Happy with how I look
Slow at schoolwork	Happy with my height and weight
Forget what I learn	Like my body the way it is
Don't do well at classwork	Like the way I look
Trouble figuring answers	Wished I looked different[a]
Just as smart as others[b]	Good looking
Total 11	Total 20
Social	Behaviour
Hard to make friends	Don't like the way I behave
Not many friends	Usually do the right thing
Like to have more friends	Act in ways I know I'm supposed to
Do things by myself	Get in trouble for things I do
Wished more people liked me	Do things I know I shouldn't
Popular	Find it hard to behave
Total 11	Total 14
Sport	General self-esteem
Do well at all sports	Unhappy with myself[a]
Good at sport	Don't like the way I'm leading my life
Could do any sport	Happy with myself
Better than others at sport	Like how I am
Like to play rather than watch	Happy with the way I am
Good at new games	Way I do things is fine
Total 23	Total 19

[a] John expressed a dislike for the curls in his hair.
[b] Smart for John meant being dressed smartly, not intelligent, as Harter intended it to mean.

John also showed satisfaction in his kindness, helpfulness, honesty and what Harter described as general self-worth. The realms of self-construing where John expressed dissatisfaction included his behaviour, schoolwork and social relationships. John's view of self appeared both discriminating and sophisticated. He acknowledged his struggle to master schoolwork, recognized a concern about his behaviour and doing things he knew he shouldn't and finally he demonstrated a profound unease about his ability to get along with others.

11.3.3   Social Relationships

Often a consequence of dyslexia is alienation from others. John's view of himself contains a theme about loneliness and the wish for more friends. Poignantly the behaviour log at school makes many references to John's rejection by his peer group. Table 11.4 provides some examples of how the

Table 11.4 Some comments from the behaviour log which illustrate John's reported effect on classmates (names changed to preserve confidentiality)

Makes Billy show off
Sabotaged Darren's drawing
Class became noisy, having been excited by John
Called several people's mums a fat bitch, silly cow, fat slag
Tried to push others off grassy mound
Enticed others but no one joined in
Other children asked me to send John to another class
Telling tales – the whole of the class atmosphere changed
Calls others rude names
Mocked others, upsetting them
Others disturbed by John's language and behaviour
Children complained about John
Prevents others from working
No child is impressed by John's antics
Other children swore – John's behaviour is apparently affecting one or two others
Tried to incite others
Class became high due to John's behaviour

teachers described John's behaviour in relation to classmates and how in turn they reacted to John. This portrayal points an unwavering finger at John as the source of trouble. It captures the teachers' feeling of John being the creator of other children's discomfort and their ultimate rejection of him.

John's actions might be seen as validating the view he has of himself – they confirm his academic inadequacy, behavioural nonconformity and social alienation. However, failure to play 'a social role' with others at school seems to have encouraged John to gravitate towards others outside school who survived on what might be called the fringes of socially acceptable behaviour. Being a 'misfit' within one social domain (school) may have fostered the search for relationships where he could play a social role; where he could be understood by others; where his 'socially inappropriate behaviour' could not only be validated but elaborated. In such ways his incompetence could be transformed into an asset. So outside school John sought friendships with other boys who were similarly in trouble. Enmeshed within a group of like-minded individuals John could conduct behavioural experiments – acting in antisocial ways – with a fair degree of anticipation that his efforts would be applauded and gain social acceptance.

In an attempt to understand how John perceived himself in relation to the other two boys who were on the roof with him, he was asked to undertake a ranking exercise. The names of the three boys involved – John, Alan and Carl – were written on separate cards and John was asked to place them in

Table 11.5 John's ranking of the three boys against social activities

	Rank		
Social activity	1	2	3
Who's best at football?	Alan		
Who gets into most trouble?	Alan	Carl	John
Who's good at schoolwork?			
Who gets teased most?	John	Carl	Alan
Who gets his own way?	Alan		
Who messes about at school?	Carl	Alan	John
Who bullies others?	Alan		
Who worries most?	Carl		
Who gets upset?	Carl		
Who dares others to do things?	Alan		
Who gets into fights?	Alan		
Who is most bad-tempered?	Alan		
Who gets bored?	Carl	John	
Who gets others into trouble?	Alan		

rank order against a set of activities. The results of this stab at understanding John's social role are illustrated in Table 11.5.

Fascinatingly, John declined to place any of the three boys alongside 'good at schoolwork'. A perceived commonality was their abject failure to meet schools' expectations. Carl, the youngest of the three, was seen as the one most likely to become emotionally upset. Alan on the other hand was perceived by John to be the leader of the group (getting his own way) and the one to assert his power and domination over the other two through bullying, fighting and getting others into trouble. John ranked himself first on only one aspect, perceiving himself to be the victim of teasing. He went on to describe how Alan would bully, punch and steal things off him in order to make him do as Alan wanted. John claimed Alan was the instigator that morning, asserting that 'When we were playing that day, Alan said he were going to batter me if I didn't go up on the roof with him'. John claimed it was Alan's idea to 'play on the roof, throw stuff off, mess about and get into trouble'. John's acceptance within the group appeared therefore to be largely dependent on assuaging and currying favour with Alan. Even amongst kindred spirits his continued approval was threatened. John was possibly faced with the need to engage in ever more extreme acts in order to maintain 'credit', validate the antisocial aspect of his self-construing and hold on to what he felt was a somewhat tenuous but fundamentally important relationship. Taken in this context, the act of tipping the cement block from the roof may have made perfect sense to

John. It was an extension of previous acts which served to further define the notion of himself as a nonconformist troublemaker coupled with a prediction that such behaviour would foster a greater acceptance by other like-minded individuals, notably Alan.

The ironic tragedy in terms of social validation happened a few hours after the incident when, in police custody, John learnt that both his compatriots, as it were to save their own necks, turned against him. They claimed to have told John not to push the boulder from the roof. Ultimate rejection.

What appears legally to be a reasonably straightforward task of determining if John, at the time, knew that what he was doing was seriously wrong, turns out psychologically to be a somewhat thorny issue. There would seem to be little doubt that John knew he was engaged in behaviour that would probably get him into trouble. Indeed his very self-identity was built on the idea that he was a troublemaker and his acts and misdemeanours successfully served to validate this notion. If we act in ways governed by our self-construing, then it might be argued that John had little choice but to act in such troublesome ways. Interestingly a Kellyan position would predict that having committed the act, John would not feel necessarily guilty because he was merely acting in a way he expected of himself. Guilt, according to personal construct theory, occurs when we discover ourselves acting in ways we would not have predicted of ourselves. The problem of 'fitting' a legal definition of wrongness onto John's actions is particularly illuminating, given that John 'naturally' construed events in terms of fun and getting into trouble versus being good, compared to the legal construct of wrong versus right. If John did not construe events in the manner proposed by the legal system, how would he be expected to know about wrongness? Getting into trouble, yes – indeed he was a connoisseur of this – but knowing it was wrong, well, that's a different ball game.

To further compound the problem is the notion of acting in a way that might be described as seriously wrong. The prosecution has to demonstrate this in order to counter the presumption of *doli incapax*. The incompatibility of construing – John's construction of fun/getting into trouble versus the legal definition of wrong – still infiltrates and complicates the reasoning at this level. However, there are some additional legal constructs which might be held up to compare how John's act measures against them. These include the idea of intent versus accident; pre-planned versus an exception; and whether John considered the implications of his actions versus a consideration of only the moment in time. The legal definition focuses on an appreciation of what harm the behaviour might do to a victim, whereas it would seem John's focus and actions were directed more towards himself (seeking validation of his self-image) and towards his compatriots (seeking to secure social allegiance with Alan).

Further 'expert witnesses' were asked for by the prosecution and defence. Two saw John and another two commented on the reports. All concurred essentially with these initial findings. Disappointingly none of the reports was heard in court because of a pretrial agreement between prosecution and defence. During the trial John appeared disinterested in the proceedings, frequently occupying himself in drawing pictures. After a trial lasting four days, the jury considered the evidence for 55 minutes and then delivered its verdict of guilty.

11.4   POSTSCRIPT

Some might find themselves feeling uneasy about the foregoing account, perhaps a hint of the proverbial do-gooder's inclination to blame anybody but the little devil who threw the brick in the first place. Taking the argument further we might consider that the analysis excuses, rather than explains, some fundamentally inexcusable behaviour. What happens to the sense of personal responsibility which is central to the moral education we aim to offer young people when even the perpetrators of crimes are perceived as victims?

'It's not my fault – look at my circumstances', may not be a plea to which many might be immediately sympathetic. Indeed if judgements in cases such as John's boil down to 'Whose side are you on?', we probably have little hesitation in empathizing with the elderly victim and her family. As an afterthought we might even find ourselves harbouring suspicions that these psychologists might end up doing more harm than good when they muddy the judicial waters with their fancy jargon and faddish theories of child development! All these questions are worthy of further examination.

11.5   CHILDREN'S CULPABILITY

In order to be blameworthy in the eyes of the law, a young person has to be aware that their wrongdoing is wrong. Age is reckoned to be a rough indicator of whether a child is capable of making this sort of moral judgement in much the same way that the competence of a juvenile witness in court will be gauged in part by how old they are. However, there will be appreciable variation within as well as between age bands, so the question of whether any particular youngster knowingly misbehaved needs to be individually assessed, especially when that person is considered to be on the chronological cusp of moral awareness, at between 10 and 14 years of age.

The social context in which a crime has been committed becomes evident when more than one person is implicated in the act. If, for example, a gang of teenagers engages in a delinquent activity such as vandalizing a bus shelter, the issue of personal culpability might depend on the perceived seniority of an individual within the group. Were they older 'ringleaders' or more junior followers who had 'fallen in with a bad crowd'? Where an adult is adjudged to have played a destructive role in fostering juvenile crime it is the adult rather than the child whom we hold responsible. We despise Fagin and sympathize with Oliver.

Indeed children's legislation is designed primarily to protect children from adults rather than the other way round. For example the key principle of the Children Act 1989 that decisions be taken in the best interest of the child applies equally whether the young person has committed an assault or been himself the victim of one. In fact young people who commit offences of the person against others have often been physically maltreated themselves.

Where does this brief consideration of social and developmental aspects of juvenile crime leave us in our understanding of the individual case? Take another example:

> Ben is a 10-year-old boy recently admitted to a residential child psychiatric hospital because of concerns that his highly sexualized behaviour indicates that he has been abused within his family home. While living in the unit he makes suggestive remarks to female staff and fellow residents. This inappropriate behaviour rapidly escalates, culminating in two sexual advances on a particularly vulnerable girl patient. At a rapidly convened case conference the young man is viewed by some parties as being in need of treatment (as he is displaying the very symptoms which led to his admission to hospital in the first place) while others see him as needing to be controlled (as he has become a significant danger to others). The mood of the meeting swings dramatically, sometimes seeing him as a patient, sometimes as a perpetrator, and fails to come to any clear conclusions on his future management.

Is there a correct way to make sense of this episode? Personal construct theory argues that the same event is open to a myriad of more or less useful interpretations. The meaning of an act is not self-evident but comes from our attempts to understand. So we can choose to attribute blame to individual failings and locate the problem within the individual as when we invoke the idea of a person being inherently 'evil'. We can place greater importance on situational factors and recognize mitigating circumstances if we so wish. We may strive to get a grasp of the actor's motives in committing an offence. In essence we evolve our own personal theories to try to make sense of the puzzling activities of others. The classic courtroom confrontation offers but two stories to account for a particular episode, those told by the prosecution and the defence counsel respectively, but there are many other ways in which the tale can be told. However, it appears that the discomfort which deeds such as the sexual abuse and murder of children evoke in us makes it difficult to engage in circumspect consideration of alternative explanations. We are tempted to take up a position pre-emptively as if ours were the only view that any reasonable person could adopt. In so doing we risk forgetting that there are always other ways of construing, and fail to realize that our capacity to envisage alternatives is limited by the time we live in, the family we came from, and the very people we are.

11.6 PSYCHOLOGICAL THEORY IN THE COURTROOM

Legal decision-taking is a formidably challenging exercise. Judgements must be made which will have a major impact on the future lives of all concerned. All voices must be heard with equal respect. Furthermore, everything must be completed as quickly as possible. In essence, the pressure is on to sum up individuals and their circumstances with maximum efficiency. What psychological models are likely to be best suited to this task?

Legal judgements invariably include elements of retrospective analysis and prospective prediction. Evidence is heard and its significance weighed. The question of guilt likely needs to be addressed. Those passing sentence or making recommendations about future management try to anticipate the probable outcomes of various courses of action open to them. This time-perspective colours the ways we understand other people's actions. Looking back, human behaviour appears convincingly predictable. The apparently smooth and inevitable life-courses depicted in biographies of the great and good imply they were always destined for glory. The glaring oversights of some hapless social worker who has gravely failed to protect a child at risk of serious injury seem unforgivable when it is 'perfectly obvious' they would be harmed. But 20/20 hindsight teases us with an illusory clarity. At 2.45 p.m. the perceptive punter will be able to explain the outcome of the 2.30 race with expert confidence. He will note the impact of the going, the benefits of a draw close to the rails and of course the classic breeding of the winner on the dam's side. However, when applying these self-same canons of wisdom to name the horse that will win the 3.00 race, our expert's breezy certainty diminishes somewhat, and he begins to hedge his proverbial bets. A world that can look so reassuringly predictable in retrospect has the unnerving habit of appearing confusingly erratic when we peer in the opposite direction (Green, 1993).

A second powerful influence of perspective on the way we make sense of behaviour depends, as alluded to earlier, on our position as participant in, or observer of, the action under analysis. It is a well-established principle of social psychology that folk tend to adopt markedly different schemes when explaining their own actions compared to the system they apply to make sense of the behaviour of others. We have a penchant for putting our own failings down to passing situational factors such as an 'off-day' or adverse circumstances. However, when we offer an opinion on the likely causes of somebody else's misdemeanours we seem more inclined to evoke enduring constitutional explanations for their fallibility – they are 'a bad lot' or 'not really up to it' and so on.

An example from the classroom might be a young lad with reading problems who persuades himself that his difficulties stem from the fact that the book his teacher has provided is too boring for anyone to concentrate on for more than two minutes. His teacher's analysis of events may tend to emphasize the pupil's limited intellectual ability in other aspects of his schoolwork and a pervasive negative attitude to learning than can come across as a truculent laziness. Evidently when the child identifies circumstances, rather than some generalized personality characteristic, as the cause of his reading problem he can approach a new book with his self-esteem reasonably intact and with some hopes of a more successful outcome next time around.

Indeed the way we attribute blame when things go wrong in our lives is a key determinant of our ability to maintain morale in times of adversity. It is less immediately obvious why observers should prefer to invoke trait theories when explaining the misconduct of others. Maybe we need a robust classification system to help us to sort out the wheat from the chaff among our fellow citizens – particularly those we don't know too well. Perhaps we have a faith that the world is an inherently just place where bad people get their just deserts. Sometimes this psychological shorthand works well and enables us to see enduring patterns in another person's conduct of which they are unaware. On other occasions our need to sum up people simply and quickly drifts into the sort of harmful stereotyping on which racial prejudice thrives.

In summary therefore, as observers analysing retrospectively the misdeeds of young people in trouble with the law, our 'common-sense psychology' will incline us towards explanations that emphasize the lasting personality characteristics of the individual perpetrator. We consider criminal tendencies to be in his nature in some sense and see a constitutional basis for his antisocial conduct. We would also be encouraged to adopt this viewpoint by the prevailing political ideology in both the USA and the UK in official attitudes to juvenile crime.

Do we need professional psychologists to put us right? The British judiciary doesn't think so!

11.7 TURNER RULE

The Turner Rule is a principle by which a court can determine the admissibility of psychological evidence. It runs as follows:

> If on the proven facts a judge or jury can form their own conclusions without help, then the opinion of an expert is unnecessary. In such a case if it is dressed up in scientific jargon it may make judgement more difficult. The fact than an expert witness has impressive qualifications does not by that fact alone make his opinion on matters of human nature and behaviour within the limits

of normality any more helpful than that of the jurors themselves: but there is a danger that they may think it does. (Quoted in Mackay and Coleman, 1991)

So while a judge might be prepared to invite a psychiatrist to offer a professional opinion on the state of mind of someone acting violently under the influence of paranoid delusions, he may not take kindly to psychologists pronouncing on a matter as commonplace as misbehaving youngsters throwing stones at their elderly neighbours.

It is therefore necessary to make a convincing argument that the personal construct approach to understanding the actions of young men like John adds something useful to the untutored psychology that might otherwise be employed in deciding his fate. The personal construct analysis described lays great store on getting the 'inside story' on events. It pays attention not just to the circumstances under which a crime was committed but more importantly examines the individual's construction of that situation – how he saw it at the time. It explores in depth the miscreant's view of himself and his behaviour. Furthermore personal construct psychology frames its proposals in the form of hypotheses on how things might be understood rather than drawing dogmatic conclusions that purport to say how things actually are. Three useful possibilities emerge from adopting this attitude to the problem of deciding what to do about John:

Firstly, although our estimates about the constancy of our own and others' behaviour across time and circumstances are often misguided, we do not live in an entirely chaotic social world that is quite beyond our comprehension. The better we know people the more accurately we can predict their behaviour. That tautological assertion begs the question of what it means to know another person well. When we know not just where a person works and whom they work with but also know what they think about their job and the company they keep, we can begin to anticipate accurately their performance in post. If we can add to this understanding an awareness of their sense of self-confidence in their role, how they see their strengths and weaknesses and whether work matters much in their scheme of things, we are likely to make even more informed guesses. So an appreciation of the personal construct system of an individual provides us with a great deal of evidence, which will be pertinent to our efforts at predicting their future behaviour.

Secondly, Kelly proposed in his 'sociality corollary' that our ability to play a social role with another person depends crucially on our ability to see the world through their eyes or 'construe their construction processes' in his phrasing. For those responsible for promoting the healthy development of children – parents, teachers, social workers – this seems an eminently desirable principle. The better we understand what makes a particular child tick, the more effectively we can help them. But it also follows that if our primary concern is to control a young person's behaviour to reprimand or punish them, this task will also be more successfully achieved if the parties involved appreciate each other's perspectives. If, on the contrary, adult attempts to sort out troublesome children seem to them to be ill-informed and incomprehensible, our good intentions may well be frustrated. Punishment that makes no sense to a recipient who does not feel their voice has been heard cannot but be experienced as persecutory.

Finally, everyone agrees that something must be done to deter delinquents. Quite what must be done is, however, far from certain. While advocates of simplistic penal policies may play to appreciative galleries in the public bar or at the party conference, in practice effective remedies to counter juvenile crime are hard to find. Depressingly high reconviction rates seem to follow all forms of custodial sentence for juvenile offenders, and psychological treatments for young people exhibiting antisocial behaviour have no track record of proven effectiveness. We have no option but to keep thinking creatively about ways to judge each individual case on its merits, and personal construct theory at least offers us a framework within which to consider our alternatives.

CHAPTER 12

EXPLORING ILLNESS

Ill-conceived ideas

Children, like the rest of us, don't like feeling unwell. Their suffering is often amplified by their inexperience of illness. They don't have any articulated theories about the causes of their discomfort, and they cannot predict the future course of, for example, a common cold because they have been through that 'sort of thing' before. They might be utterly perplexed when their apparently caring parents pour vile-tasting liquids down their throats and announce that this odd-coloured 'medicine' is doing them good. Sometimes previously trusted doctors and nurses go even further and stick needles into them – to make them feel better! In short, from the child's perspective, illness is both painful and incomprehensible (Wilkinson, 1988).

It's not that children make no attempt to understand their sickness or the ill health of others. Rather they evolve their own idiosyncratic theories to make sense of their suffering instead of adopting the official grown-up medical explanations of illness. Paediatric psychologists have sought to map the stages through which the young person's thinking about ill health typically passes *en route* from utterly uncomprehending infant to relatively sophisticated adult (Bibace and Walsh, 1980). Characteristically preschool children are limited to thinking about their world in pretty concrete terms and have only a few primitive ideas about cause and effect relationships.

When a youngster is ill they might invoke a magical explanation for their misfortune. A young man, described in an American journal article, who overhearing his doctors describing his condition as 'oedema' concluded he must have 'a demon in his belly' (Perrin and Gerrity, 1981). Another basic line of reasoning might go along the lines that 'If I'm hurting this bad I must have done something really naughty to deserve it'. However, not only children choose to construe ill health as punishment for misdeeds. The 'gay plague' analysis of AIDS shares the same fundamental assumption that this is a just world we live in and pains are not generally inflicted without good reason.

12.1   GIVING APPROPRIATE EXPLANATIONS

The implications of this developmental stage approach to children's understanding of illness for the clinical management of young children's health care is that parents and medical staff are advised to frame their explanations of treatment in age-appropriate terms so that youngsters can assimilate ideas into their prevailing scheme of things. Such advice may seem banal, as anyone with a dash of common sense would pitch their conversation with a five-year-old on a different, less complex level than that they would employ with a 10-year-old.

However the Piagetian approach, as it is called, holds more subtle possibilities for effective communication with such children. When preparing a six year-old for hospital admission it is advisable to describe the process in very concrete terms – where the bed will be, what colour the nurses' uniforms are, who will stay in hospital with the child and so forth. Such information, pitched at the young person's level of understanding, can help the child immediately grasp a vision of what is to happen and be informed in their anticipations of an otherwise mysterious and frightening prospect.

By giving a child information in a form they can readily use, adults assist the young person's theory-building. If, on the other hand, a well-meaning parent offers a more abstract explanation of how the medical treatment will alleviate the child's suffering (e.g. a tonsillectomy) the odds are that the conversation will go 'over the child's head' and remain unprocessed and hence sadly unhelpful in preparing for the forthcoming experience.

The Piagetian approach also reminds adults that children's construing of illness is different from their own. In discussing a child's sickness with him or her, there is a need to know about children as well as illnesses.

A final teasing implication of this developmental stage approach is the description of a narrow band of knowing what lies beyond the child's existing level of understanding but before the point at which he or she is destined to be lost by the sophistication of an overly complex argument – outside the youngster's grasp but within his reach, to coin the poet's metaphor. If adults can construe the thinking of the young person they are counselling well enough to pitch their conversation in this transitional zone, they may enable the child to accommodate their thinking to new information in a way that moves them a step or two further up the developmental ladder (Green, 1982).

12.2   COPING WITH ILLNESS

Piaget's model is primarily a cognitive one. He argues that the developing child's ability to make sense of the world is fundamentally constrained by their level of brain maturation. There are in-built intellectual limits on their capacity to understand. However, those working with sick children rapidly note differences in the attitudes as well as the abilities of their young charges. One way of categorizing the attitude a person adopts to their illness is to construe them as exhibiting a characteristic 'coping style'. The assumption is made that we all, from an early age, develop a preferred way of getting by when confronted with life's problems. Whatever the difficulty, it can be argued that an individual will adopt an almost automatic way of coping such that their attitude might be considered more a personality trait than a chosen strategy suited to particular circumstances.

Although psychologists have produced a number of systems for classifying coping styles, the limited literature examining sick children's construal of their illnesses eventually boils down to a straightforward continuum between those who actively seek out information about their disease on the one hand and those who elect to 'switch off' and deliberately ignore their condition on the other (Kupst, 1994).

This tendency to 'attend' or 'deny' puts quite contrary demands on carers. Do parents research books or consult the Internet to enable their child to get better informed about an illness, or do they continue to live family life 'as normal' with no acknowledgement of their child's ill health? By and large it appears young people who adopt an active coping style manage hospital admissions for surgery better than those who 'cross that bridge when they come to it'. They tend to experience less pre-admission anxiety, are more cooperative within hospital and report less post-operative pain (Schultheis, Peterson and Selby 1987).

The following case vignette illustrates the disadvantages of adopting an 'I don't want to think about it' approach to a painful medical procedure:

> Cheryl is a nine-year-old girl recently diagnosed as suffering from leukaemia. She doesn't discuss her condition or its treatment at all within the family and is

applauded for this 'stiff upper-lip' approach by her father who uses the same coping style himself. Cheryl gives every sign of carrying on regardless, her morale remaining high as she deals with most aspects of her treatment regime with robust good humour. However, a central element in her therapy involves regular infusion of drugs through a 'portacath' inserted just below her neck. Cheryl never mentions her feelings about this procedure but becomes very agitated and uncooperative at home when awaiting the ambulance that takes her to hospital on the 'portacath' day. When her turn for treatment comes she resists efforts to help her keep control of the process (e.g. to say when the needle goes in) and kicks out and swears at her mum and the nursing staff who subsequently find themselves having to manhandle Cheryl to ensure she receives the treatment she needs to combat a life-threatening disease.

No one concerned gets any satisfaction from this sequence of events. Cheryl feels frightened and humiliated. Nursing staff are very uncomfortable at physically imposing treatment on an unwilling young patient. Cheryl's mother dreads these 'portacath' days on which she is subjected to abuse and assault from her daughter, but also helps hold her down while she screams in pain. However Cheryl point-blank refuses to discuss other ways of preparing for, or coping with, this evidently troubling component of her care.

At first sight it seems evident that Cheryl's dominant coping style of denial is equipping her poorly for managing a key aspect of her treatment. However, would it be desirable to try and turn her into an active coper, even if it were achievable? Would there be more therapeutic mileage in working with her preferred way of getting by when under stress (e.g. by distracting her in the clinic room) than challenging the only way she knows how to cope just when her very life is under threat?

A further uncertainty is added by the finding that patterns of coping might be determined by the situation as well as the person. Young cancer sufferers, for example, report a higher level of denial on 'coping style' questionnaires than members of matched control groups with other health disorders. Furthermore 'switching off' as a way of dealing with the overwhelming anxieties of discovering you have cancer is a more common way of coping directly after initial diagnosis than at the later stages of treatment. Maybe, therefore, there is something natural and adaptive in Cheryl's attitude to her disease and its treatment.

The psychology of children with illness is not a psychology of abnormal children but of normal children reacting to a quite abnormal situation (Eiser 1990). It therefore makes sense to conduct research into the experiences of sick children who share the same diagnostic label and symptomatology and must cope with common treatment regimes (e.g. children with diabetes who need to control their diet and receive daily injections of insulin).

12.3   UNIQUE EXPERIENCE OF ILLNESS

All these approaches to children's understanding of illness make sense. Without doubt it is important to consider the age and intellectual competence of the individual, their preferred coping style and the particular characteristics of their disease and its treatment. However, what is missing from these models is a way of appreciating the unique way in which each young person constructs their experience.

In Kelly's view there are external realities with which we have to contend in which ill health can surely by numbered. However, individuals do not all wrestle directly with the same objective challenges. They interpret their worlds. Thus some people's colds always seem worse than others'! Hence sharing a diagnosis with another person gives no guarantee that their experience of illness will be identical. Diagnostic labels probably mean a lot more in the doctor's construct system than in their patient's – or certainly mean something different to the two parties. Therefore it might be apposite to view sick children as 'unique protagonists each on their own unique journey', to use Phil Salmon's (1985) persuasive phrase.

Inevitably individual children's ways of understanding their predicament will be limited, perhaps by factors associated with their biological maturity, but also by the small but expanding repertoire of constructs that they have available to try to make sense of their lives. They will seek to make sense of illness in the same way they seek to make sense of other events they confront. They cannot consult a medical textbook to find out what's going on when they get ill. They have to work it out for themselves in their own idiosyncratic way.

Sometimes these 'childish' constructions are a source of amusement for adults and are portrayed as visible failures to understand. Personal construct psychology asserts that if only we could see things through the eyes of the individual child, their versions of what it means to be unwell would make perfect coherent sense. However, that is a very big 'if only'.

12.4   UNDERSTANDING THE CHILD'S VERSION

Charlie's story gives an idea of how apparently 'senseless' actions of a sick adolescent can become comprehensible once we get access to the 'inside story'.

Charlie was a 13-year-old boy who had suffered since his birth from a congenital urinary problem. This meant that he was prone to infections which had a cumulatively deleterious effect on his health. Despite being old enough and apparently wise enough to appreciate the dangers he faced if he picked up infections, Charlie persistently took avoidable risks and ignored his parents' sound advice about wearing suitable clothing when going out in the cold and wet. He seemed to court illness by waiting for his school bus dressed in shirtsleeves during a bleak Yorkshire winter. Charlie's exasperated parents couldn't decide whether he was stubborn or stupid.

Charlie didn't much enjoy his psychological consultations but he was able to produce a number of constructs to describe himself (such as 'likes football', 'gets called lazy' and so on). In an effort to discover which of these ideas mattered most to him Charlie completed a resistance-to-change grid (Hinkle, 1965). Firstly, all of his constructs were laid out on a sheet of paper with a preferred and unpreferred pole clearly marked (e.g. 'likes football' versus 'boring creep'). Then every construct was paired with every other construct and Charlie asked to answer the following unusual question:

- If you had to move from your present position on one of these two scales towards the end you like least, on which would you choose to stay put?

This exercise results in a league table of constructs from those on which the individual is relatively happy to move in their less prepared direction up to those on which they are most resistant to change. Hinkle argued that we resist change on our most 'superordinate' constructs – those that matter most to us as individuals. Top of Charlie's league table came a construct concerning his health ('feeling well' versus 'getting sick') and one about feeling normal ('being just like everyone else versus 'being different'). However it was the latter construct that was the more resistant to change. In other words, if faced with a choice of being socially or physically handicapped, Charlie would prefer sickness to the social stigma of standing out from the crowd. Hence if the other school hard-men eschewed warm winter clothing, so did he.

12.5   SHARING AN UNDERSTANDING OF CONSTRUING

What are the therapeutic explanations of taking seriously Kelly's celebration of the uniqueness of individual experience for those charged with the care of sick youngsters? Maybe the clearest message is that as much attention should be paid to helping the doctor understand the child as is paid to trying to enable the child to understand the doctor. It is appropriate to think hard about the explanations given to young people about the medical treatment they receive. It is important that they find procedures and interventions predictable and to feel some sense of control over events. Where possible children should be helped to appreciate the motives of those who cause them discomfort.

As children grow older, clinicians should also aspire to give them choices so they can give informed consent and enter a genuine collaboration with their carers. It is important to achieve clarity in the explanations given to children and to seek to be as transparent as possible in conveying our understanding of their illness and its treatment. In so doing the application of Kelly's sociality corollary is halfway towards being achieved. At the risk of repetition this corollary states that *'To the extent that one person construes the construction process of another, they may play a role in a social process involving the other person'*.

Health care is unarguably a social process. Personal construct analysis highlights a recognition that doctor–patient communication is a two-way traffic system. There is good sense in training health personnel to improve their broadcasting skills and educating patients, of whatever age, to be attentive receivers of important medical messages. But how should the views of children be conveyed in the other direction? Health professionals in training are required to parade their constructs about illness in public examination. They are tutored in how best to get their ideas across to patients. In contrast, sick children have no comparable preparation for playing their part in a medical consultation. Few can, or will, articulate their views on their condition with any confidence, and so probably 'know' much more than they can easily tell. Most will have relied on a parent to represent their case to a doctor (a bit like a lawyer in the courtroom) and hence held only the most perfunctory of conversations directly with healthcare staff. It is therefore going to take a deal of time and invention if sick children are to be encouraged to relate their own stories of illness.

However, it is likely to prove a worthwhile effort because the doctor who ignores their patient's perspective jeopardizes the effectiveness of treatment just as securely as the patient who ignores their doctor's advice. For example research with children who wet their beds (Butler, Redfern and Forsythe, 1990; Butler, Redfern and Holland, 1994) has indicated that an understanding of the meaning enuresis has for the particular child will both improve the accuracy of predictions of their probable response to treatment, and open up therapeutic avenues to enable the individual to consider some of the social and psychological implications of becoming dry.

12.6   NEGOTIATING PERSPECTIVES

The central tenet of personal construct theory is that there is no single veridical way of making sense of any event (including the phenomenon of ill health). There are a myriad of possible different theories and interpretations, all of which may be judged more or less useful depending on the job to be done. The physician's job of 'treating illness' is different from the young patient's job of 'growing up with illness'. The manual needed to control symptoms differs from the map required to get on with life. Both tasks are crucial. Both construct systems need to be fitting to their purpose. So recognition and negotiation of a necessary difference in perspective is required for the business of effective health care to be completed.

The same principles apply within families. Parents, siblings and sufferer have different jobs to do and need to evolve construct systems fitting to their respective responsibilities (Sloper and White, 1996). You do not have to share another person's view of the world to get on with them, Kelly argues, but how successfully you can cooperate on any joint enterprise does depend on how well you can read and respect each other's scripts.

12.7   COMMONALITY OF CONSTRUING

Acknowledging the uniqueness of individual experience does not deny the usefulness of classifying sick children according to their similarities so that the health resources they need can be most effectively organized. Kelly argued that this necessary grouping might as well be achieved by putting together individuals who share a common view of the world, as by aggregating individuals that are commonly viewed by the world.

Rather than categorize sick youngsters together according to diagnosis – children with asthma, suffers from cystic fibrosis, those with enuresis and so forth – an alternative might be to bring together or consider groups of young patients with a particular coping style, such as those who seek to deny the implications of their illness, or those who become sensitive and vigilant about symptoms (e.g. Fritz and Overholser, 1989). When young people who have taken part in group psychotherapy are asked what profited them most from their sessions together, a frequent reply is the sense that they are not alone in their thoughts and feelings – others hold similar views. So self-help groups or peer-tutoring arrangements (where an older child helps a younger partner learn to better understand his or her condition) take advantage not just of the similar circumstances with which a cluster of children are confronted but also some of the shared attitudes they are likely to adopt towards their predicament (Shute and Paton, 1990). For example, a pair of adolescents with diabetes must both have to inject themselves with insulin on a regular daily basis, but might also both find themselves feeling highly resentful about the inflexibility of this regime and how it precludes them from 'hanging loose' like other teenagers.

12.8   ILL HEALTH AND IDENTITY

The development of an individual's sense of their unique identity is widely construed as the major psychological task of adolescence (Erikson, 1968). To achieve this goal successfully it has been suggested that the young person must negotiate an increasingly autonomous relationship from their parents, begin to define themselves as an adult through some productive work effort, and construe themselves as sexually mature in a physical and social sense. Ill health may complicate all these aspirations.

If the developmental drives of adolescence usually have a centrifugal impact on the family system, illness is likely to exert a quite contrary pull on family members to stick together (Rolland, 1987). The young person's physical condition may compel them to rely on their parents in a way that under other circumstances might not be considered age-appropriate (in getting help with bathing, for example). Parents' anxieties (that for example a teenager with diabetes may lose consciousness) may make 'letting go' of an adolescent son or daughter problematic for fear that this offspring will come to avoidable harm if left unsupervised.

Ill health can confuse the developing individual's sense of their own sexuality. Sometimes a disease or its treatment will have a direct impact on growth and the timing of puberty (e.g. some cancer treatments). More commonly a young person who has experienced illness or injury has concerns about their physical attractiveness and may be very self-conscious about, for instance, their weight, or physique. Frequently ill health places constraints on the opportunities young people have to mix with peers and engage in group activities such as sports or other leisure pursuits, and so the individual feels less socially prepared for the challenge of courtship. They don't feel ready in the sense that both their own sexuality and that of potential partners remains a mystery. It is, of course, arguable that uncertainty and discovery are intrinsic characteristics of all new relationships. That promise of excitement is why people choose to pursue fresh liaisons in the first place. However, personal construct theory reminds us that while we may sometimes opt for the adventurous alternative through which our views of ourselves and others can be elaborated, we can also choose to stick with what we know and find predictable. Ill health does not often bring out the bold explorer in any of us, whatever our ages.

Illness can have major vocational implications. Schooling may well be disrupted, so reducing the person's prospects of academic success. This can have a direct effect on grades achieved in public examinations and hence restrict access to further training opportunities (Madan-Swain and Brown, 1991). More subtly, scholastic underachievement will influence the individual's emergent sense of competence and self-efficacy. Physical ill health may also block a number of potential career routes. Poor eyesight, asthmatic reactions to dusty conditions, limited mobility and so on will all close off certain occupational possibilities. For young people with a life-threatening disease such as cystic fibrosis whose families dare not adopt a long-term perspective on adult life-plans, the issue of what job the child may want to do when they grow up just does not arise. For all these reasons the stepping stone to adulthood that the first wage packet represents may prove beyond the easy reach of young people whose development has been complicated by significant experience of illness.

Furthermore recent socio-economic changes in the USA and UK (such as a much higher proportion of young people entering higher education and escalating house prices) have compelled many young adults to remain reliant on their parents throughout their twenties (Settersten, Furstenberg and

Rumbaut, 2005). This developmental phase has been dubbed 'emerging adulthood' and can represent a particular challenge for groups of young people, such as those who have been brought up in care for example, who lack the support structures on which their peers can draw when negotiating this uncertain transition to fully functioning adulthood. While sufferers from chronic childhood illness often have very well-established family and professional support networks their educational achievements have frequently been compromised by their condition. It is also important to remember the financial price that many families pay for devoting themselves to the care of a sick child. Unsurprisingly young adults who have experienced serious illness have been identified as an 'at risk' group by social scientists monitoring the impact of contemporary societal changes on growing up as a member of what Douglas Copeland christened 'Generation X' (Osgood *et al.*, 2005).

This analysis of the way in which ill health can interfere with the process of identity development applies whether the individual has suffered from chronic illness from an early age, or is obliged to reconstruct their emergent sense of identity when experiencing major ill health for the first time in adolescence. This task of redefinition is daunting at any point in a person's life (after a stroke in a late-middle age for example) but perhaps the teenager, whose sense of identity remains plastic and somewhat confused anyway, has even more on their plate.

Two brief case examples illustrate how hard it can be for adolescents whose development has been compromised by ill health to construct a satisfactory sense of self:

> Neil has suffered from the unusual skin complaint, epidermolysis bullosa (basically thin skin) throughout his life. At age 16 he can reflect poignantly on how growing up with chronic illness has stopped him from 'living out the other parts of my life'. He is socially anxious, friendless and highly self-critical, reserving his strongest condemnation for the person he is, rather than the condition he's got. He can be very hurtful and mocking towards his parents on whom he remains very reliant. Neil cannot walk very far unaided, needs assistance with the administration of some skincare medication, and generally has a poorly developed capacity to look after himself (he won't shop independently, cannot make himself a meal, etc.). His troubled attitude towards his mother and father could be characterized as resentful dependence. He is taking some GCSEs but appears uncommitted to further education. He scoffs at the thought that any girl might be prepared to go out with him.

> Steve was 17 when he suffered a closed head injury in a motorcycle accident, after which he was hospitalized for over eight months. He subsequently has a number of gross physical and psychological handicaps including hemiparesis and spasticity, slow slurred speech and pronounced sexual disinhibition. Before his accident Steve was an apprentice mechanic – an occupation he is

no longer equipped to pursue. Twelve months after receiving the injuries that have palpably ended his motorcycling days for ever, he continues to describe himself as 'a biker through and through'. However he also reflects sadly that most of the time he can barely recognize himself in the way he feels and reacts. He is lost within his own skin. Steve's parents want to encourage their previously freewheeling son to resume an independent social life, but dread the consequences of Steve's disinhibited impulses for his own and other people's safety.

What can a personal construct approach offer to young people in such dire straits? To paraphrase Kelly, 'It's not what your illness or injury has made of you that matters, but what you make of it.' There are realities of treatment regimes and painful symptomatology that need to be confronted, but when Kelly asserted that everything which exists can be re-construed, he meant everything. What does it mean personally to discover you have diabetes? What implications does having 'petit mal' epilepsy have for how you construe yourself? These are questions to be personally considered and reconsidered. There is no 'that's it' finality imposed by medical diagnosis.

Personal construct psychology emphasizes the importance of developing a schema to allow the individual to anticipate events. One consequence of the appropriate mourning for 'what might have been' (in Steve's bike fantasies, for example) is that the person with health problems may have a very well-articulated sense of the person they could/should have become.

For constructive adaptation to the world they actually live in, they need to create a similarly detailed map of their current possibilities. Just like Fransella's group of stutterers who needed help to think of themselves as fluent speakers before they could make best use of technical speech therapy advice (Fransella, 1972), young people who are unwell may need reminding that sickness does not write your life script for you. History is not destiny, though it can feel that way as the following case study illustrates:

> Kevin had suffered from a neck cancer at age six that had been quickly diagnosed and effectively treated. After some reconstructive surgery the only notable consequence of his illness was some relatively minor scarring, and the prospects for his future physical and psychological well-being looked good. This optimistic prognosis was born out until at about age 13 when, after a long period of emotional stability, Kevin became increasingly moody and ill-tempered both at home and in his school where he was implicated in some uncharacteristic episodes of bullying. His evident unease whenever cancer was mentioned on a TV programme suggested there was more to this behavioural pattern than teenage angst.

> Kevin was able to explain to his parents and therapist that he had been getting harshly teased by other boys at his school. They had challenged him about

the scars on his upper back and when Kevin had tried to explain that these were caused by his earlier treatment for cancer they had branded him a liar. The same tormentors subsequently took to calling Kevin 'cancer boy' at every opportunity. These experiences had led Kevin to reappraise his opinion of the implications that having had cancer as a child would have on his future. He was now convinced that his chances of happiness and self-respect had been permanently blighted like the effect a heavy frosting can have on a tender young plant.

In personal construct terms Kevin had experienced a nasty case of invalidation (when the older boys disbelieved his account of his illness) and adapted a pre-emptive construction of his future life-chances (utterly ruined by cancer). However, in telling his tale he started a conversation with his parents and therapist that opened up alternative understandings of his circumstance. This audience could validate his experiences not only of having had cancer but also of having been so badly treated by the lads who teased him so mercilessly. Feeling better appreciated allowed Kevin himself to consider whether there was indeed only one sad and constricted script his life could follow. The following extract from the letter written by Kevin's therapist as a record of these discussions reflects the healthy all-round 'loosening' of previous constructions that had taken place:

Dear Kevin

When we first met, the story I heard about you went along the lines that you were a bit of a terror; had a bad temper you couldn't control; couldn't put your feelings into words; and even felt that your chances in life had been ruined by having cancer as a child. I don't think of you that way at all now. If I were telling your tale I'd notice quite different qualities in you. I'd start by talking about your emotional maturity. I've been really taken by the way you've been able to talk about what you're going through. It's helped me and your Mum and Dad understand more and I suspect it's helped you make better sense of things too.

I've also appreciated the uncommon level of provocation that you've had to endure. It's bad enough to be teased about scarring, but to have kids disbelieve your explanation about having had surgery for cancer just stunned me. This makes your recent achievements in controlling your angry feelings all the more impressive.

You've also showed in your comments an unusual wisdom and ability to reflect (I know you like that word). I've sometimes noticed this strength in other young people who have had cancer as children. It's as if the experience can help you realise what matters in life a bit more quickly than others of your age.

Although the style of this therapeutic letter owes an evident debt to the narrative school of systemic therapy (Drewery, Winslade and Monk, 2000), the reconstructive theme is pure Kelly.

12.9 CONCLUSION

The sociologist Goffman famously subtitled his treatise on stigma, 'The management of spoiled identity' (Goffman, 1963). The optimistic message of personal construct theory is that 'spoiled' is a construct open to revision, not an immutable life sentence. However, our views of ourselves are socially as well as personally constructed and children's self-concepts are substantially influenced by their understandings of how other people react to them. So it is important for health professionals to ensure that they see the person beyond the diagnosis.

The risks involved in children failing to acknowledge the consequences of their illnesses might easily be recognized, such as when an adolescent with diabetes undertakes a bout of prolonged exercise without considering the impact on their blood sugar levels. But there are parallel dangers when adults construe young people as nothing but a diagnostic category. Even in a condition such as autism that so impairs the social development of the individual, the concerned outsider who pays close attention and listens carefully can get to appreciate the singular characteristics of each evolving person. The neurologist Oliver Sacks (1995) displays just such an attitude of respectful curiosity towards the patients he meets and describes in his books and films. You always get the sense of being introduced to an individual, rather than encountering a syndrome. If medical consultations never go beyond diagnostic labels we should perhaps be concerned for the psychological well-being of the doctor as well as for their patients. As Kelly wryly observed, 'hardening of the categories' can be an awfully debilitating condition!

CHAPTER 13

CONSTRUING WITHIN THE FAMILY

In a sense we are always interviewing a child in the context of his or her family. As human beings we develop in a supremely *social* way, internalizing from the earliest age the local version of what the world is like from those around us. Such primary constructs as warm versus cold, pain versus comfort, tastes nice versus nasty and frustrated versus pleased seem to be 'wired in' but are soon joined by an increasingly elaborate set of dimensions governing and defining interactions with the world and between self and others. As language develops, these meanings are labelled according to the social traditions and personal constructions of the child's principal carers. However, from the beginning, children are far from passive as they grapple with their environment and select labels according to their unique developing personal construct system. The child's identity is actively carved out through the earliest years but who we are is not simply an individual matter. We are defined and define ourselves in relation to members of the family and other figures in our lives in a dialectic of social and personal processes.

The child also meets with us in the context of a more immediate situation in which the family will usually be playing a central part. He or she may be with us because a parent is worried, concerned or angry. An adolescent, attempting to be more independent, may want help without the family knowing about it, but he or she will have strong ideas and feelings about what Mum or Dad would think and do were they to know. Others, such as a teacher, may be concerned about a young person, but a parent or carer's potential position towards the issue has a vital influence on what is happening currently and how things will develop over the coming months. The origin of the issues themselves will very often reside in problematic family situations such as break-up, abuse and neglect, sibling issues or attachment difficulties. If the child has particular developmental or psychological difficulties, these in turn will affect family relationships with associated stress, jealousies and rivalries.

Involving other family members in work with children and young people is therefore a matter of central concern which brings with it many complex issues and opportunities. These need handling with great sensitivity and awareness of a number of people's feelings in addition to the child in question's well-being.

The spirit, values and methods of personal construct theory have much to contribute to this work. Its stress on each person being likened to a scientist, inquiring, exploring and making hypotheses is perhaps particularly appropriate in reflecting the essence of childhood, as the child progressively struggles to make sense of the physical and social world. The whole approach from George Kelly's writings onward is imbued with a sense of play and playfulness and the outstanding contributions of Don Bannister, Phillida Salmon and Tom Ravenette on children are particularly good examples of this.

13.1 ENGAGING ALL FAMILY MEMBERS

In my own work, I have sought to extend PCT's emphasis on respecting and working with each individual to *doing* this simultaneously with all the people in a situation. Too often, in clinical or educational settings, professionals are drawn into taking sides, being *for* the child and against the parents or vice versa. Families in difficult situations typically become very polarized and to join only one part usually has the effect of exacerbating the conflict and impeding resolution. Indeed many problems can be effectively prevented in daily life by maintaining a stance of supporting all the people in a situation. From a PCT perspective, each person's point of view, although it may have become extreme and rigid, has a truth within it and a contribution to make in resolving problems. There are, of course, limits to this, such as where violence and abuse are involved, but this positive and accepting stance is invaluable in meeting any situation and in engaging the various parties concerned.

How to engage and convene families in the myriad situations with which one is confronted is beyond the scope of this chapter. However, in general, flexibility, offering choice and being able to meet with people together or in different combinations are useful principles. The interviewer also has an important point of view and will actively influence the process to maximize the opportunity for flexibility and choice on behalf of the individuals in the situation. Who to meet with and when are best negotiated with each family afresh, often using the telephone, rather than using standardized appointment letters. Who is in the situation and their attitude to the work can then be established early on and an invitation made to meet all together or in particular combinations. If one member is strongly dictating the format, as in the earlier example of the teenager insisting on one-to-one work, one may have to accept this, but one may be able to make a bargain for a session with other members of the family. Sessions may be divided in which individuals or subgroups are seen with the clear understanding that confidentiality holds for each encounter. There are many advantages to meeting with significant people in a young person's life reaching agreement as to how to proceed with a piece of work.

Interviewing children with other members of the family has many advantages. By focusing from the start on each member as a whole person, with a wealth of experience and a contribution to make, we can begin to counter destructive and conflicting processes in which people are regarded as 'nothing but a problem'. This often requires that the interviewer is quite active in steering the conversation and postponing the consideration of issues. It allows the detailed knowledge base of each member to be tapped. For example, a brother or sister may have something to say about a shy child's interests, allowing a conversation to be started and an alliance made. Adults often gain a lot from hearing a new sort of conversation between the interviewer and the child taking place. Parents often said to me, 'I didn't know she thought and knew all that!' Alternatively, if the child is very shy or unwilling to co-operate, a joint session allows a conversation to begin in which the child is participating to the extent that they are listening. I found that children are often incredibly grateful when they see that somebody is interested in grasping thorny differences and conflicts in a way that is supportive and respectful of each person. Perhaps the most important advantage of the family interview is that it allows direct observation of interactions and relationships to be made, what we might call *construing in action* as opposed to relying on a child or adult's *representation* of situations.

Set against these advantages, there are of course hazards and disadvantages. People, especially young people, will often be inhibited in sharing and elaborating their views in the presence of family members. It can also have pitfalls, especially if it results in the child feeling less understood or if he or she feels that the interviewer has taken a one-sided position, for example in siding with a concerned parent's version of events. Families typically contain strong power hierarchies in which a particular way of looking at things predominates with alternative views being suppressed, rejected or ridiculed. For a young person to be exposed to a parent's anxious concern about the child's mental health or a diatribe of moral criticism can be devastating and should be avoided if possible (although this of course may be happening on a regular basis outside the session). In cases of abuse, a young person may have things to say which would be dangerous to share, which would be met my invalidating denials or lead to retributions later. In such situations, opportunities are given to meet with family members separately and this can be done by dividing a session into parts or arranging to see people in different appointments, settings or on the telephone. In this situation I may comment, 'I will use what everyone has told me to work out the best way of understanding and helping the situation.'

In less problematic circumstances, the effect of power differentials will often be strongly in evidence or exercising themselves in more subtle or invisible ways. These may be founded on age, gender or status, such as where children are discriminated as birth children versus half-, step or adopted siblings. There may be children who differ in terms of how favoured they are by a more powerful member, or cross-generational coalitions in which an adult and young person unite in criticism of another adult or child. Powerful external figures such as separated parents or grandparents may be having a strong influence.

To stress the value of each individual participant (whether present or in the background) is usually the best stance to take in addressing these situations. The power differentials are gently countered by allowing the less powerful voices, usually the youngest, to be expressed first and enabling these to continue to be heard. This starts with the first greeting (see Appendix 13.A) where the interviewer may squat to meet a young child at eye level and take an interest in their play or drawings, pacing him- or herself in a very responsive and friendly way. Finding each person's name is important here, especially how people like to be addressed and what other people closest to them call them. Names are closely associated with core identities. I offer my own first name as representing a close and trusted ally. Some families of course may be embarrassed if they stress status issues and sometimes end up calling me 'Dr Harry!'

13.2   SETTING AND MATERIALS

The setting in which the interview takes place is important and will often be seen by children as an extension of the interviewer as a person. Carefully selecting toys and materials suiting children of all ages is fundamental. Over the years, in the Child and Adolescent Mental Health Service where I worked, I accumulated a collection which evolved through the preferences of the children themselves, some of which are drawn in Figure 13.1. Brightly coloured materials and pencils are immediately attractive to younger and older children. For sullen adolescents, I found that 'executive toys' were useful. After a while they found it hard to resist picking up the 'oil mill' or the 'Rubik snake', for example, and beginning to fiddle with them. Once play is established, this signals the young person's willingness to begin to participate and collaborate. This applies to the adults too and one knows things are going well when the parents begin to play or draw themselves!

Perhaps the simplest toy of all is the soft multicoloured juggling ball. This may be gently offered to a very young or disabled child for them to grasp. Can they catch it when dropped into their hand from just an inch or so above? What do they do if offered a second one when they are already holding the first? Their level of development and skill can be established and matched as the balls can be used from these simplest skills to the advanced physical skill of juggling or the social ability to pass one back and forth or roll it along the floor to each other. I might teach the child a new trick at the appropriate level. I am establishing a relationship in which we are going to learn together and have some fun.

Toy figures and animals can be used to enact situations or make up new stories. Particularly useful was the 'Wise Mouse'. Over the years Mousey became very experienced at working with and helping all sorts of children. I would suggest that the child put the puppet on their hand and listen to see if he had anything to whisper in their ear. 'Mousey may say something really useful to you to help you or your family because he's really wise!' I would give them the choice to keep what he said to themselves or share it with us.

Figure 13.1 A Selection of Harry's Toys drawn by Kiran Roy (14) and Rohan Roy (11) including juggling balls, rubber juggling eggs, transformer, oil mill, the Wise Mousse, walking rabbit, various animals and Rubik snake.

13.3   INTERESTS

Asking children about their interests, recent experiences and who is in the family is a nice way for people to begin to get to know each other. This is not simply to facilitate the interview – it is a window into the child's world of construing and identity. The child's particular way of phrasing things and the concrete experiences they have had should be carefully noted. This requires tremendous concentration and presence of mind and details should be written down if in danger of being forgotten. If the immature phrasing that children use is paraphrased into adult language in the interviewer's mind, much of the personal meaning will be lost or changed.

The little gems reflecting the child's actual experiences may be used again and again later and in future interviews and gradually expanded into fuller accounts. The younger child's attention span is much shorter and there will often be no second chance if the interviewer forgets or mishears a contribution. I often found these conversations were like 'juggling' four or five different topics or snippets, recycling and returning to them, dwelling on them a little longer if the child has more to say and moving on, preventing an embarrassing (for the child) silence at any point. In this way rapport and involvement are developed.

With each topic, one can move around and make sequential contact with different members of the family. For example, 15-year-old Sandra, reluctant to speak, says she has been at school that day. I ask, 'Have you got some nice friends there?' She says, 'Some'. 'Who's your best friend at the moment?' 'Linda'. I turn to her parents, 'Who were your best friends when you were Sandra's age?' and then immediately back to the children. 'Do you know who your parents' best friends were?' In this way a topic of conversation is maintained and elaborated involving all the people in the room.

A parent will often want to 'help' the child here, but suitable gestures and expressions (indicating great interest in the parent too) will often prevent the conversation with the child being disrupted. The conversational competence of the adult compared to the child is a strong pressure for the interview to revert to adult talk. The interview is steered so that members are contributing more equally or with the children's voices predominating. It is useful to keep everyone involved and 'spot around', involving different members, maybe using humour and word-play. The interviewer should be alert to any member losing interest.

Children's spontaneous comments are always likely to reflect their construing and choices more than material given in response to questions. These should therefore be particularly acknowledged and responded to usually immediately. One can always come back to the previous topic and one may find a way of knitting topics together or, failing that, listing them. 'So you were learning about electricity in school today, you two went fishing on Saturday and you're going to the caravan next weekend – what a lot of different things you are doing, that's great!' This method generates richness and excitement, an enjoyment of life that in itself can begin to reduce the size of the presenting problem in people's minds and counter the associated 'stuck-ness' and frustration. The child's spontaneous interests (however seemingly insignificant) are a reflection of their core constructs and are therefore a source that can be used to make inroads into the problem area. Milton Erickson presents a lovely case of how he helped an 11-year-old boy with severe reading difficulties by using his and his father's interest in fishing and looking at maps and talking about where they had been:

> We got out a map of the West and we tried to locate the towns. We weren't reading the map, we were looking for the name of towns. You look at maps, you don't read them. I would confuse the location of certain cities and he would have to correct me. I would try to locate a town named Colorado Springs and be looking for it in California and he had to correct me. He rapidly learned to locate all the towns we were interested in. He didn't know he was reading the names. We had such a good time looking at the map and finding good fishing spots. He liked to come and discuss fish and the various kinds of flies used in catching fish. We also looked up different kinds of fish in the encyclopaedia. (Haley, 1973)

13.4 WORRIES AND DIFFICULTIES

When we begin talking about the difficulties that led to the interview it is good to think in terms of who is *worried* about what (see Appendix 13.A). Life invariably involves worries. We all have them and we can leaven the frightening emotions of anger and disappointment and the child's feeling of failure and blame that are associated with the complaint in this way. A parent usually wants to speak at length about the history of the difficulties. The interview is steered and slowed down so the child understands each step. We look at examples and incidents that the child can remember and therefore give his or her account of their experience. Animals and puppets can be used to enact events and feelings. What they were trying to do or what they could do to make things go better or differently bring agency and choice points into the scenarios. Watzlawick and colleagues' brilliant work concerning the division of issues into problems, attempted solutions, goals, steps and views of what would help remain invaluable in this context (Watzlawick, Weakland and Fisch, 1974). Questions derived from such categories are outlined in Appendix 13.A.

Because constructs are two-ended, one can always move over to the more hopeful and creative end of the dimension. So if a child is seen by a parent as naughty, we can spend more time thinking about what they *do*, could do or used to do when they behave well, even if it is for only brief times. As time goes on, the focus on progress or improvements is useful. Following Fay Fransella's 1972 notion that stuttering is highly elaborated and fluency for the stutterer is much less highly construed, we spend time on and elaborate the non-problem pole of the construct. For example, if the child has been much less anxious we might continue with such questions as, 'I wonder how that happened?' and 'Do you know how you managed that?' (see Appendix 13.A).

How much we focus on the presenting problem is a matter of judgement in each individual case. Parents generally expect their concerns to be met and may become frustrated if they do not experience the content of the session to be relevant. I remember with a shudder a parent who sharply instructed a young child to stop playing and put the toy down, 'so that they could listen'. It is necessary, especially in current busy services, to be clear why one is meeting and agreeing what the criteria of success in terms of problem resolution might be. However, in my experience, I usually found that the central work did not necessarily involve focusing on the problem as presented or referred. These difficulties were nearly always embedded in relational issues, such as those listed at the beginning of the chapter. When these are addressed or eased, they will often 'spontaneously' improve. The same applies to therapeutic goals. After they have been agreed (loosely or in detail, as seems appropriate to the situation), we do not have to keep revisiting them. They will often 'do their work' of themselves if everyone agrees that they are a desirable aim. It is important that the work itself is not too much associated in the child's mind with the 'problem'. The sessions should be primarily enjoyable and interesting for the child or their cooperation will be lost and resistance damaging to the therapeutic process will arise.

13.5 WORKING WITH CONSTRUCTS

Constructs are often misunderstood as being intellectual or verbal. PCT sees the cognitive, emotional and behavioural aspects of construing as one whole thing. When a teenage girl says, 'My father is a bastard', whilst clenching her fist, the idea, the feeling and the action are all part of the construct. With younger children particularly, constructs will be observed in expressions, tones of voice and actions as much as in words. Gathering these constructs allows the interviewer to understand the child's experience more and more fully.

Constructs may be 'elicited' or 'supplied'. The child's own explanations are always better indicators of his or her construing but they may need help in finding words that fit the experience. These should only be offered tentatively, ensuring that the child acknowledges their suitability before assuming understanding. Other members of the family will often supply a word, assuming they understand. The interviewer should check, 'Are you sure that is what you meant?' or giving some alternatives for them to choose from. Chronic lack of mutual understanding through this kind of assumption characterizes many family difficulties.

All the methods introduced elsewhere in this book, such as 'Tell me three things about', 'The Portrait Gallery' and 'The Drawing and its Opposite' (see Chapter 4) are readily usable in family sessions. Also, as described in Chapter 6, methods of exploring any construct according to its position in the hierarchical construct system are very useful as conversational methods in the family context. The laddering method allows fascinating similarities and differences in superordinate construing between members to be explored. We may ask typical laddering questions along the lines of:

1. 'Which would you prefer to do: your mum's job or your dad's job?'

2. 'How come you prefer that?'

3. 'I wonder how he/she came to choose that job?'

Pyramiding 'down' the hierarchy to more concrete constructs is particularly important in child work. For example, if a boy says 'he went out' at the weekend, it is worth spending time finding out the details of when, who he was with, what they did and what it was like. When, next time, one recalls, 'Last time you told me about that time when you went into the fields on Saturday with your friend Jim and had some fun climbing a tree', the boy will remember because the concrete images are evoked. He will then feel more valued and understood.

Each construct carries a story and each story carries further constructs. In this way the interviewer unfolds in a 'zigzag' a series of constructs and events as in Figure 13.2. This also allows us to move from more standardized or professional constructs (such as 'problem' versus 'behaving well') to progressively more unique and personalized construing.

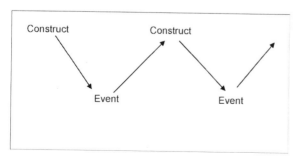

Figure 13.2 The zigzag interview.

13.6   QUALITATIVE GRIDS

Just as we can have repertory grids with numbers in them, with children (and adults) we can use qualitative grids in which they write or draw pictures in the squares. An example of this is the perceiver-element grid or PEG illustrated in Figures 13.3 and 13.4. The names of the family members (or others) are written down the left-hand side as perceivers and, along the top, the same names are put in as elements who are perceived or construed. The PEG can be filled in by individuals or the family can fill one in (say a 4 × 4 one on a large sheet of paper) as a group exercise. In a fascinating piece of work, Lucille Giles (2003) got family members to draw pictures of each member and of the family as a whole using the PEG method to investigate similarities and differences, agreements and disagreements and relational patterns.

In the example here, I asked two brothers, Kiran (aged 14) and Rohan (11), known as Ro, to think about a particular recent situation. They chose an event from a few days before which had led to some tension. Each was given a 2 × 2 PEG to fill in separately. They were told they could put words, pictures or cartoons in the squares as they chose. Each therefore had the chance to put in how they felt about and construed themselves and the other and how they guessed the other had construed self and other in the situation. They were then asked to fill in a second PEG after we had all had a discussion about the situation and each explained what he had put in the first grid.

	(a) KIRAN	(b) ROHAN
(a) KIRAN	Rohan said he needed to get up early, but wouldn't get up so I arroused him with the drum	I think Ro knew he needed to get up but he is lazy.
(b) ROHAN	I think Ro saw me as an idiot. but in his heart knew he had to get up.	I think he just wanted to be lazy and saw himself better than anyone else.

Figure 13.3 Perceiver-Element Grid – Kiran. Here Kiran (14) completes his initial PEG describing how he sees himself and his brother and his guess about how his brother sees both of them during an incident that led to an argument.

Figure 13.4 Perceiver-Element Grid–Rohan. This is Rohan's (11) second PEG after they had both drawn initial PEGs about the incident and then discussed them together.

Figure 13.3 shows Kiran's first PEG. He aroused his brother by playing Ro's drums, just next to his bed, loudly, after his mother had asked him to wake Ro up else he'd be late for school. He calls his brother lazy and guesses that Ro sees himself as 'better than anyone else'. In his initial PEG (not shown), Ro draws his brother drumming, with the caption 'rubbish'. He describes himself as having been 'happy and mellow until (sic) my brother woke me up'. For his brother's view of himself he draws a triumphalist 'he-man' figure and correctly saw Kiran as seeing him as 'lazy'. The incident therefore seems to involve some rivalry between them and evokes Ro's central concern currently of learning to play the drums well (as opposed to 'rubbish') – he had just received the drum kit a few days before!

Figure 13.4 show Ro's PEG completed after the discussion. He now recognizes that Kiran was doing 'his duty' and that he was 'happy' that Kiran woke him up. He still sees his brother as a bad drummer and that Kiran saw him as 'lazy'. In Kiran's second PEG (not shown) he says, 'I now think Rohan was very tired and because of that quite grumpy, so I do sympathize a bit.'

Although relatively simple, the method can bring forth surprisingly rich material. I asked them what they thought of the exercise. Kiran said that the most useful square was, 'The one how you think they feel, so you kind of imagine yourself in their position'. It is therefore a powerful method for promoting sociality and interpersonal understanding in a way that children find interesting and fun.

13.7   A CASE EXAMPLE

I worked with 11-year-old Stuart for 18 months. He had been getting into a lot of trouble with rages and violence towards his older and younger brothers. Indeed this continued to escalate through early phase of my work with him. He was caught stealing from a house and was accused of having sex with a 10-year-old girl. This required a professionals' meeting which included his mother, maternal grandparents, social workers and members of the youth offending team.

Stuart's father took little interest in him and had in fact been physically abusive towards him as a baby, leaving the family while Stuart was still a toddler. His mother married again, but this man proved also to be violent. He was in Stuart's life between the ages of four and seven. Stuart was said to have been close to his stepfather before he left. I worked with Stuart for three sessions during this time to address his bed-wetting.

Stuart did not want to come but was quite thoughtful in the session and agreed to come for some further meetings. He was due to start secondary school in a few weeks' time. He said that he and his two brothers were 'friends' and all played football in a team. The first few meetings were slow-going and once, when I went to the waiting room, Stuart was sitting there alone. His mother had left him there, saying that she would pick him up at the end of the meeting. I worked with them together and separately and met with one of his brothers too on some occasions.

Figure 13.5 shows a 'bow-tie' diagram (Procter, 1985, 2005) of the construing and action between Stuart and his mother which captures the conflicting and escalatory relationship between them. His mother said that Stuart strongly reminded her of his biological father, in his expressions and mannerisms as

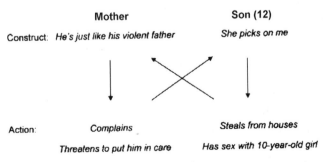

	Mother	Son (12)
Construct:	*He's just like his violent father*	*She picks on me*
Action:	Complains	*Steals from houses*
	Threatens to put him in care	*Has sex with 10-year-old girl*

Figure 13.5 'Bow-tie' diagram of construing between Mother and Robert.

well as his behaviour. The actions governed by this construing, complaining at him and even saying that he would 'have to go into care' if he carried on, were seen by Stuart as *unfair* picking on him all the time, in contrast to her treatment of his brothers. His resultant rages and destructive behaviour were seen by his mother as 'To get at me' and 'He's angry with me'.

These sorts of patterns are often not easy to shift but I was able to develop a good relationship with both of them over the months. Their relationship seemed intense and a bit like a marriage with Stuart assuming a 'macho', 'head-of-the-household' kind of role. His older brother seemed to cope by keeping a low profile and concentrating on his academic work. One day they saw Stuart's father in town. His mother said to Stuart, 'Hey, that's your father, shout at him that he's a "wanker".' Stuart then shouted this rude word at his father.

My work with them followed the approaches described in this chapter. I was particularly concerned to have them see the good and positive sides of people, in each other and in the two father figures in the past. This proved very difficult, but I persisted. 'There must have been something good in him, or you wouldn't have got together with him!' I also said this at the professionals' meeting, saying how important it was that Stuart be able to find something in his biological father to positively identify with. At the next professionals' meeting, which took place after Stuart had quite suddenly started to shape up and improve, his grandfather explained, 'I listened carefully to what you said last time. I was waiting for the right opportunity and when we were playing football recently, I said to Stuart, "If you could play football half as well as how your father used to play, you'd be a real star!"' Stuart had apparently been quite dumbfounded by this remark and it was from this point on that he made a radical change in his whole attitude and behaviour. I believe a core, superordinate construct, defining his identity and role and kept in place by his mother's validation of it, was finally able to shift. Men, himself as a man, could now be seen as something more than violent and abusive. I assume that my own influence as a positive and warm male figure played a part in this process too.

I continued to work with them for a few more weeks. At follow-up a year after finishing the work Stuart was maintaining his improved behaviour. The case illustrates the importance of careful work with a young man's construing of himself and key figures, but also of supporting and working with his mother. She had experienced considerable loss and rejection herself and working with her construing of herself and Stuart was, I believe, a vital part of the progress that we were able to achieve.

APPENDIX

Useful questions in interviewing children

Greeting

Hello, are you Sam? My name's Harry, it's really nice to meet you!
That looks really interesting. What's happening there?
What would you have been doing at school today?

Interests

What do you like doing best? How do you spend your free time?
What did you do last weekend?
Who is your teacher? Is she a nice chap?
What do you like best? What are you best at?
Who are your best friends? What do you like doing together?
What does your dad do for his work?
Have you been to your mum's place of work?

Family

Who lives in your home?
What's your sister's name? Do you two get on well together?
What do you call your mum's mum? Does she live near you?
Who's your favourite grandparent?
Has your mum any brothers and sisters?
Where does she come – is she the oldest, middle or youngest?
What's it like to be the oldest?
How often do you see your dad?
What do you enjoy doing together?

Worries

Who's been worrying most in your family recently? Who next? Who the least?
Who have you been worrying about most often?
What will Mum say she's been worrying about? Is she right?
What is it that's bothering you at the moment?
Can you give me an example? What happens?
Where does this happen most, at home or at school?
When is it worst – morning, afternoon, evening or at weekends?
Is it sometimes worse, sometimes better?
How long does it go on for? Who was there?
Why do you think it's happening?
Is there anything else you're unhappy about?

Attempted Solutions

What do you do to try and make things better?
Did that work? What else have you tried?
What do you think Mum should do with two boys who are fighting?
What does Dad say?
Does your friend know about this?
What does she say to you?
When he shouts at Mark, what does Mum do?
What would happen if he did nothing?

Relationships

Tell me three nice things about your dad.
What was he cross about?
Who gets the most upset? Tom, James or Sharon?
Do you agree with her?
Would it be different if you lived with your dad and you saw your mum on a Saturday?
How do your sister and your mum get on?
Which two people argue the least?
What was life like when you were five?
Have you heard about your dad's life when *he* was 12?
If this wasn't happening would you be closer?
Who in the family is still missing Nan the most? Who else is?
When you are sad, who is the best person to talk to about it?

Goals

When have you been happiest in the last week?
Tell me about a time when things were okay.
If you had three wishes what would you wish for?
If things changed a teeny-weeny bit what would be different?
When things are better, what will you want to do instead?

Therapy

Who wanted you to come and see me?
Who was the keenest that you come, you or your mum?
Have you seen anyone like me before?
How can we make things happier?
Would you like to come and talk again with me?
How do you feel this meeting's going?

Progress

How's it been better?
Do you know how you managed it?
What would make it worse again?
What would have to happen to make it worse again?

Evaluation

When you first came what were you worried about?
Is it better now, worse or the same?

CHAPTER 14

AN EVIDENCE BASE

14.1   A FASHIONABLE CONCEPT

There is a contemporary drive within the health business to try to ensure that treatment decisions are informed by the best available scientific evidence. So, when government makes major decisions regarding the investment of public funds in providing psychotherapeutic services, those choices will be heavily influenced by the results of published outcome research in the field. At a more local level, patients increasingly (and appropriately) expect to be told details of the success rates of the alternative treatments considered suitable for their conditions. A primary component of the continued professional development that all clinicians are required to undertake is that they 'keep up to date' with relevant research findings. In many ways these tactics parallel the way in which the wise consumer might go about buying a car. Check out prices and performance data. Discover the relative breakdown rates of the models you have in mind by consulting independent trade magazines. See how happy previous buyers of the various products have been with their purchase. 'Caveat emptor' is a piece of advice that has never gone out of fashion. Why would the commissioners and consumers of psychological help for young people do otherwise?

So how does personal construct therapy compare to the competition? Can it be considered, in the current American parlance, an 'empirically supported treatment'? Before offering a candid overview of what is, and isn't, known about the effectiveness of some of the interventions described in this book, it will probably be helpful to explain briefly the rationale and preferred methodologies adopted by proponents of evidence-based practice.

The proverbial gold standard of therapy outcome research is the randomly controlled trial (RCT). As the name suggests, participants in the trial are randomly allocated to either the treatment or a control group. The logic of this design is that if the members of the two groups are well-matched and assigned by chance alone then any differences in outcome can be reasonably attributed to the treatment provided. The model works well in pharmaceutical research when no one involved (participant, prescriber or researcher) can identify whether the drugs being taken are placebo versions or the real Mc-Coy – until of course the code is broken at the evaluative stage of the analysis. This 'double-blind' ideal is not so easily achieved in outcome research for psychological interventions.

The strategy of trying to control the possible influence of non-treatment variables on therapy outcomes is also reflected in the care researchers take to employ the most valid and reliable measures available and to standardize the service that therapists provide to participants in the study (by for example following a published protocol). This attention to detail is time-consuming and expensive so the kind of compellingly large-scale randomly controlled study that might deliver a definitive judgement on the efficacy of a particular intervention for a psychological problem is, in practice, very rarely conducted. Instead knowledge is reckoned to accumulate slowly as a series of (hopefully) well-conducted trials are reported and reviewed by members of the scientific community. At this point it becomes possible to conduct a 'meta-analysis' that employs recognized statistical strategies (based on the common metric of the effect size) for combining data from a series of studies to present a systematic summary of the available research evidence (Glass, 1976). A meta-analytic review of outcome research in personal construct therapy was published by Linda Viney and colleagues in 2005 (Viney *et al.*, 2005). It is not a long document . . .

The reviewers conducted an extensive search of all published interventions that compared a group of individuals receiving PCT therapy with a comparison group that had either received an alternative treatment or acted as no-treatment controls. For the purposes of this study the authors did not insist that allocation to the PCT variant or its alternative had been randomly decided. They identified only one study concerning young people. This was an evaluation of a personal construct group conducted with troubled adolescents aged between 12 and 15 years old in Australia (Truneckova and Viney,

2003). Outcome was assessed both by changes in interpersonal construing picked up from repertory grids and self-characterizations and standardized questionnaires concerning levels of disruptive behaviour completed by the parents and teachers of the young people who participated in the project. Those who were randomly allocated to the PCT group were reported to have benefited from a significant treatment effect on these behavioural measures compared to the no-treatment control group. However, as the authors of this study take pains to explain, finding improvements compared to a control group of adolescents who were basically left to their own devices is not compelling evidence of effectiveness. What might that group have achieved had they received a similar level of special attention or indeed participated in an alternative form of therapy group? It is also important to acknowledge that this project was conducted and evaluated by a couple of unabashed PCT enthusiasts. The so-called 'allegiance' of therapists and researchers to particular psychotherapeutic schools has been consistently related to reports of treatment efficacy (Luborsky *et al.*, 1999).

The current state of outcome research examining the efficacy of personal construct interventions with young people therefore falls well short of both the quantity and quality of studies that would be necessary to gain recognition as an empirically supported treatment as judged by the standards of the American Psychological Association. However, before disgruntled readers start to abandon the good ship *HMS Kelly* in droves, there are a few more arguments worth considering . . .

14.2   WHOSE EVIDENCE?

There is an adage, oft-repeated in the world of treatment research, that 'absence of evidence is not evidence of absence'. This serves as a timely reminder to the scientific community not to discount as ineffective any therapy that has not been subjected to adequate research scrutiny. However, in the field of psychological intervention with young people, the absence of evidence is not restricted to such relatively local lacunae. In a comprehensive and critical review of treatments for children and adolescents published under the engagingly straightforward title of 'What works for whom?' in 2002, Fonagy and his co-authors (Fonagy *et al.*, 2002) acknowledged that they had been unable to identify many studies that were designed to prioritize young people's constructions of their difficulties and assess therapeutic outcome from their perspective. Rather the field is characterized by research designed according to adult constructions of children's problems (most often psychiatric diagnostic categories) and evaluated by soliciting feedback from adults (such as parents or teachers) rather than young people themselves. Readers will probably not be surprised to discover that when studies have taken the care to compare parent and self-report responses to questionnaires concerning children's experiences, they rarely tell an identical tale. And why would they?

So it transpires that the question 'What works for whom?' carries a double meaning. The first carries the intended message that it is important to weigh the available evidence concerning the efficacy of specific interventions for a range of common psychological problems of childhood. The second asks more provocatively why no one seems to have tried very hard to seek the real consumer's opinion that ought to lie at the heart of this enquiry. The repeated theme of this book is that young people are competent, indeed expert, commentators on their own condition if only they are given the respect and opportunity to express their opinions. Personal construct theory provides a framework and a philosophy to anyone (be they researcher, clinician or teacher) who wants to take up the challenge of tapping this potential.

14.3   QUALITY CONTROL

If we liken psychotherapy to pharmacotherapy, it makes sense to take measures to ensure that psychological interventions are delivered in a standardized form in much the same way that tablets are. So, much care is taken in large-scale outcome studies to produce treatment manuals that are closely scripted to contain all the technical components considered necessary to deliver a specified product. Furthermore the performance of therapists involved in treatment trials is regularly sampled to check that everyone is 'adhering' to the same protocol. The logic of adopting this strategy is the familiar research goal of seeking to control as many of the many variables that might contribute to the outcome of an intervention as possible so that the impact of the primary factor under examination (i.e. the brand of treatment adopted) can be most accurately evaluated. If therapists were allowed to do their own thing the picture would get very murky, very quickly.

So there seems a good case for getting clinicians to 'sing from the same hymn sheet', to employ an overused analogy. However, a somewhat different musical metaphor casts this passion for constancy in a different light – the therapist as Elvis impersonator! People are inspired by the Great Originals in any walk of life and seek to emulate their heroes (and heroines). They buy football shirts; amass large record and book collections; join fan clubs; log-in to websites; and even attend master-class workshops. Ultimately (recognizing that imitation is both a sincere and rewarding form of flattery) some even manage to make a living out of mimicking their particular gods and goddesses. Fair play – you know what to expect if you buy tickets for an Abba tribute band performance. But there is something lost as well as something gained from the hard won predictability of this enterprise . . .

Performers who choose this repetitive and constrained form of expression must suppress their personal creativity almost entirely. They cannot even sing with their own voices. It would be considered foolhardy, at the very least, to stray from the inherited repertoire. Do therapists following the diktats of treatment manuals ever experience comparable artistic frustrations?

Like all analogies the 'therapist as Elvis impersonator' metaphor has its limitations. While musicians will no doubt respond to the interpersonal chemistry that develops between artist and audience, there is not room for the moment-to-moment adjustments that characterize sensitive therapeutic conversations. Attentive listening rather than virtuoso performance is the hallmark of the skilful psychotherapist. If adherence to a predetermined script interferes with our capacity to hear what our young clients have to say for themselves, the alliance between help seeker and help provider may be jeopardized. Adopting the credulous attitude that Kelly recommended in our discussions with young people means allowing them some editorial control over the treatment manual.

An allied concern about reliance on treatment manuals relates to the psychological inflexibility traditionally associated with rule-following behaviour. Many readers will be familiar with the 'Jobsworth' phenomenon – as in 'It would be more than my job's worth to allow you to park here/speak to Mr X/submit an incomplete form' or any other divergence from the official protocol. The reason these exchanges feel so frustrating is that we realize that a spot of straightforward adaptation to the particular circumstances at hand could make life so much easier for all concerned. Rather than attribute this rigidity to the unattractive personality characteristics of the Jobsworth, we may be wiser to recognize that all behaviour learned on rule-following lines will prove resistant to change in the light of altered environmental contingencies (Hayes *et al.*, 2006). If a psychotherapist's contextual sensitivity is impaired by a preoccupation with following a rule-governed script she risks losing touch with her clients on a number of levels.

14.4   THE THERAPEUTIC ALLIANCE

The most powerful predictor of the outcome of psychological interventions (excluding client-related factors) is not the technical nature of the therapy provided but the quality of working relationship established between the parties involved (Wampold, 2001). It is arguable that this notion of a therapeutic alliance is even more central to effective work with young people than it is with adults. Children rarely refer themselves for help. Adolescents may feel disaffected with the adult world at large. Often whole families need to feel engaged in the treatment process. Dropout rates from therapy are disarmingly high (Shirk and Karver, 2003). So it is perhaps unsurprising that a large-scale randomized study of interventions for 600 US adolescent drug abusers found that neither the dose nor type of treatment provided predicted differences in outcome, but measures of working alliance did – albeit to a modest degree (Tetzlaff *et al.*, 2005). Although the number of research studies investigating relationship variables in child and adolescent therapy is very much smaller than the evidence available concerning adults, findings suggest that similar factors contribute to the development of a strong alliance (Green 2006). Consumers of all ages appear to appreciate a treatment programme that is customized to their own circumstances and congruent with their own values and ideas (Norcross, 2002).

14.5   NOTHING SO PRACTICAL AS A GOOD THEORY ...

In the preface to Volume One of the *Psychology of Personal Constructs*, Kelly confessed that his *magnum opus* had not really turned out as he had initially planned. He had wanted to pass on to novice therapists the tricks of the trade that he had acquired over years of hard-won clinical experience. It was to be a guide to practice – what we might now term a treatment manual. However, when Kelly attempted to convey technical advice in this format he was unimpressed by his own efforts, which he dismissed as 'a morass of tedious little maxims'. His analysis of the problem was both candid and profound: 'It was no good – this business of trying to tell the reader merely *how* to deal with clinical problems; the *why* kept insistently rearing its puzzling head' (Kelly's italics)

Kelly's solution was to present his theory (at some considerable length) in Volume One of the *Psychology of Personal Constructs* that he subtitled 'A Theory of Personality' and to consider the therapeutic implications of his ideas (with similar attention to detail) in Volume Two that was subtitled 'Clinical Diagnosis and Psychotherapy'. This sequence represents the natural order of things to a reader of Kelly. First do your best to appreciate your client's sense of himself and his world. Then seek to understand the directions in which he would like to take his life in the future. Finally negotiate some opportune psychological experiments that seem well-suited to his ambitions. Interestingly it seems it is not only personal construct psychotherapists who are attracted to this approach to their chosen business. When the US organization Consumer Reports (roughly equivalent to *Which* magazine in the UK) surveyed a large sample of individuals who had made use of the services of a clinical psychologist or similar practitioner (Seligman, 1995), most expressed satisfaction with the care they had received. When asked what had helped they highlighted the way in which good therapists took time to understand them as individuals and could then drew upon an eclectic range of treatment techniques as they deemed appropriate.

In so far as personal construct psychology has devised a unique set of techniques they are essentially methods of enquiry designed to answer the 'Why?' question rather than 'how to do it' procedures for treating particular clinical problems. Kelly left his successors to discover for themselves how to translate the therapeutic implications of his theory into effective clinical practice. Some (including this book's authors on occasions) might wish that he'd swallowed his pride and written down a few more of those 'tedious little maxims' to light the way more obviously, but there are opportunities as well as frustrations that flow from the stance Kelly chose to adopt.

There are no a priori constraints on the interventions at the therapist's disposal. Kelly himself was prepared to pinch treatment techniques from almost anywhere – dream analysis, systematic desensitization, psychodrama. It is entirely consistent with the personal construct approach that these decisions about which methods to adopt should be informed by the published evidence. However, Kelly's view was that it is only once that choice has been made that the real science begins. The precise outcome of any particular intervention cannot be guaranteed. Clients conduct their own experiments and draw their own conclusions. Assuredly psychologists and their like can contribute to the venture. We can assist in the design of pertinent and reasonably safe experiments – an ethical responsibility that those who work with young people tend to feel keenly. We can display concerned curiosity when the data starts to roll in. We may even offer some alternative interpretations of the results. But ultimately ours is a strictly supporting role. The young people with whom we work are the senior research partners in the enterprise and it is the evidence of their unique experiences that will prove the ultimate test of our theories.

14.6   WHOSE CONSTRUCTS?

Personal construct theory is a reflexive psychology that purports to explain the conduct of psychologists as well as that of the children they study. How might Kelly have understood the workings of the Task Force of Clinical Child Psychologists who decide on behalf of the American Psychological Association which treatments shall be deemed 'empirically supported'? He would certainly have noted that they meet the personal construct definition of a group as a collection of individuals who see their world in a similar way. Indeed the Task Force has worked hard to develop a high degree of commonality in their construing of the particular elements on which they have been asked to pronounce. They seem broadly to agree among themselves about judgements such as what constitutes a 'well-conducted group design' or an 'established alternative treatment'.

They have even worked out their own rules of thumb to help the group decide if a treatment has demonstrated that it works 'well enough' to merit their endorsement, much like the judges at an agricultural show coming to a consensus on which bunch of carrots should be awarded the gold medal. But the respective merits of various vegetables and psychotherapies do not simply stand around waiting to be recognized; they need to be personally and socially constructed. Other individuals and groups will see these phenomena through different eyes. For example, while the Task Force may gauge the effectiveness of a psychological intervention for enuresis by the number of published randomly controlled trials in which it outperformed a no-treatment control, a mother may be more interested in whether her son stops wetting the bed. The most important criterion of success to the lad himself may be when he stops being teased at school. Each of these alternative constructions is valid, yet outcome research is usually designed to accommodate the priorities of psychologists rather than of those who use their service. Perhaps the American Psychological Association should have commissioned a gang of teenagers to come up with a few ways to evaluate psychological treatments for common adolescent problems. Might have made interesting reading.

14.7 CONCLUSIONS

So in summary the evidence base for the effectiveness of personal construct interventions with young people is distinctly limited at present. RCTs may not be the only way to assess the efficacy of psychological treatments but the logic of their design is undeniable. It will be interesting to see if the research wing of the personal construct community can muster its forces in the coming years to commission and conduct more good-quality outcome research in the field. Kelly had a term for the sort of scientists who were so certain of their convictions that they never dared to test them – hostile construers. It is characteristic of all good experiments that nobody really knows quite how things are going to turn out.

Of course PCT research with young people must also stay true to its basic tenets. Adopting the credulous position means that children's priorities and opinions will be afforded much greater respect when research studies are designed than is currently the case. Kelly's principled decision to concentrate on the *why* rather than the *how* of therapeutic practice means that personal construct theory will inform rather than dictate treatment decisions. It is therefore probably unwise to hold your breath while awaiting publication of the authoritative treatment manual!

As ever, the proof of the pudding will be in the eating.

REFERENCES

Andrews, B. (1998) 'Self esteem'. *The Psychologist* 10, 339–342.

Arsenio, W. & Lemerise, E. (2001) 'Varieties of childhood bullying: values, emotion processes and social competence'. *Social Development* 10, 59–73.

Badanes, L., Estevan, R. & Bacete, F. (2000) 'Theory of mind and peer rejection at school'. *Social Development* 9, 271–283.

Bandura, A. (1977) 'Self efficacy: towards a unifying theory of behavioural change'. *Psychological Review* 84, 191–215.

Bannister, D. (1962) 'The nature and measurement of schizophrenic thought disorder'. *Journal of Mental Science* 108, 825–842.

Bannister, D. (1963) 'The genesis of schizophrenic thought disorder: a serial invalidation hypothesis'. *British Journal of Psychiatry* 109 680–686.

Bannister, D. (1977) 'The logic of passion' in D. Bannister (ed.), *New Perspectives in Personal Construct Theory*. London: Academic Press.

Bannister, D. (1983) 'Self in Personal Construct Theory' in J.R. Adams-Webber & J.C. Mancuso (eds), *Applications of Personal Construct Theory*. Toronto: Academic Press.

Bannister, D. (1985) 'Foreword' in R.A. Neimeyer (ed.), *The Development of Personal Construct Psychology*. Lincoln, NE University of Nebraska Press.

Bannister, D. & Agnew, J. (1977) 'The child's construing of self' in J. Coles & A.Landfield (eds),*Nebraska Symposium on Motivation 1976*. Lincoln, NE University of Nebraska Press.

Bannister, D. & Fransella, F. (1986) *Inquiring Man: The Psychology of Personal Constructs*. 3rd edn. London: Croom Helm.

Baron-Cohen, S., Tager-Flusberg, H. & Cohen, D. (2000) *Understanding other Minds. Perspectives from Developmental Cognitive Neuroscience*. Oxford University Press.

Batson, C., Ahmad, N., Lishner, D. & Tsang, J. (2002) 'Empathy and altruism'. in C. Snyder & S.Lopez (eds), *Handbook of Positive Psychology*. New York: Oxford University Press.

Baumeister, R. (2005) 'Rejected and alone'. *The Psychologist* 18, 732–735.

Beck, A.T., Rush, J., Shaw, B. & Emery, G. (1979) *Cognitive Therapy for Depression*. New York: Guilford Press.

Berger, M. (2006) 'A model of preverbal social development and its application to social dysfunction in autism'. *Journal of Child Psychology and Psychiatry* 47, 338–371.

Bibace, R. & Walsh, M. E. (1980) 'Development of children's concepts of illness'. *Pediatrics* 66, 912–917.

Biringen, Z., Fidler, D., Barret, K. & Kubicek, L. (2005) 'Applying the Emotional Availability Scales to children with disabilities'. *Infant Mental Health Journal* 26, 369–391.

Briscoe, C. (2006) *Ugly*. London: Hodder & Stoughton.

Bronowski, J. (1973) *The Ascent of Man*. London: BBC Publ.

Burnham, J. (1992) 'Approach–method–technique: making distinctions and creating connections'. *Human Systems* 3, 3–26.

Burnham, J. (2000) 'Internalized other interviewing: evaluating and enhancing therapy'. *Clinical Psychology Forum* 140, 16–20.

Burr, V. (1995) *An Introduction to Social Constructionism*. London: Routledge.

Butler, R.J. (1985) 'Towards an understanding of childhood difficulties' in N. Beail (ed.), *Repertory Grid Technique and Personal Constructs*. London: Croom Helm.

Butler, R.J. (1994) *Nocturnal Enuresis: the Child's Experience.* Oxford: Butterworth Heinemann.

Butler, R.J. (1996) *Sports Psychology in Action.* Oxford: Butterworth Heinemann.

Butler, R.J. (1997) *Sports Psychology in Performance.* Oxford: Butterworth Heinemann.

Butler, R.J. (1999) *Performance Profiling.* Leeds: The National Coaching Foundation Press.

Butler, R.J. (2001) *The Self Image Profiles for Children and Adolescents.* London: The Psychological Corporation.

Butler, R. J. (2006) 'Investigating the content of core constructs'. *Personal Construct Theory & Practice* 3, 27–33.

Butler, R. J. & Hardy L. (1992) 'The Performance Profile: theory and application'. *Sport Psychologist* 6, 253–264.

Butler, R.J. Redfern, E.J. & Forsythe, W. I. 1990 'The child's construing of nocturnal enuresis: a method of enquiry and prediction of outcome'. *Journal of Child Psychology and Psychiatry* 31, 447–454.

Butler, R.J. Smith, M. & Irwin, I. (1993) 'The Performance Profile in practice'. *Journal of Applied Sports Psychology* 5, 48–63.

Butler, R.J. Redfern, E.J. & Holland P. (1994) 'Children's notions about enuresis and the implications for treatment'. *Scandinavian Journal of Urology and Nephrology* 163, Suppl. 39–48.

Butler, R.J. & Green, D. (1998) *The Child Within: The Exploration of Personal Construct Theory with Young People.* Oxford: Butterworth Heinemann.

Butler, R.J. & Gasson, S.L. (2004) *The Self Image Profile for Adults.* London: The Psychological Corporation.

Butler, R.J. & Gasson, S.L. (2005) 'Self esteem/self concept scales for children and adolescents: a review'. *Child & Adolescent Mental Health* 10, 190–201.

Butt, T.W., Burr, V. & Epting, F. (1997) 'Core construing: discovery or invention?' in R.A. Neimeyer & G.J. Neimeyer (eds),*Advances in Personal Construct Theory.* New York: Springer-Vol.

Coopersmith, S. (1981) *Coopersmith Self Esteem Inventory.* Palo Alto, CA Consulting Psychologists Press.

Dalton, P. & Dunnett, G. (1992) *A Psychology for Living: Personal Construct Theory for Professionals and Clients.* Chichester: Wiley

Davies, B. & Harre, R. (1990) 'Positioning: the discursive production of selves'. *Journal for the Theory of Social Behaviour* 20, 43–63.

Department of Health (1989)*The Children Act.* London: Department of Health.

Department of Health (2001) *The Expert Patient: A New Approach to Chronic Disease Management in the 21st Century.* London: Department of Health.

Deutsch, D. (1997) 'The final prejudice'. *The Libertarian Enterprise* 25

Dickinson, C. (2007) 'Mothers' perspectives on the development of attachments in autism: a qualitative study' in D. Clin (ed.), *Psychology thesis.* University of Leeds. (Unpublished).

Donaldson, M. (1984) *Children's Minds.* London: Fontana.

Drewery, W., Winslade, J. & Monk, G. (2000) 'Resisting the dominant story: toward a deeper understanding of narrative therapy' in R. Neimeyer & J. Raskin (eds), *Constructions of Disorder: Meaning-making Frameworks for Psychotherapy* Washington: American Psychological Association.

Dunn, J. (1993) *Young Children's Close Relationships. Beyond Attachment.* London: Sage.

Edwards, B. (1988) *Drawing on the Artist Within.* Glasgow: Fontana.

Eiser, C. (1990) *Chronic Childhood Disease: An Introduction to Psychological Theory and Research.* Cambridge: Cambridge University Press.

Elliott, C.D. (1983) *British Ability Scales*. Windsor: NFER-Nelson.

Emler, N. (2001) *Self-Esteem: the Costs and Causes of Low Self-worth*. York: Joseph Rowntree Foundation.

Epting, F.R. (1984) *Personal Construct Counselling and Psychotherapy*. Chichester: Wiley.

Epting, F.R. (1988) 'Journeying into the personal constructs of children'. *International Journal of Personal Construct Psychology* 1, 53–61.

Erikson, E.H. (1968) *Identity, Youth and Crisis*. New York: Norton.

Fekadu, D., Alem, A. & Hagglof, B. (2006) 'The prevalence of mental health problems in Ethiopian child laborers'. *Journal of Child Psychology and Psychiatry* 47, 954–959.

Fonagy, P., Target, M. & Cottrell, D. (2002) *What Works for Whom? A Critical Review of Treatments for Children and Adolescents*. London: Guilford Press.

Fransella, F. (1972) *Personal Change and Reconstruction: Research on a Treatment of Stuttering*. London: Academic Press.

Fransella, F. (1995) *George Kelly*. London: Sage.

Fransella, F. (2003) *International Handbook of Personal Construct Psychology*. Chichester: Wiley.

Fransella, F. & Bannister, D. (1977) *A Manual for Repertory Grid Technique*. London: Academic Press.

Fransella, F. & Dalton P. (1990) *Personal Construct Counselling in Action*. London: Sage.

Fransella, F. & Neimeyer, R.A. (2003) 'George Alexander Kelly: the man and his theory' in F. Fransella (ed.), *International Handbook of Personal Construct Psychology*. Chichester: Wiley.

Fraser, S., Lewis, V. & Ding S. (2004) *Doing Research with Children and Young People*. London: Sage.

Fritz, G.K. & Overholser, J.C. (1989) 'Patterns of response to childhood asthma'. *Psychometric Medicine* 51, 347–355.

Giles, L.D. (2003) 'Use of drawings and reflective comments in family construct development'. *PhD thesis*. Open University, Milton Keynes. (Unpublished).

Glass, G. (1976) 'Primary, secondary and meta-analysis of research'. *Educational Researcher* 5, 3–8.

Goffman, E. (1963) *Stigma: Notes of the Management of Spoiled Identity*. New York: Prentice-Hall.

Graham, J. & Cohen, R. (1997) 'Race and sex as factors in children's sociometric ratings and friendship choices'. *Social Development* 6, 355–372.

Green, D. (1982) 'Moral development and the therapeutic community'. *International Journal of Therapeutic Communities* 3, 209–217.

Green, D. (1993) *Constructs in the courtroom*. Paper presented at the Xth International Personal Construct Congress. Townsville, Australia.

Green, D. (1997) 'An experiment in fixed role therapy'. *Clinical Child Psychology and Psychiatry* 2, 553–564.

Green J. (2006) Annotation the therapeutic alliance – a significant but neglected variable in child mental health treatment studies journal of child psychology and psychiatry 47, 5, 425–435.

Greene, S. & Hogan, D. (2005) *Researching Children's Experience*. London: Sage.

Haley, J. (1973) *Uncommon Therapy—The Psychiatric Techniques of Milton H. Erickson*. Norton New York.

Harter, S. (1985) *Manual for the Self Perception Profile for Children*. Denver, CO University of Denver Press.

Harter, S. (1999) *The Construction of the Self*. New York: Guilford Press.

Hartley, R. (1986) 'AT Imagine you're clever'. *Journal of Child Psychology and Psychiatry* 27, 383–398.

Hay, D., Payne, A. & Chadwick, A. (2004) 'Peer relations in childhood'. *Journal of Child Psychology and Psychiatry* 45, 84–108.

Hayes, S., Luoma, J. & Bond, F. (2006) 'Acceptance and commitment therapy: model, processes and outcomes'. *Behaviour Research and Therapy* 44, 1–25.

Hepburn, A. (2005) '"You're not taking" me seriously": ethics and asymmetry in calls to a child protection helpline'. *Journal of Constructivist Psychology* 18, 253–274.

Higgins, E.T. (1989) 'Self-discrepancy theory: what patterns of self beliefs cause people to suffer?' in L. Berkowitz (ed.), *Advances in Experimental Social Psychology*. San Diego: Academic Press.

Hinkle, D. (1965) 'The change of personal constructs from the viewpoint of a theory of construct implications'. Unpublished PhD thesis, Ohio State University.

Hughes, H.M. (1984) 'Measures of self concept and self esteem for children aged 3–12 years: a review and recommendations'. *Clinical Psychology Review* 4, 657–692.

Hughes, M. (1986) *Children and Number: Difficulties in Learning Mathematics*. Oxford: Basil Blackwell

Jackson, S.R. (1988) 'Self characterisation: dimensions of meaning' in F. Fransella & L. Thomas (eds),*Experimenting with Personal Construct Psychology*. London: Routledge Kegan Paul.

Jackson, S.R. & Bannister, D. (1985)'Growing into self' in D. Bannister (ed.), *Issues and Approaches in Personal Construct Theory*. London: Academic Press.

James, W. (1892) *Psychology: The Briefer Course*. New York: Holt.

Johnson, M. (2000) 'The view from the Wuro: a guide to child rearing for Fulani parents' in J. DeLoache & A. Gottlieb (eds), *In a World of Babies. Imagined Childcare Guides for Seven Societies*. Cambridge: Cambridge University Press.

Kellett, M. & Nind M. (2003) *Implementing Intensive Interaction in Schools*. London: David Fulke.

Kelly G. (1955) *The Psychology of Personal Constructs*. New York: NortonVols.

Kelly, G. (1969a) 'Sin and psychotherapy' in B. Maher (ed.), *Clinical Psychology and Personality: The Selected Papers of George Kelly*. New York: Wiley.

Kelly, G. (1969b) 'The language of hypothesis: man's psychological instrument' in B. Maher (ed.), *Clinical Psychology and Personality: The Selected Papers of George Kelly*. New York: John Wiley.

Kelly, G. (1969c) 'The autobiography of a theory' in B. Maher (ed.), *Clinical Psychology and Personality: Selected Papers of George Kelly*. New York: Wiley.

Kelly, G. (1970) 'Behaviour is an experiment' in D. Bannister (ed.), *Perspectives in Personal Construct Theory*. London: Academic Press.

Kelly, G.A (1980) 'psychology of the optimum man' A.W. Landfield & L.M. Leitner (eds), *Personal Construct Psychology: Psychotherapy and Personality*. New York: Wiley.

Klion, R.E. & Leitner, L.M. (1985) 'Construct elicitation techniques and the production of interpersonal concepts in children'. *Social Behaviour & Personality* 13, 137–142.

Kupst, M.J. (1994) 'Coping with paediatric cancer: theoretical and research perspectives' in D.J. Bearson & R.K. Mulheard (eds), *Pediatric Psycho-oncology: Psychological Perspectives on Children with Cancer*. Oxford: Oxford University Press.

Lansdown, G. (2005) *The Evolving Capacities of the Child*. Florence: UNICEF Innocenti Research Centre.

Leitner, L. & Thomas L. (2003) 'Experiential personal construct psychotherapy' in F. Fransella (ed.), *International Handbook of Personal Construct Psychology*. Chichester: Wiley.

Luborsky, L., Diguer, L. & Seligman, D. (1999) 'The researcher's own therapy allegiances: a "wild card" in comparisons of treatment efficacy'. *Clinical Psychology: Science and Practice* 6, 95–106.

Maccoby, E. (1998) *The Two Sexes. Growing up apart, Coming together*. Cambridge, MA Harvard University Press.

Mackay, R.D. & Coleman, A.M. (1991) 'Excluding expert witness: a tale of ordinary folk and common experience'. *General Law Review* 800–810.

Madan-Swain, A. & Brown, R.T. (1991) 'Cognitive and psychological sequelae for children with acute lymphocytic leukaemia and their families'. *Clinical Psychology Review* 11, 267–294.

Mair, J.M.M. (1977a) 'Metaphors for living' in A.W. Landfield (ed.), *Nebraska Symposium on Motivation 1976*. Lincoln, NE University of Nebraska Press.

Mair, J.M.M. (1977b) 'The community of self' in D. Bannister *New Perspectives in Personal Construct Theory*. London: Academic Press

Mair, M. (1986) 'Obituary: Don Bannister'. *Bulletin of the British Psychological Society* 39, 305.

Mancuso, J.C. & Adams-Webber J. (1982) *The Construing Person*. New York: Praeger.

Marshall, W., Anderson, D.& Fernandez, Y. (1999) *Cognitive Behavioural Treatment of Sexual Offenders*. London: Wiley.

McCoy, M.M. (1977) 'A reconstruction of emotion' in D. Bannister (ed.), *New Perspectives in Personal Construct Theory*. London: Academic Press.

McWilliams, S. (2004) 'On further reflection'. *Personal Construct Theory and Practice* 1, –7.

Meeuwesen, L. & Kaptein M. (1996) 'Changing interactions in doctor–parent–child communication'. *Psychology and Health* 11, 787–795.

Mosley, J. (2002) *Quality Circle Time in the Primary Classroom*. Wisbech: LDA Publ.

Natinal Autistic Society website www.nas.org.uk

Neimeyer, G.J., Bowman, J.Z. & Saferstein, J. (2005) 'The effects of elicitation techniques on repertory grid outcomes: difference, opposite and contrast methods'. *Journal of Constructivist Psychology* 18 237–252.

Neimeyer, R.A. (1985) *The Development of Personal Construct Psychology*. Lincoln: University Nebraska Press.

Neimeyer, R. & Harter, S. (1988) 'Facilitating individual change' in G. Dunnett (ed.), *Working with People: Clinical Uses of Personal Construct Psychology*. London: Rout ledge.

Norcross, J.C. (2002) *Psychotherapy Relationships that Work*. New York: Oxford University Press.

Osgood, W., Foster, M., Flanagan, C. & Gretschen, R. (2005) *On Your Own Without a Net: The Transition to Adulthood for Vulnerable Populations*. Chicago: University of Chicago Press.

Perner, J., Ruffman, T. & Leekam, S. (1994) 'Theory of mind is contagious: you catch it from your sibs'. *Child Development* 65, 1228–1238.

Perrin, E.C. & Gerrity, P.S. (1981) 'There's a demon in your belly: children's understanding of illness'. *Pediatrics* 67, 841–849.

Procter, H.G. (1985) 'A construct approach to family therapy and systems intervention' in E. Button (ed.), *Personal Construct Theory and Mental Health*. Beckenham: Croom Helm.

Procter, H.G. (2005) 'Techniques of Personal Construct Family Therapy' in D. Winter & L.Viney (eds), *Personal Construct Psychology: Advances in Theory, Practice and Research*. London: Wiley.

Ravenette, T. (1977) 'Personal construct theory: an approach to the psychological investigation of children and young people' in D. Bannister (ed.), *New Perspectives in Personal Construct Theory*. London: Academic Press.

Ravenette, T. (1980) 'The exploration of consciousness: personal construct interventions with children' in A.W. Landfield & L.M.Leitner (eds), *Personal Construct Psychology: Psychotherapy and Personality*. New York: Wiley

Ravenette, T. (1988) 'Personal construct psychology in the practice of an educational psychologist' in G. Dunnett (ed.), *Working with People: Clinical Uses of Personal Construct Psychology*. London: Routledge.

Ravenette, T. (1997) *Selected Papers: PCT and the Practice of an Educational Psychologist*. Farnborough: EPCA Publ.

Ravenette, T. (2003) 'Constructive intervention when children are presented as problems' in F. Fransella (ed.), *International Handbook of Personal Construct Psychology*. Chichester: Wiley.

Rolland, J.S. (1987) 'Chronic illness and the life cycle: a conceptual framework'. *Family Process* 26, 203–221.

Ronen, T. (1996) 'Constructivist therapy with traumatised children'. *Journal of Constructivist Psychology* 9, 139–156.

Ross, N. (2003) '"Tell us what you think!": children's explanations of attendance at CAMHS'. *Clinical Psychology* 31, 9–12.

Rowe, D. (1983) *Depression: The Way Out of Your Prison*. London: Routledge & Kegan Paul.

Rowe, D. (2003) 'Personal construct psychology and me' in F. Fransella (ed.), *International Handbook of Personal Construct Psychology*. Chichester: Wiley.

Rutgers, A., Bakermans-Kranenburg, M., van Lizendoom, M. & van Berckelaer-Omnes, I. (2004) 'Autism and attachment: a meta-analytic review'. *Journal of Child Psychology and Psychiatry* 45, 1123–1134.

Rutter, M. & Yule W. (1975) 'The concept of specific reading retardation'. *Journal of Child Psychology and Psychiatry* 16, 181–197.

Rutter, M. & Yule, W. (1979) 'Reading difficulties' in M. Rutter & L. Hersov (eds), *Child Psychiatry: Modern Approaches*. Oxford: Blackwell.

Sacks, O. (1995) *An Anthropologist on Mars: Seven Paradoxical Tales*. London: Picador.

Salmon, P. (1970) 'A psychology of personal growth' in D. Bannister (ed.), *Perspectives in Personal Construct Theory*. London: Academic Press.

Salmon, P. (1976) 'Grid measures with child subjects' P. Slater (ed.), *The Measurement of Intrapersonal Space by Grid Technique*. Chichester: Wiley.

Salmon, P. (1985) *Living in Time*. London: Dent.

Salmon, P. (1995) *Psychology in the Classroom: Reconstructing Teachers and Learners*. London: Cassell.

Salmon, P. & Claire, H. (1984) *Classroom Collaboration*. London: Routledge & Kegan Paul.

Sarason, B., Sarason, I. & Gurung, R. (2001) 'Close personal relationships and health outcomes: a key to the role of social support' in B. Sarason & S.Duck (eds), *Personal Relationships: Implications for Clinical and Community Psychology*. Chichester: Wiley.

Schultheis, K., Peterson, L. & Selby, V. (1987) 'Preparation for stressful medical procedures and person + treatment interactions'. *Clinical Psychology Review* 7, 329–352.

Seligman, M. (1995) 'The effectiveness of psychotherapy: the consumer reports study'. *American Psychologist* 50, 965–974.

Sereny, G. (1995) *The Case of Mary Bell: A Portrait of a Child Who Murdered*. London: Pimlico.

Settersten, J., Furstenberg, F. & Rumbaut, R. (2005) *On the Frontier of Adulthood: Theory, Research and Public Policy*. Chicago: University of Chicago.

Shirk, S. & Karver, M. (2003) 'Prediction of treatment outcome from relationship variables in child and adolescent therapy: a meta-analytic review'. *Journal of Consulting and Clinical Psychology* 71, 452–464.

Shute, R. & Paton, D. (1990) 'Childhood illness—the child as helper' in H.C. Foot, M.J.Morgan & Shute R. (eds),*Children Helping Children*. London: Wiley.

Slade, A. (2005) 'Parental reflective functioning: an introduction'. *Attachment and Human Development* 7, 260–281.

Sloper, P. & White, D. (1996) 'Risk factors in the adjustment of siblings of children with cancer'. *Journal of Child Psychology and Psychiatry* 37, 597–607.

Smith, D.J. (1994) *The Sleep of Reason: The James Bulger Case*. London: Century.

Smoller, J. (1987) 'The etiology and treatment of childhood'. *Networker* 69–71.

Stager, S. & Young R.D. (1982) 'A self concept measure for pre-school and early primary grade children'. *Journal of Personality Assessment* 46, 536–543.

Stefan, C. (1977) 'Core role theory and implications' in D. Bannister (ed.), *New Perspectives in Personal Construct Theory*. London: Academic Press.

Sutton, J., Smith, P. & Swettenham, J. (2001) '"It's easy, it works, and it makes me feel good"—a response to Arsenio and Lemerise'. *Social Development* 10, 74–78.

Tafarodi, R.W. & Swann, W.B. (1995) 'Self-liking and self-competence as dimensions of global self esteem: initial validation of a measure'. *Journal of Personality Assessment* 65, 322–342.

Tetzlaff, B., Kahn, J. & Godley, S. (2005) 'Working alliance, treatment satisfaction, and patterns of post-treatment use among adolescent substance users'. *Psychology of Addiction Behaviours* 19, 2005 199–207.

Thompson, G.G. (1968) 'George Alexander Kelly (1905–1967)'. *Journal of General Psychology* 79, 19–24.

Tomm, K. (1988) 'Interventive interviewing: part 111. Intending to ask lineal, circular, strategic, or reflexive questions'. *Family Process* 27, 1–15.

Truneckova, D. & Viney, L. (2003) 'Evaluating personal construct group work with troubled adolescents'. Unpublished manuscript, University of Woolongong.

Tschudi, F. (1977) 'Loaded and honest questions: a construct theory view of symptoms and therapy' in D. Bannister (ed.) *New Perspectives in Personal Construct Theory*. London: Academic Press.

Viney, L., Metcalfe, C. & Winter, D. (2005) 'The effectiveness of personal construct psychotherapy: a meta-analysis' in D. Winter & L. Viney (eds), *Personal Construct Psychotherapy: Advances in Theory, Practice and Research*. London: Whurr.

Volkmar, F., Lord, C. & Bailey, A. (2004) 'Autism and pervasive developmental disorders'. *Journal of Child Psychology and Psychiatry* 45, 135–170.

Wampold, B. (2001) *The Great Psychotherapy Debate: Models, Methods and Findings*. New Jersey: Lawrence Erlbaum.

Watzlawick, P., Weakland, J. & Fisch, R. (1974) *Change: Principles of Problem Formation and Problem Resolution*. New York: Norton.

Wheen, F. (2004) *How Mumbo-Jumbo Conquered The World: A Short History of Modern Delusions*. London: Harper Perennial.

Wilkinson, S.R. (1988) *The Child's World of Illness*. Cambridge: Cambridge University Press.

Wing, L. (1981) 'Asperger's syndrome: a clinical account'. *Psychological Medicine* 11, 115–129.

Winter, D.A. (1992) *Personal Construct Psychology in Clinical Practice: Theory, Research and Application*. London: Routledge.

Young, B., Dixon-Woods, M., Windridge, K.C. & Heney, D. (2003) 'Managing communication with young people who have a potentially life threatening chronic illness: qualitative study of patients and parents'. *British Medical Journal* 326, 305–308.

AUTHOR INDEX

SUBJECT INDEX

Items in **bold** are the original corollaries